SONG OF EXILE

Purdue Studies in Romance Literatures

Editorial Board

Íñigo Sánchez Llama, Series Editor
Elena Coda
Paul B. Dixon
Beth Gale

Patricia Hart
Gwen Kirkpatrick
Allen G. Wood

Howard Mancing, Consulting Editor
Floyd Merrell, Consulting Editor
Joyce Detzner, Production Editor
R. Tyler Gabbard-Rocha, Production Editor

Associate Editors

French
Jeanette Beer
Paul Benhamou
Willard Bohn
Thomas Broden
Gerard J. Brault
Mary Ann Caws
Glyn P. Norton
Allan H. Pasco
Gerald Prince
Roseann Runte
Ursula Tidd

Italian
Fiora A. Bassanese
Peter Carravetta
Benjamin Lawton
Franco Masciandaro
Anthony Julian Tamburri

Luso-Brazilian
Fred M. Clark
Marta Peixoto
Ricardo da Silveira Lobo Sternberg

Spanish and Spanish American
Catherine Connor
Ivy A. Corfis
Frederick A. de Armas
Edward Friedman
Charles Ganelin
David T. Gies
Roberto González Echevarría
David K. Herzberger
Emily Hicks
Djelal Kadir
Amy Kaminsky
Lucille Kerr
Howard Mancing
Floyd Merrell
Alberto Moreiras
Randolph D. Pope
Elżbieta Skłodowska
Marcia Stephenson
Mario Valdés

 volume 84

SONG OF EXILE
A Cultural History of Brazil's
Most Popular Poem, 1846–2018

Joshua Alma Enslen

Purdue University Press
West Lafayette, Indiana

Copyright ©2022 by Purdue University. All rights reserved.

∞ The paper used in this book meets the minimum requirements of American National Standard for Information Sciences—Permanence of Paper for Printed Library Materials, ANSI Z39.48-1992.

Printed in the United States of America
Template for interior design by Anita Noble;
template for cover by Heidi Branham.
Cover image:
Wounded Land (2016) by Alaina Enslen, courtesy of www.alainaenslen.com

Cataloging-in-Publication Data is on file at the Library of Congress

This book is dedicated to Susan Quinlan, Robert Moser, Amélia Hutchinson, and to the entire Department of Romance Languages at the University of Georgia.

Contents

- ix **Acknowledgments**
- 1 **Chapter One**
  "Minha terra tem palmeiras" : A Brief Introduction to Brazil's Most Popular Poem
- 11 **Chapter Two**
  "Adeus Coimbra inimiga": Precedents and Contexts
- 27 **Chapter Three**
  "Onde canta o rouxinol": Early Portuguese Responses
- 55 **Chapter Four**
  "Onde canta o periquito": The First Republic to the Vargas Era (1889–1945)
- 79 **Chapter Five**
  "Minha terra só tem tanques": The Military Regime (1964–1985)
- 99 **Chapter Six**
  "As sirenes que aqui apitam": Twenty-First-Century Songs of Exile (1999–2015)
- 121 **Chapter Seven**
  "Sou ali": Variations by Female Authors (1867–2015)
- 143 **Chapter Eight**
  "As aves que aqui twittam": Twitter, Instagram, and Beyond
- 151 **Chapter Nine**
  The Word, the Database, and the Algorithm
- 157 **Afterword**
  Literary Research as Data Art: An Experiment in Critical Reading (Manuel Portela)
- 165 **Appendix**
  Table of 500 Texts
- 201 **Notes**
- 213 **Works Cited**
- 229 **Index**

Acknowledgments

Since beginning this project in earnest in 2014, there have been many mentors, colleagues, and friends to help and encourage me along the way, across numerous institutions, disciplines, and different continents. But, at the top of the list, I must first mention someone who is not only all of these, but also family too: the artist extraordinaire, Alaina Enslen, whose stunning visual narratives and talent have been integral to the success of the project's exhibitions, and whose critical perspectives and daily conversations on the topic have helped me to organize the analyses presented herein.

Secondly, I express my sincere gratitude to my post-doctoral advisor Manuel Portela, whose state-of-the-art Materialities of Literature program at the University of Coimbra leads in so many creative and innovative ways in the most critical discussions of digital humanities, electronic literature, and new media today. I feel very fortunate to have had his mentorship over the years and for his initial acceptance of my post-doctoral proposal in 2015, which paved the way for this book to be written. The year I spent as a fellow in Coimbra was crucial to the completion of my research, to the development of its methodological approach, and to the initiation of the related data art exhibition series. As evidence of his important role, Portela's thoughtful contextualization of this study can be found as the Afterword to this book.

Near the top of the list, I must also express my heartfelt gratitude to my friend and colleague, the poet-scholar Nuno Miguel Neves, who volunteered his talents and hundreds of hours of his personal time to help create our first exhibition at the University of Coimbra's Museum of Science. Appreciation is also due to Jorge Simões, whose material and logistical support were essential to the exhibitions, and to the graduate students of the Materialities of Literature program, many now with PhD in hand and doing great work around the world

I would like to thank Carlota Simões, Teresa Girão, and the rest of the excellent staff of the Museum of Science at the University of Coimbra for agreeing to host our first exhibition sight unseen, for their keen interest, patience, and careful oversight, and for the exhibition's subsequent success, which led directly to an exhibition at FOLIO 2016 in Óbidos, yet another in Lisbon, and to its

Acknowledgments

nomination for an APOM 2017. Appreciation is similarly due to Ana Maria Calçada and Celeste Afonso of FOLIO, to our friends Marcela Dantés and Leo Lott whom we met there, and to Michael Baum and the Luso-American Development Foundation for a travel grant to make our participation at FOLIO possible, along with Luis de Carvalho of the Reitoria of the University of Lisbon, for his interest in a third exhibition at the Caleidoscópio in summer 2017. Without these exhibitions, this book would have never taken on the dimensions it has. The time taken to conceptualize and craft the artisanal installations and other visualizations, far from distracting me from the writing, made the organization of the data exponentially more efficient.

I would like to thank Pedro Martins, Catarina Maçãs, and Adriana Barbosa from the Computational Design and Visualization Lab of U Coimbra's Department of Informatics Engineering. Barbosa's prototype website has opened the door to the next stage of the project. Likewise, an honorable mention is due to Silvana Guimarães, editor of the Brazilian online literary journal, *Germina: Revista de Literatura e Arte*. The journal's website dedicated to variations of "Canção do exílio" was an important catalyst in the early stages of this project. It is my hope that my collaborations may continue with both the Computational Design and Visualization Lab in Portugal and *Germina* in Brazil.

Among those colleagues closer to home, I must especially thank the engineer Ledlie Klosky and the mathematician Jocelyn Bell for our brainstorming sessions which helped to articulate early versions of the categories of analysis. I would also like to thank my colleagues in West Point's Department of Foreign Languages, especially Rebecca Jones-Kellogg and Olivier Tonnerre, for their encouragement; Emma Dugas, a gifted student, for her early assistance; and the departmental leadership, Rickie McPeak, Gregory Ebner, and John Baskerville, for their unfailing support over the years.

To those many colleagues at home and abroad, anonymous and otherwise, who have encouraged me along the way, who read chapters or offered feedback at conferences, lectures, and other events, especially Susan Quinlan, Christopher Lewis, Vinícius Carvalho Pereira, Rex Nielson, João Queiroz, Cris Lira, Emanuelle Oliveira Monte, and Anita de Melo, among others (you know who you are), I also thank you.

Chapter One

"Minha terra tem palmeiras"
A Brief Introduction to Brazil's Most Popular Poem

"Canção do exílio" is by far the most popular poem of all time in Brazil. Written in Coimbra, Portugal in 1843 by the Brazilian student Antônio Gonçalves Dias, thousands of authors, canonical and otherwise, have imitated its Romantic verses to glorify the wonders of the Brazilian nation, its culture and geography, while just as many have parodied it to criticize Brazil, exposing a litany of the nation's issues. Yet, only in recent years, with the widespread availability of computational tools for textual analysis and the development of searchable online archives, has it become possible to take a comprehensive view of the poem's rich intertextual history. Based on the analysis of 500 intertexts spanning more than 170 years, this book explores the evolution of "Canção do exílio" in Brazilian print culture, cataloguing the networks of its re-inventions across generations and discussing its importance as Brazil's most popular poem.

Published in 1846, "Canção do exílio" is indeed the author's debut work, the first to appear among all others in the volume, *Primeiros cantos*. Gonçalves Dias would go on to publish a number of other books of poetry, such as *Segundos cantos* and *Últimos cantos*, though *Primeiros cantos* would remain his most influential work. No other work, not even the popular epic poem *I-Juca-Pirama*, published in the 1850s, comes close to repeating its success.[1] Filled with poems such as "O canto do índio" and "O soldado espanhol," *Primeiros cantos* bodes content associated with the particular mix of peoples and politics involved in the European colonization of the Americas. Many, but not all, poems, in the form of national allegory, recount stories of love, deceit, revenge, and violence, most with an Indianist hue, and the volume opens with none other than "Canção do exílio."

Chapter One

A defining work of Brazilian Romanticism, "Canção do exílio" came along just at the right moment in national history to establish itself as Brazil's most emblematic poem. It appeared in the same decade as the crowning of a young Dom Pedro II (1841), and as the nation was taking its first prodigious steps toward unification after independence (1822). Soon after its publication, a burgeoning print culture (the printing press had only officially arrived in Brazil in 1808) carried the poem's simple, yet powerful Romantic message of national unity far and wide, while the crown also sought to unify an expansive geography, diverse populace, and competing political ideologies. As the government successfully quelled numerous regional revolts, Dom Pedro II would also champion important societies, such as the Instituto Histórico e Geográfico Brasileiro (established 1838), wherein he would commission Brazil's intellectual class to write the nation's history, proposing the narrative of an official national identity supportive of the monarchy.

Replete with images of the nation as a tropical paradise, founded in well-established colonial discourses, the flowers, birds, lovers, and palms at the heart of "Canção do exílio" articulate Brazil as both an Edenic garden and as a great nation in waiting. Over the centuries since, the continued hope among Brazilians of the realization of this long-foretold utopia, together with its repeated frustration, have all but guaranteed the permanency of the poem in the national imaginary. Other features of the text, especially the memorability of its simple rhymes and phrasing, based on the popular Portuguese "redondilha maior" form, and its Romantic appeal to patriotism, further propelled it to become what it is today: one of the most imitated poems in the world. The poem is reproduced below with its original orthography.

> Canção do exílio
>
> Minha terra tem palmeiras,
> Onde canta o Sabiá;
> As aves, que aqui gorgeião,
> Não gorgeião como lá.
>
> Nosso céo tem mais estrellas,
> Nossas varzeas tem mais flores,
> Nossos bosques têm mais vida,
> Nossa vida mais amores.

"Minha terra tem palmeiras": A Brief Introduction

> Em scismar—sósinho—á noite—
> Mais prazer encontro eu lá;
> Minha terra tem palmeiras,
> Onde canta o Sabiá.
>
> Minha terra tem primores,
> Que taes não encontro eu cá;
> Em scismar—sósinho—á noite—
> Mais prazer encontro eu lá;
> Minha terra tem palmeiras,
> Onde canta o Sabiá.
>
> Não permitta Deos que eu morra,
> Sem que eu volte para lá;
> Sem que desfructe os primores
> Que não encontro por cá;
> Sem qu'inda aviste as palmeiras,
> Onde canta o Sabiá. (Gonçalves Dias 9–10)

A comparative endeavor, "Canção do exílio" expresses the author's longing to return home from his studies in Coimbra while proposing that Brazil is better than Portugal in almost every way. This comparison, symbolized by how the Brazilian thrush ("o sabiá") sings more beautifully than the birds in Portugal, instigated a need to reply to Gonçalves Dias's assertions almost immediately. Before long, the poem was reverberating across the Lusophone world by way of foreign and national voices alike.

Among the busy streets of nineteenth-century Rio, the many Portuguese immigrants who set up shop there were among the first to respond to "Canção do exílio." The poem's exilic theme and Portuguese form struck a chord with these first-generation immigrants, prompting them to compose their rebuttals, such as António José Ferreira's "A saudade da pátria (imitação)" from 1847. His response begins, "Minha terra tem loureiros / Onde canta o rouxinol, / Por dias de primavera / De manhã e ao pôr do sol" ("A saudade" 43). This verse would eventually inspire its own branch of imitations. Two years later, in 1849, the Angolan poet, José Maia de Ferreira, published responses to "Canção do exílio" in his nation's first volume of published poetry, *Espontaneidades da minha alma*, such as "A minha terra" and "Benguelinha." And, in 1850, Hypollito Pereira Garcez wrote a pastiche of the original about his home, the Luso-Indian outpost of Goa. The Azores too would have a response for Gonçalves Dias in the early years of the poem's reception. In 1860, Antero Quental wrote his own variation entitled "A. M. E."; however, the poem's most enduring influence has been in Brazil.

In late May 2016, amidst the impeachment proceedings of Dilma Rousseff, I received a message from a colleague who, aware of my research, shared with me a telling tweet. Summing up the ubiquity of "Canção do exílio," she wrote: "It never ends! Põe esse tweet no teu trabalho. É perfeito" (Melo). She then included the following, written by @temerpoeta, a faux-Michel Temer personality tweeting satirical poetry in the politician's name: "Minha terra tem Calheiros / Onde cantam os Jucás / das aves que aqui gorjeiam / a mais linda é satanás." This tweet, based on the first stanza of the original, was shared more than 6,000 times in a matter of days and replaces Gonçalves Dias's "sabiá" and "palmeiras" with the names of two high-profile politicians heavily involved in the impeachment crisis (Renan Calheiros and Romero Jucá). It ends with an allusion to President Michel Temer as the devil himself. My friend closed her message with a powerful thought, "O Brasil é mesmo uma poesia de Gonçalves Dias até no inferno." This last observation conveniently makes an important point for us about the influence of the original in popular culture. Since its publication in 1846, "Canção do exílio" has become a palimpsest upon which successive generations write and re-write the nation's history and culture, at times utopic, at others dystopic, within the context of their own time. The poem and its intertexts are, in effect, Brazil as text-in-motion, a cyclical drama, encapsulating a multitude of forms and voices evolving over the decades alongside Brazil's crises in counterpoint to the utopia proposed by the original. Writers across Brazil, from the favelas of Rio to the villages of the Amazon, continue to reinvent the poem as both a foil to criticize the nation's failtures or as a psalm to champion its virtues, real or imagined.

Until recently, traditional text-based research of all types has been bound by an individual's capacity for reading. For this reason, it has most often focused on, and directly resulted in, comparatively small numbers of canonical texts.[2] Such directed, deliberate focus, termed "close reading" by students of literature, has been the norm for centuries; but now with the aid of computational tools, researchers can digitally explore millions of texts simultaneously and, with the right algorithms and queries, tease out specific topic-based data to build corpora, exponentially increasing our capacity for macro-level

"Minha terra tem palmeiras": A Brief Introduction

analysis.[3] Based on Franco Moretti's approach to literature, termed "distant reading,"[4] this study employs a systematic method for identifying instances of significant words and phrases from the original in other works, resulting in the creation of a main body of 500 intertexts of varied size and provenance.

"Canção do exílio" has been retrofitted over the decades to almost every possible scenario. It reappears in nineteenth-century political discourse and popular music, with its earliest imitations, such as Ferreira's mentioned above, published not even a year after its debut. Weaving its lines into the fabric of Brazilian identity, the text accompanies the evolution of the nation's print media and popular culture throughout the nineteenth and twentieth centuries. Variations commonly appear in newspapers and deal with almost every subject under the sun. Government corruption, dictatorships, state-sponsored violence, systemic racism, poverty, education, inequality, environmental atrocities, and other issues all play a part alongside more lighthearted subjects such as Carnaval, the "jogo do bicho," the Palmeiras soccer club, and even northern Brazil's *technobrega* club scene, constituting a grand exhibition of Brazilian culture put on display through the aggregate reading of the poem's textual progeny.

Echoes of "Canção do exílio" are indeed everywhere in Brazil, yet the true dimensions of the poem's vast cultural influence have never been captured in the scholarship. This book represents the first comprehensive attempt to map the contours of this vast network of intertextual data. The basic analogy conceptualized for this study is borrowed from DNA sequencing. In effect, each word in the poem represents a specific link in a chain of words that, when strung together, constitute the original. In the poem's intertexts, portions of this sequence of words remain identifiable in varying degrees of modification. With this basic idea in mind, a few categories of analysis have emerged for identifying and categorizing similarities and differences with the original, both quantitative and qualitative. These categories of analysis—*Significant Words, String Similarity, Syntactic Templates, Word Tokens,* and *Modal Analysis*—are briefly described below and developed in greater detail over the course of the study.[5]

> a) *Significant Words,* based on word frequency analysis, are the most repeated nouns among the intertexts, which together outline the general structure of a network. These *Significant*

5

Words establish nodes of contact with the original and across the intertexts wherever they appear. The three most repeated nouns among all the texts are "terra," "palmeiras," and "sabiá."

b) *String Similarity Test*, a purely computational endeavor, produces a coefficient of textual relatedness with "Canção do exílio" for each variation, or intertext. *String Similarity Tests* compare two distinct sequences of characters (in our case, two literary texts) and then calculate the amount of modification needed to transform one sequence into the other to determine their similarity. As a companion to more traditional hermeneutics, the results of the test are expressly used in the discussion of twenty-first century variations, a period which has witnessed an exponential increase in the production of variations, and in the related exhibition series, *Bird-watching: Visualizing the Influence of Brazil's "Song of Exile"* (see Afterword for more information on the exhibition series).

c) *Syntactic Templates* are grammatical structures established in the original, such as "Minha terra tem palmeiras," from which variations typically generate related texts. In these templates, the syntax of the original remains intact while *Significant Words* are altered, such as in Jô Soares's opening line from his 1992 "Canção do exílio às avessas," a satirical poem about the resignation of President Fernando Affonso Collor de Mello. The variation begins, "Minha Dinda tem cascatas," as "Dinda" and "cascatas" replace "terra" and "palmeiras" in reference to Collor de Mello's mansion in Brasília where he officially resided as President (Soares 15).

d) *Word Tokens*, readily associated with *Syntactic Templates*, are words (such as "Dinda" and "cascatas" above) that replace *Significant Words* from the original. For example, the word "palmares" in Oswald de Andrade's 1925 "Canto de regresso à pátria" is a subtle token under the type "palmeiras" with post-colonial ramifications, setting the stage for his irreverent modernist parody, discussed in Chapter 4 ("Canto" 144).

e) *Modal Analysis*, a notion loosely adapted from the Greek musical modes, is a means to categorize the general sentiment of a text through close readings. Defining each variation in one of three sentimental modes—Positive, Negative, or Other—this approach, turning on the original's nationalist focus, allows for greater specificity in our analysis than the broad strokes portrayed by the designation of parody or pastiche. The characteristics of each of these modes will be clearly defined throughout the course of the book in relation to historical groupings of texts.

"Minha terra tem palmeiras": A Brief Introduction

Although this study is focused on texts written posterior to the original, Chapter 2 explores precedents and texts contemporary to the original as it defines how it will apply the concept of intertextuality. As the chapter explains, "Canção do exílio" is part of a long tradition of Luso-Brazilian texts predating its publication which articulate similar themes of longing and patriotic fervor. A discussion of examples from colonial Brazil, the Portuguese Age of Discoveries, and texts written by Gonçalves Dias's contemporaries in both Coimbra and Brazil strengthens our understanding of the historical force of the original's enduring narrative, explaining how it comes from centuries of well-established negotiations of identity.

After this brief historical contextualization, Chapter 3, entitled "Onde canta o rouxinol," analyzes in detail the earliest responses to Gonçalves Dias's text, introducing heretofore unexplored nineteenth-century poems, and focusing on a core group of texts written by Portuguese immigrants in Rio. Beginning with A. J. Ferreira's "A saudade da pátria (imitação)" from 1847, this chapter considers several direct responses to Gonçalves Dias's proposition that Brazil was better than Portugal. Articulating "loureiros" and the "rouxinol" in place of the original's "palmeiras" and "sabiá," the former pair of tokens is a frequent fixture of these Portuguese responses, inspiring its own branch of imitations and leaving a distinct mark on the responses of the nineteenth century. The rest of the chapter follows the "rouxinol" well into the twentieth century as it depicts the evolving relations between Portugal and its former colony, Brazil.

Chapter 4, entitled "Onde canta o periquito" in reference to the mascot of the Sociedade Esportiva Palmeiras, focuses on the period between 1889 and 1945, encompassing a discussion of the varied texts from the First Republic through the end of the Vargas dictatorship. From Carnaval and guaraná to the national anthem and the renovations of downtown Rio, the texts from the first half of this period (1889–1930) demonstrate the entrenchment of the poem in Brazilian culture while its use in newspapers and periodicals expands in stride with print culture and the early industrialization of the economy. In the latter half of the period (1930–45), the politics of the Vargas regime and the resulting populist efforts toward the homogenization of national culture serve as a backdrop for a discussion of the numerous satires and pastiches from Modernists, musicians, and other cultural commentators of the time.

The next significant group of texts emerges from the years of the military regime (1964–85), a tumultuous period in Brazilian history. In Chapter 5, "Minha terra só tem tanques," themes of international duress and state-sponsored oppression maintain a significant presence in "Canção do exílio" variations as the analysis focuses on the decades-long military regime (1964–1985), a tumultuous period in Brazilian history. Of the thirty-nine texts analyzed in this chapter, twenty-three of them cast Brazil in a negative light, conveying the dark realities of a dystopic nation under intense pressure. During this period, Brazilian identity is in crisis and, as these texts seek to make sense of the historical moment, they confront the utopic ideals of Gonçalves Dias's foundational myths. The frustration of the original's paradise is palpable as the nation's identity flirts with dissolution. Looking back to the texts from the decades immediately preceding the coup of 1964, the evidence of a crisis in the making becomes clear while a brief presentation of post-dictatorship texts shows how the traumatic scars of the military regime remain ever-present in the nation's zeitgeist.

Chapter 6, "As sirenes que aqui apitam," focuses on the significant number of "Canção do exílio" variations being published today. Sparked by the advent of the internet in the late 1990s, roughly half of all texts under analysis in this book were produced during the twenty-first century. These more recent texts discuss the most important issues currently facing Brazil. Namely, they concern themselves in a pronounced fashion with themes of political corruption, failed stewardship of the environment, violence, and poverty. Given its articulation of Brazil as a garden paradise, the original is particularly adaptable to environmental questions while also showing incredible versatility in its application to other contexts as many of these texts turn Gonçalves Dias's Romantic nationalism on its head.

Building on themes presented in the previous chapter, Chapter 7, "Sou ali," discusses how, in a book primarily organized by a principle of intertextual connections, the relationship between gender and authorship is a surprising narrative that emerges upon closer analysis. In contrast to their historical exclusion, women authors now have an almost equal share in the "Canção do exílio" narrative tradition. Since women authors account for only 5 of

"Minha terra tem palmeiras": A Brief Introduction

258 texts written prior to 2000 and 98 of 242 written subsequently, this chapter underscores the democratizing power of new media as it compares the themes of female-authored texts with the balance of the others while also exploring earlier texts, such as Honorata Minelvina Carneira de Mendonça's "Saudades da minha terra" from 1867.

Chapter 8, "As aves que aqui twittam," brings our reading and analysis up to date, focusing on the original's continued reinvention on Twitter and Instagram. Based on thousands of tweets collected in a matter of months in late 2015, this chapter explores how Brazil's millennial generation has hijacked the original, taking it down unexpected and disruptive paths, detaching it almost entirely from its nationalist underpinnings and recasting it as a humorous and irreverent internet meme. An analysis of the photographs associated with the poem on Instagram and Flikr also renders results worthy of discussion, as the interplay of photography and text offers new possibilities for literary studies. As we explore the colors and images connected with the poem, in contrast to the tweets, we will see how the nationalist narrative continues.

A reading at the "middle distance," as Marti A. Hearst has described a similar approach ("Exploratory Text Analysis"), this book's experimental methodology is not focused on the author nor the literary canon, but on a history of words, and those in a specific order, making possible a new reading of the cultural influence of one of the world's most popular poems. But, if a book is "a temporary intervention in a living field of language, images and ideas" (Drucker 175), that fact is never more obvious than in a study such as this. Although more comprehensive than any has ever been on the topic before, this analysis is based on the premise of an organic and ever-growing body of interrelated texts with a limitless horizon. No one will ever track down all the "Canção do exílio" variations—past, present, or future—despite technology's promise. Nor will we ever exhaust all the ways that the influence of this text and its intertexts may be studied, individually or as a group. In this light, the final chapter draws some general conclusions about the study while Manuel Portela's Afterword considers the project in relation to the Digital Humanities, visualization and the Bird-watching exhibition series, pointing toward the proposed creation of a digital environment for the continued dynamic exploration of this important narrative tradition in Brazilian culture.

Chapter Two

"Adeus Coimbra inimiga"
Precedents and Contexts

In Machado de Assis's short story "O espelho," written in the late 1800s, the protagonist Jacobina advances a theory in which every human has two souls, one facing inward and the other outward. One night, in the presence of four or five others, Jacobina is challenged to present his theory in the context of the metaphysical discussions of the evening. Although he had until that moment remained "calado, pensando, cochilando," he takes over the conversation with his radical theory, "Em primeiro lugar, não há uma só alma, há duas." "Duas?" the others inquire. "Nada menos de duas almas. Cada criatura humana traz duas almas consigo: uma que olha de dentro para fora, outra que olha de fora para dentro" (155). In Jacobina's theory, the exterior soul, as he termed it, influences the interior soul, shaping it through its gaze. This process "que Jacobina não hesita em localizar no olhar, torna-nos permanentemente sujeitos e objetos de significação atribuída" (Villaça 101–02). Jacobina explains further, "Quem perde uma das metades, perde naturalmente metade da existência; e casos há, não raros, em que a perda da alma exterior implica a da existência inteira" (Machado de Assis, "O espelho" 155).

Jacobina, a military officer, then recounts how overwhelming loneliness and solitude once put his whole existence in jeopardy. Left alone on a farm in the countryside, his exterior soul, the one defined by the social aspects of his identity (objects, relationships, etc.), began to fade. In desperation, he sought a solution to his crisis and eventually found one: his military uniform. "Cada dia, a uma certa hora, vestia-me de alferes, e sentava-me diante do espelho, lendo, olhando, meditando; no fim de duas, três horas, despia-me outra vez. Com este regímen pude atravessar mais seis dias de solidão, sem os sentir" (Machado de Assis, "O

Chapter Two

espelho" 162). This act, reminding him of his respected role in society, breathed new life into his exterior soul, making it possible for him to survive the ordeal.

In the words of María Jesús Martínez Alfaro in "Intertextuality: Origins and Development of the Concept," texts do not function "as self-contained systems but as differential and historical, as traces and tracings of otherness, since they are shaped by the repetition and transformation of other textual structures" (268). Broadly speaking, every text is an intermittent articulation of ideas formed within a complex web of (con)texts stemming back to prehistoric drawings and early human mark making. Thus, adapting Jacobina's theory, words also have two souls and the basic meaning of any given text, like Jacobina's interior soul, is dependent upon and constantly shaped and re-shaped by all those other word-texts that exist alongside it, by those that came before it, by those that will come after and by its own repetitions through time.

In the 1960s, when Julia Kristeva introduced the term intertextuality for the first time, she was in many ways putting a new spin on an old idea, but with the pronounced possibility of new analytical rigor. Turning it into a spatialized process, intertextuality represents a post-modern constructivist approach to understanding the production of meaning. In "Word, Dialogue, and Novel," Kristeva's original hypothesis on intertextuality visualizes a matrix in which a series of discrete texts or words—the latter defined as the "minimal textual unit"—enter into dialogue with one another through their temporal and spatial relations: "The word as minimal textual unit thus turns out to occupy the status of mediator, linking structural models to cultural (historical) environment, as well as that of regulator, controlling mutations from diachrony to synchrony" (37).

> Defining the specific status of the word as signifier for different modes of (literary) intellection within different genres or texts put poetic analysis at the sensitive centre of contemporary "human" sciences—at the intersection of *language* (the true practice of thought) with *space* (the volume within which signification, through a joining of differences, articulates itself). To investigate the status of the word is to study its articulations (as semic complex) with other words in the sentence, and then to look for the same functions or relationships at the articulator level of larger sequences. Confronted with this spatial conception of language's poetic operation, we must first define the

"Adeus Coimbra inimiga": Precedents and Contexts

> three dimensions of textual space where various semic sets and poetic sequences function. These three dimensions or coordinates of dialogue are writing subject, addressee, and exterior texts. The word's status is thus defined horizontally (the word in the text belongs to both writing subject and addressee) as well as vertically (the word in the text is oriented towards an anterior or synchronic literary corpus) … The notion of intertextuality replaces that of intersubjectivity, and poetic language is read as at least double. (36–37)

As originally conceived in the text above, intertextuality was at once already a visual mode of thought. Despite her initial rendering in purely narrative form, one must only briefly consider the language Kristeva employs in order to appreciate intertextuality's inherent visuality as a Cartesian plane. She describes "the word's status" "horizontally" and "vertically." She writes of the movement of the word within these "axes" as it is transmitted linearly *from* "writing subject" *to* "addressee," the addressee (or reader) possessing the lens of interpretation. Kristeva then conceives of a "semic complex" as a frame of reference for capturing a word's historical and cultural evolution within and across these texts and contexts, a word's "synchrony" and its "diachrony." She also uses such visual terms as "dialogical space," "dimensions," "spatial," and "spatialized," when describing the interactions between author, text, and reader.

The two axes of Kristeva's intertextual machine—the horizontal and vertical—represent the two dimensions of a Cartesian plane, or the "coordinates of dialogue," as she calls it. The horizontal line is the space of the text, as it is transmitted from writing subject to addressee. The vertical column is the position of the text ordered chronologically within a plane hypothetically containing all texts: every text a line, every line in time. Still, Kristeva writes not just of these two axes, but also of dimensions. The word functions in three dimensions in the process of transmission: "subject—addressee—context," but these three "dimensions" are of a single hypothetical reading. Thus, there are many more than just three dimensions to intertextuality. In fact, and this is important, if we were to count each and every reading as a dimension, then they are limitless. In this "semic complex," it falls to the reader to give meaning to the text, who positions each word within her own dynamic textual matrix. With each subsequent reading, she reconfigures her Cartesian plane of intertextuality, re-inventing every time a new set of dialogical truths to be negotiated with those of other readings, whether dramatically or only slightly different than the previous set. Although a bit overwhelming in theory, it is this limitlessness that makes dialogue possible, since with every reading new perspectives may emerge. As every reading (and writing) re-configures each reader's Cartesian plane of dialogue, our collective multiplicitous perspectives dangle in mobile-like confusion, tinkling, and clanging against one another when in conversation.

In contrast to formalism, intertextuality represents a post-structural approach to the production of meaning, considering the whole of textual production as one grand novelistic enterprise (Bakhtin). Like the theory of the two souls, this is a bold concept which attempts to describe the spatial relations between all texts ever written, articulating each as part of what one might call a *grand ubertext*, a text that simultaneously contains all other texts. But, even as its totality diffuses any original, such as "Canção do exílio," of its force and power, the implications of intertextuality lay the foundations for the networking of the poem with others. In this light, "Canção do exílio" emerges as a provisional text, or a *strategic urtext*, from which to pinpoint a non-essential origin for the elaboration of a body of texts for analysis. A term partially inspired by Gayatri Spivak's notion of "strategic essentialism," a *strategic urtext* represents a discrete text in which can be located, in chronological terms, the earliest occurrence of a specific pattern of words. In the case of "Canção do exílio," this pattern of words and phrases, borrowed and transformed to varying degrees in subsequent texts, can be used to identify the contours of a vast network of influence that carries at its core questions of Brazilian history, identity, and culture.

Still, while this provisional positioning places "Canção do exílio" as an original, a first of many, intertextuality also reminds us that nothing is created *ex nihilo*, and that "Canção do exílio" carries the marks of other texts. Thus, despite its singular influence, "Canção do exílio" is not unique, and an account of the literary (con)texts from which it emerged will help to illuminate this fact. Anterior texts from writers in both Portugal and Brazil gaze upon and course through the interior soul of "Canção do exílio," triangulating and shaping its historical influence. Heavily indebted to the international discourses of Romanticism, "Canção do exílio"

"Adeus Coimbra inimiga": Precedents and Contexts

is a late articulation of nationalistic tendencies in Brazil under development since the arrival of Cabral and with precedents in Portugal. In fact, all the prominent features of "Canção do exílio" in both form and content have their roots in earlier texts. These features are surmised in the glorification of Brazil's flora and fauna over that of other nations, especially Portugal. This glorification, bound to a Eurocentric gaze of the colonial other, communicates the "ripeness" of Brazil for colonization, re-writing the territory's history as a European imposition while romanticizing its pre-colonial past. The poem accomplishes this re-writing by drawing upon traditional Portuguese forms and tropes, especially the *redondilha maior*, and *saudade*, a characteristic longing for home. These features find ample representation in both Portuguese and Brazilian literature as examples from both countries abound.

Gonçalves Dias's poem famously begins "Minha terra tem palmeiras," and Alfredo Bosi, in *Colony, Cult, Culture*, provides an etymological explanation for the metonymic relationship of "terra" with the idea of nation. "The words *culture, cult* and *colonization* all derive from the Latin verb *colo*, whose past participle is *cultus* and whose future participle is *culturus*. In the language of Rome, *colo* signified *I live on, I occupy the land*, and by extension, *I work on and cultivate the land*" (27). As expressed in their shared etymological root, traditional cultures arose from the relationship of a people with their land, or "colo," consolidated through "cultus" or religious rites. Colonization, of course, entails the imposition of one people's culture over another along with the occupation of its land. As Bosi reminds us, "colonization is a totalizing process whose dynamic forces can always be found at the level of *colo*: in the occupation of new land, the exploitation of its resources, and the submission of its inhabitants" (*Colony* 31).

The first three words of "Canção do exílio," "Minha terra tem," grounded in the discourses of colonization, exploration, and the acquisition of land and power, configure prominently in the dialectics of Brazil's post-colonial identity. In fact, "terra" is the most frequently repeated noun in all 500 interrelated texts under analysis in this book. Appearing 1245 times in 407 of the 500 texts, "terra" is three times more frequent than the second most frequent noun, "sabiá." A pivotal component of the most common three-word phrase in the 500 texts, "terra" typically appears after the word "minha" (repeated a comparable 1205 times) and before the verb "tem" (1486 times). These three words forming the opening line of "Canção do exílio" are part of a centuries-old dialectic of identity politics. The phrase's syntactical structure, placing the emphasis on "land," evokes subsequent descriptions of what it possesses or "has" and establishes the role of all nouns in the original as signifiers for what the land or, by extension, the nation is.

The absence of adjectives in "Canção do exílio," an attribute first noted by Aurélio Buarque de Holanda, further emphasizes the role of nouns as the primary descriptive variables (33). While Brazil holds more "estrelas," more "flores," and more "amores," the poem's nouns describe the general nature of the Brazilian land, not from an Indianist perspective (as one might expect in the period), a voice entirely absent from the poem, but from a colonial one through the differentiation of Brazil by degrees from Portugal. Portugal simply does not possess the same quantities of beauty and charm as Brazil and, reproducing the imperial logic of colonialism, more—whether it be land and power or, in this case, flowers and loves—is always better. Portugal is therefore rendered inferior. José Guilherme Merquior, in his essay "O poema do lá," in dialogue with Holanda, writes: "O Brasil, na 'Canção do exílio', não é *isso* nem *aquilo*; o Brasil é sempre *mais*" (qtd. in Castro Rocha, *O exílio* 130). João Cezar de Castro Rocha, expanding on Merquior's analysis, points out the patent circularity of the logic of nationalism inherent in "Canção do exílio" where Brazil is articulated as "more" only because it is the poet's homeland: "Trata-se somente da operação mental do poeta que compara os elementos comuns à pátria e aos demais lugares, julgando-os superiores sempre que podem encontrá-los 'lá', isto é, em sua terra, pois ele se encontra temporariamente desterrado" (*O exílio* 129).

Not surprisingly, in Portuguese literature, the concept of nation is also so connected to the word "terra" that one sees a similar pattern in *Os lusíadas*, despite it being an epic about the sea. In Camões's long-form poem, "terra" is one of the two most frequently repeated nouns alongside "gente," the former appearing 271 and the latter 281 times (in the singular or plural). In third place is the noun "mar" with 214 appearances. Of course, at the heart of the Portuguese prowess over the seas was the search for new routes to distant lands where the peoples were to be controlled and colonized. The word "terra," not by chance, is also one of the three most frequent nouns in Brazil's foundational

"Adeus Coimbra inimiga": Precedents and Contexts

document, the letter written in April 1500 by the accountant and Cabral's scribe, Pero Vaz de Caminha (discussed in greater detail in Chapter 3). In Caminha's letter, "terra" appears 46 times. The other two most frequent nouns are "todos," appearing 57 times, mostly in reference to the indigenous, and "capitão," appearing 50 times in reference to Cabral. As Bosi observes, "It is not coincidental that whenever the various types of colonization are distinguished, so are two processes: that which attains to the populating of the colony and that which refers to the cultivation of the land" (*Colony* 27). Both *Os lusíadas* and Caminha's letter highlight the intentions of the Portuguese colonizers while portending those of Brazil after independence.

Similar to his Brazilian predecessors and contemporaries, such as Gonçalves de Magalhães, José de Santa Rita Durão, and Manuel Botelho de Oliveira, Gonçalves Dias dreamed throughout his short career of composing Brazil's nationalist epic, a would-be response to Camões's *Os lusíadas*, the definitive Portuguese long-form poem in the tradition of Homer. This was the author's explicit hope for his Indianist poems such as *I-Juca-Pirama*, published in 1851, and *Os timbiras*, published a few years later. The author's contemporary, José de Alencar, in his "Carta ao Dr. Jaguaribe" (published as an appendix to *Iracema*), famously praised him for these efforts. He proposed that Gonçalves Dias had become "o poeta nacional por excelência; ninguém lhe disputa na opulência da imaginação, no fino lavor do verso, no conhecimento da natureza brasileira e dos costumes selvagens" (81). In the words of Darlene Sadlier, Gonçalves Dias's Indianist poems played the role of empowering "a population that over the centuries was seen and described but never heard" (140). Nonetheless, Indianism was ultimately an oversimplified misappropriation of indigenous culture, despite the best intentions of its authors.

Bosi describes Indianism as being motivated by the egoism of nationalism: "Para a primeira geração romântica, porém, presa a esquemas conservadores, a imagem do índio casava-se sem traumas com a glória do colono que se fizera brasileiro, senhor cristão de suas terras e desejoso de antigos brasões" (*História concisa* 106). Due in part to the incompatibility of a would-be nationalist epic founded in the narratives of indigenous peoples who were silenced, enslaved, and slaughtered in order to create that very same nation—much of their culture extinguished by those doing the myth-making—none of these long-form Indianist poems would have the same permanency that Camões's *Os lusíadas* had for Portugal. On the other hand, the diminutive "Canção do exílio," a seemingly inevitable evolution of Caminha's narrative, would be more suitable as an expression of its nation's mythic foundations.

In the fictional imaginary of "Canção do exílio," Brazil is not a nation with a complex pre-colonial history in confrontation with European colonization. It is a paradisiacal land on the verge of re-invention, an unnamed, uncomplicated, and beautiful land. It is a virgin territory ripe for occupation and development, awaiting colonization like a blank page. For this reason, despite his later Indianist attempts, Gonçalves Dias had already invented Brazil's hallmark nationalist text when he wrote "Canção do exílio" and, not coincidentally, from the same locational perspective (Portugal) as those who had named and colonized it. As will be shown, the thousands of subsequent imitations and parodies leave no doubt of the central position of "Canção do exílio" in the articulation of this idealistic national ethos, an ethos defined by an unending Cabralian journey of re-discovery and a perpetual re-staging of his arrival in hopes of one day re-inventing Brazil and ridding it of the ills and egoism stemming from that first encounter. In this vein, commenting on the journey of Mario de Andrade's *Macunaíma*, Castro Rocha observes, "Logo, para ser *bem* brasileiro é necessário nunca encontrar *o* brasileiro ... já que através de operações tais como o modo comparativo aperfeiçoado por Gonçalves Dias, *o incaracterístico se torna estimulante, favorecendo uma constante auto-apresentação*" (*O exílio* 131).

Long before "Canção do exílio" was written, many other Brazilians had already attempted to capture this same ethos. Half a century before the publication of Gonçalves Dias's poem, Santa Rita Durão would compose his own "braziliada," his term for an epic poem about the European discovery of Brazil. Francisco Adolfo de Varnhagen in *Florilégio da poesia brasileira* attributes the following words to the eighteenth-century poet: "Os sucessos do Brasil não mereciam menos um poema que os da Índia. Incitou-me a escrever este o amor da pátria" (343). In consequence, *Caramuru*, the poet's only published work, appeared in 1781, narrating the Brazilian landscape at the moment of Cabral's

"Adeus Coimbra inimiga": Precedents and Contexts

arrival in the Americas. With themes similar to those found in "Canção do exílio," Santa Rita Durão writes: "Da nova região, que atento observa / Admira o clima doce, o campo ameno / E entre arvoredo imenso, a erva fértil / Na viçosa extensão do aúreo terreno" ("Descobrimento" 352). This is just one example of how Santa Rita Durão's poem evokes the leitmotiv of an exceptionally fertile and beautiful land, its inviting climate and docile fields awaiting the inevitable plow of the colonizer. In Santa Rita Durão, the fact that the land is also described as "golden" might likewise bely the capitalistic impetus behind the colonial enterprise, alluding not only to the color of the fields, but veiling what the Portuguese hoped they would find beneath.

In the poetry of Manuel Botelho de Oliveira, at times written with the pseudonym Anônimo Itaparicano, one finds other literary precedents for Gonçalves Dias's glorification of Brazilian flora and fauna. In his "Descrição da ilha de Itaparica," the poet describes the nationalist resolve of his verse: "Cantar procuro, descrever intento / Em um heroico verso e sonoroso / Aquela, que me deu nascimento, / Pátria feliz, que tive por ditoso" (Oliveira, "Descrição" 157). Afterwards, he explains that, had he been born in any other land, he would exalt it with equal zeal. Foreshadowing the same tautological trope found in "Canção do exílio," he offers the following words of advice: "Nunca queiras, leitor, ser delinquente, / Negando a tua pátria verdadeira; / Que assim mostras herdaste venturoso / Ânimo heroico, peito generoso" (157). Later, in the fourth stanza, he explains, "Em o Brasil, província desejada / Pelo metal luzente, que em si cria, / Que antigamente descoberta e achada / Foi de Cabral, que os mares descorria … / Jaz a ilha chamada Itaparica, / A qual no nome tem também ser rica" (158). The poem goes on to describe in detail the natural wonders of the island, including numerous fruits, trees, birds, and other wildlife.

In another of the author's poems, "A ilha da Maré," about an island off the coast of Bahia, Oliveira provides an equally long and exuberant exposé of the beauties of the title's namesake, finishing the poem with a lighthearted slight to the Portuguese: "Tenho explicado as frutas e legumes / Que dão a Portugal muitos ciúmes; / Tenho recopilado / O que o Brazil contém para invejado" ("A ilha" 142). As will be discussed in the next chapter, this assertion of the superiority of Brazil, evident in its literature since colonial times, and an essential element of "Canção do exílio," would be vehemently opposed by the Portuguese immigrants' nineteenth-century responses to Gonçalves Dias.

By the time "Canção do exílio" was composed, Brazil's oedipal impetus to rail against imperial powers despite its continued dependency was already a clearly defined tradition in its literature. The Brazilian-born Gregório de Matos, in the seventeenth century, long before the consolidation of any national identity, demonstrated this tendency while also presaging Gonçalves Dias's dialectic of "cá" / "lá" (Portugal / Brazil). Coming to the end of his university career at Coimbra, Matos, a master of satire, expresses his desire to return home to Brazil. Beginning his poem with the same two-word phrase as does the traditional student song, "Balada dos estudantes," one might imagine that Gonçalves Dias perhaps sang this tune too on occasion alongside his classmates in the "cidade do conhecimento." The musical allusion in the title of Gonçalves Dias's original, articulating his poem as a "canção," along with the shared experience of a Coimbra education, further draws the texts together. Matos's poem begins: "Adeus Coimbra inimiga, / Dos mais honrados madrasta, / Que eu me vou para outra terra / Onde vivo mais à larga" ("Adeus" 20). Another "canção" written by Domingos Caldas Barbosa likewise employs the "cá" / "lá" dialectic, and in a mode much closer to "Canção do exílio." Citing Barbosa's eighteenth-century "Doçura de amor" in which the poet, while abroad in Lisbon, compared a tempered "cá" (Portugal) with a "lá" (Brazil) "mais doce," Castro Rocha places this iconic adverbial play at the heart of Brazil's search for an identity ("A lírica" 363–68). Coincidentally, in 1892, a certain Brazilian author using the initials B.C.S. would publish "Adeus a Coimbra" in which he references "Canção do exílio" while saying his own goodbyes to the storied university town, yet he seems to prefer Coimbra over Brazil: "Vou partir! Adeus Coimbra … / Quanto me custa deixar-te … / Oh! formosa Lusa Athenas / Não deixarei de amar-te … À sombra das palmeiras / Dessas terras de lá … Meu peito te enviará / Ecos de minha paixão / Donde trina o sabiá" (105–06).

Alongside his Romantic contemporaries, Gonçalves Dias also further guaranteed the permanence of the "sabiá" within the lexicon of Brazilian literature. In 1836, a decade before the publication of *Primeiros cantos*, the iconic bird had already made

"Adeus Coimbra inimiga": Precedents and Contexts

appearances in the work of Gonçalves de Magalhães. In his monumental *Suspiros poéticos*, this first-generation Romantic published "O dia 7 de abril em Paris" wherein the songs of the "colibri" and the "sabiá" are explicitly associated with a Eurocentric longing for the Brazilian paradise. For this reason, according to Castro Rocha, "Canção do exílio" can be read as a simplified, if more impactful, re-writing of "O dia 7 de abril em Paris": "o '*mimoso* colibri' ou o 'sabiá *canoro*' transformam-se simplesmente no 'Sabiá'" (*O exílio* 129). As Domingos Gonçalves de Magalhães describes his sadness for being away in France, he writes, "Mas em vão, que nos ares ambruscados / O mimoso colibri não adeja, / Nem longe do seu ninho o canto exhala / O sabiá canoro. [...] Quiçá na ausência da querida Pátria / Pudesse, inda que rouco, / Mais um hino ajuntar aos outros hinos" ("O dia" 327). In the same volume, the "sabiá" makes an appearance in at least four other poems. These are "O vate," "A tempestade," "Por que estou triste?" and a poem dedicated to Dona Joanna Marques Lisboa.

The "sabiá" makes a number of Romantic cameos in Joaquim Norberto de Souza Silva's *Modulações poéticas* from 1841, too, where its song represents the longing for lost loves and lost innocence. In "Uma Tarde em Nighteroy," Souza Silva writes, "Saudoso o sabiá nos ares solta / Gratas modulações, ternas endeixas" (147). Thus, when Gonçalves Dias penned the iconic phrase, "Minha terra tem palmeiras / Onde canta o sabiá," he was simply re-emphasizing an already well-established theme of exile from an Edenic Brazil, abundantly represented in both colonial poetry and the work of his Romantic predecessors and symbolized by the song of the "sabiá." Yet, an aspect much less explored in the criticism is that his exposure to popular Portuguese verse while in Coimbra also played an influential role in the composition of "Canção do exílio."

Despite the somewhat novel appearance of the "sabiá," an American species of bird, Gonçalves Dias's expressions of "saudade" and use of the Portuguese meter "redondilha maior" make "Canção do exílio" almost indistinguishable from much of popular Portuguese poetry of the time. Its style and even certain turns of phrase are, to put it bluntly, cliché, finding abundant representation in the period. In his prologue to *Primeiros cantos*, Gonçalves Dias confesses as much at least in terms of form: "adotei todos os ritmos da metrificação portuguesa, e usei deles como me pareceram quadrar melhor com o que eu pretendia exprimir" (5). In Portugal, at the time, dozens of publications were filled with similar themes of longing. The dislocation of young men to Portugal's urban centers—Porto, Coimbra, or Lisbon—in search of employment or learning, or at times their enlistment in the military and overseas expeditions, among other reasons, were common enough occurrences to serve as the impetus for the expression of a perpetual longing for home in the Portuguese imaginary. Likewise, the bucolic imagery expressed by these Portuguese poets often concentrated on the flora and fauna of a native region or town, further approximating Gonçalves Dias's poem.

In 1842, only one year before "Canção do exílio" was written, Gonçalves Dias's friend and collaborator, the poet A. M. Couto Monteiro wrote a short piece entitled, "Coimbra." This poem contains a refrain repeated numerous times which, unlike Matos's poem, exalts the famed college town: "Louçã, formosa Coimbra, / Linda flor de Portugal, / Belezas que os Céus te deram, / Na terra não tem rival" (52). In these superlative verses, it is impossible to ignore Couto Monteiro's *saudade*, an untranslatable noun that, among other emotions, evokes a bittersweet longing for bygone times, origins, and absent loved ones. This expression of *saudade* was quite common among many other Portuguese poets who, with equal zeal, defended their hometowns with superlatives, as the best, the most beautiful, the greatest, etc. Coincidentally, this short poem also shares a number of descriptive nouns in common with "Canção do exílio," such as "flor," "céus," and "terra." These general terms, all found in the second verse of "Canção do exílio," were extremely common in the anthologies of popular Portuguese poetry of the nineteenth century.

Written in Porto in September of 1843, only a few short months after "Canção do exílio" (but years before its actual publication), Evaristo Basto's "A partida" also displays many similar features in common with "Canção do exílio." Composed in the same "redondilha maior" form, where each line contains seven syllables, the beauties of the Douro region are described in detail for the reader. As Basto reminisces about the joys and innocence of his youth, he laments his necessary departure and longs for a return to the simplicity and natural beauty of home. He also employs the same images and terms as Gonçalves Dias to express these sentiments.

"Adeus Coimbra inimiga": Precedents and Contexts

A partida
Cara estancia onde eu nasci,
Berço meu que me embalaste,
Puro céu que me cobriste,
Doce mãe que me criaste.

Teixo que a sombra me deste,
Em dias de sol ardente,
Verdes prados que eu corria,
Que eu saltava alegremente.
Fontinha que tantas vezes
Me mataste a dura sede,
As brancas pombas que eu tinha,
Que eu caçava em minha rede.
Gorjeio das avesinhas,
Doce harmonia do céu,
O sino da minha terra,
Lindas margens, Douro meu.

Cara estância, prados, rio
Berço, céu, frondoso teixo,
Doce mãe, pombinhas, fonte,
Tudo alfim, saudoso eu deixo!

Beneath a Portuguese "céu," under the shade of the "teixo" tree, and listening to the "gorjeios" of the "avesinhas," the poet immediately evokes for the attuned reader the "palmeiras," "sabiás," and "céu" of Gonçalves Dias's Brazil. If the singing birds are not a direct enough hit with "Canção do exílio," as the poem employs the same terminology ("gorjeios") and, for the birds ("avesinhas"), albeit in the diminutive, then the phrases "minha terra" and "Douro meu" further demonstrate an intertextual affinity between the two poems.

In fact, the theme of longing for home was so common by the time that *O bardo* was published, an anthology of Portuguese poetry printed in Porto in 1851, that the editor, Faustino Xavier de Novais, satirizes the theme in the volume's versified introduction. Considering his publication commonplace, he opens it with these lines: "Eis aí mais um jornal / De versos, à luz do dia! / E ninguém tome isto a mal; / Haja, ao menos, de poesia / Abundância em Portugal" (3). Later in the introduction, the poet conveys some of the most common tropes that readers should expect to find in the volume: "D'afamados escritores / Pilharei *lanças, arnezes, / Estrelas, prados e flores*; / Roubarei até mil vezes / A paciência aos meus leitores" (4). The italics in the original denote these terms' prevalence at the time and, of course, "estrelas," "prados," and "flores" are also key elements of Gonçalves Dias's poem: "Nosso céu tem mais estrelas, / Nossas várzeas têm mais flores, / Nossos bosques têm mais vida, / Nossa vida mais amores" (9–10).

Published in *O bardo* by a certain R. V., "Saudades do Tejo: canção" is an 80-line poem that describes the author's childhood memories along the banks of the Tagus River. As the poet describes how he, as a youth, bathed in its waters and sailed in its currents, the poem repeats the phrase, "Rio da minha saudade!" Then, in the last stanza, he employs another familiar rhetorical device. Specifically, the poet, similar to Gonçalves Dias, fast-forwards to the hypothetical scene of his death in which he would return to the river of his youth: "Tenho Saudades do Tejo, / Não morrerei senão lá; / É de fogo o meu desejo, / Nas águas se apagará!" (R.V. 291). In this scene, a final return to the Tagus becomes the fulfillment of the poet's earthly desire, allowing him to extinguish, or "matar," as the colloquial phrase goes, at long last, his "saudades" of home.

A hallmark of Gonçalves Dias's poem, this hypothetical scene of death is another common trope of the period and, when there is no prospect of return, the thought of death, often appearing in the final lines, becomes a reason for lament. Such was the case in "Recordação da infância," written by Luiz Augusto Xavier de Palmeirim in 1845. Found in the first volume of *Lisia poética*, the poem closes with the following lines: "Morra pois ... distante dela, / Mas não ouça ecos da serra, / Trazer-me na viração, / Saudades da minha terra" (160). The village bell, signaling the return of the writer, whether in the spirit or in the flesh, also configures prominently in João de Lemos's "O sino da minha terra," written in 1843, but published in *O trovador* in 1848: "Se ainda aqui vier morrer, / Chora no meu funeral, / E se for em terra alheia, / Repete o alheio sinal. / Tange, tange, augusto bronze, / Teu som casado comigo, / Inda na morte me agradas, / Inda ali sou teu amigo" (25). As noted by Castro Rocha, Gonçalves de Magalhães's "Adeus à Europa" also shares this similarity with "Canção do exílio" (*O exílio* 132), ending with the verse: "Adeus, ó terras da Europa! / Adeus, França, adeus, Paris! / Volto a ver terras da Pátria, / Vou morrer no meu país" (Gonçalves de Magalhães, "O dia" 368).

"Adeus Coimbra inimiga": Precedents and Contexts

Thus, the last verse of "Canção do exílio" is clearly inspired by contemporaneous texts in both Portugal and Brazil: "Não permita Deus que eu morra / Sem que eu volte para lá; / Sem que desfrute os primores / Que não encontro por cá; / Sem que ainda aviste as palmeiras / Onde canta o sabiá" (Gonçalves Dias, "Cancao" 2).

In the seventeenth century, by way of religious allegory, Matos's "Em quarta feira de cinzas," written with his brother Eusébio, tells the story of a sailor in search of a promised land. Having overcome the perils and temptations of sin and worldliness, represented by the tempests of a perilous sea, the unnamed sailor's arrival to a new land is a metaphor for admittance into celestial paradise: "Se acaso, de mundano mar batido, / Atento o teu baixel chega a tal terra, / Nesta terra há de ser bem recebido; / Que nesta terra todo o bem se encerra" ("Em quarta-feira" 126). In this poem, Matos's sailor seeks God's protection as the ship searches for safe harbor beyond Africa's Cape of Good Hope: "Caminha para a terra sem mudança; / Passa este mar de culpas desastrado; / Chegarás logo ao Cabo da Boa Esperança, / De tantos navegantes desejado" (125). The opening lines of the closing stanza of "Canção do exílio" echo with a similarly religious anxiety. In comparing "Canção do exílio" with this poem, certain re-occurring nouns, especially "terra" and "Deus," are also hard to ignore. Grounded in the Judeo-Christian tradition of the Exodus, both texts are not only bound to the Israelites' comparable search for Zion, but they also harbor the same belief in a God-given entitlement. Specifically, the land, whether Canaan, India, or the Americas, to include its people and its resources, despite to whom it may have belonged prior, now belongs to these newly arrived believers.

In a much more distant antecedent, hearkening back to the Age of Discoveries, Camões's "Sôbolos" locates the protagonist's misfortunes in an allegorical Babylon and his ideal past in a lost Zion (the same Promised Land referenced in Matos). "Sôbolos rios que vão / Por Babylonia, me achei, / Onde sentado chorei / As lembranças de Sião," Camões writes ("Sôbolos" 101). The poem then closes with the following lines: "Ditoso quem se partir / Para ti, terra excelente, / Tão justo e tão penitente, / Que depois de a ti subir, / Lá descanse eternamente!" (117). It makes sense that the word "terra" dominates not only Matos's and Gonçalves Dias's narratives, but also Camões's and Caminha's, as it does in Genesis, considering the thematic of colonization and conquest at play, whether explicit or implied.

Chapter Two

From Camões to Gonçalves Dias, all of these depictions of longing underscore a hope for a felicitous reunion, a dramatic end to a hero's successful journey, as death becomes the gateway to the poet's definitive and final return to paradise, national, religious, or otherwise. Camões's adaptation of the Biblical theme of Jewish exile so foundational to Judeo-Christian cultures courses through centuries of Portuguese literature, making its way into Brazilian literature. Propagated by the Crusades, by sailors' long absences, and symbolized by the frustrated Messianic return of Sebastião, this tradition survives transplanted still today, especially within the intertexts of "Canção do exílio." Thus, when considering its many antecedents, "Canção do exílio" reads as just one text among many. A diminutive response to Camões and other writers from Portugal, it articulates post-colonial attitudes founded in an anxiety of comparison, tapping into centuries-old themes of longing for a paradisiacal home. But, if just one among many in Portugal, once published in Brazil, "Canção do exílio" would take on a life of its own, one probably unimaginable to the young aspiring writer at the time.

Chapter Three

"Onde canta o rouxinol"
Early Portuguese Responses

For the ever-expanding horizons of the Portuguese Empire, descriptive correspondence was an important early colonial enterprise. Narratives written to the king from voyages abroad were composed with an Adamitic zeal, adhering to the logic that naming led to *de facto* dominion over those things named. For example, after describing interactions with the indigenous, their appearance, and behavior, Cabral's scribe, Caminha, writes from the newly christened Terra da Vera Cruz in 1500: "Parece-me gente de tal inocência que … imprimir-se-á facilmente neles qualquer cunho que lhe quiserem dar." Afterwards, he turns his gaze to the land while broaching issues of keen interest to the king, such as the possible existence of gold and the adequacy of the land for colonization: "Esta terra, Senhor, parece-me … muito grande … não podíamos ver senão terra e arvoredos … Nela, até agora, não pudemos saber que haja ouro." Then, like "Canção do exílio," Caminha's letter concludes with a comparison of Portugal with the newly encountered continent: "Contudo a terra em si é de muito bons ares frescos e temperados como os de Entre-Douro-e-Minho, porque neste tempo d'agora assim os achávamos como os de lá." Caminha's favorable assessment as scribe set the stage for the colonization of Brazil.

Three decades later, in 1532, King João III of Portugal wrote to Martim Affonso, a sixteenth-century Portuguese explorer who would eventually rule over the São Paulo region (then known as São Vicente) as its first captain. The king, increasingly interested in the business of Brazil's initial colonization, was anxious to learn more about what he had seen during his voyage. At the time, Affonso found himself in charge of a fleet exploring the coastline. King João III writes to him with a request for more information: "Havendo de estar lá mais tempo, enviareis logo uma caravela com

Chapter Three

recado vosso, e me escrevereis muito largamente tudo o que até então tiverdes passado, e o que na terra achastes" (João III 193). At the end of their journey, a travelogue was produced, written by his brother, Pero Lopes de Souza. The document described their journey from Lisbon to Fernando de Noronha and then down the coast to the River Plate. *Diário da navegação da armada que foi à terra do Brasil*, later published in 1839 by the Brazilian historian Francisco Adolfo de Varnhagem, may not be as graceful or compact as Caminha's letter, but it is with narratives like these two and others from the sixteenth century that "Canção do exílio" finds the moorings of its comparative dialectic and colonial subtext. Once received by the king, these letters from "além-mar" were as good as deeds. Imperial plans could be made, territories divided, peoples subjugated, crops planted, minerals and other commodities extracted, and general instructions for exploration expounded, all in an effort to enrich and expand the empire.

Three hundred years later, in the early nineteenth century, as colonies gained independence across the Americas, the Romantics would turn this mode of descriptive narration on its head, symbolically reclaiming the ownership of newly independent nation-states as they rewrote history from a local perspective, albeit an elite one. Laden with the same imperialist anxiety for possession, poems like "Canção do exílio" still approximate the enthusiasm of the explorers. As Gonçalves Dias assumes Caminha's gaze, he tells us that "lá" in Brazil, everything is wonderful: the birds' songs more beautiful, the fields more abundant, the stars brighter. Yet, the impulse to describe everything "lá" no longer serves colonial interests. Unlike Caminha and Affonso, Gonçalves Dias, as a self-described exile in Portugal, does not write to the king; instead, he implicitly challenges him and what was the Portuguese empire. The land is now "minha," declares the Brazilian, and the gardens, the flowers, the stars, "nossos." Brazil in all its exuberance now belonged to the newly independent Brazilians.

When Gonçalves Dias's *Primeiros cantos* reached Portugal in 1847, making the journey back across the Atlantic, the critics received his first volume of poetry with praise. Famously, the nineteenth-century Portuguese novelist and historian Alexandre Herculano, in "Futuro literário de Portugal e do Brasil," wrote a glowing review: "*Os primeiros cantos* são um belo livro; são

"Onde canta o rouxinol"

inspirações de um grande poeta. A terra de Santa Cruz, que já conta outros no seu seio, pode abençoar mais um ilustre filho" (98). Herculano's reference to Brazil by its original colonial name points to the post-colonial dynamic at the heart of Romantic poetry, opening the way for Herculano to praise all those American poets who glorify their own land and not Europe: "Quiseramos que as *Poesias americanas* ... ocupassem [em *Primeiros cantos*] maior espaço ... Esse Novo Mundo ... é assaz rico para inspirar e nutrir os poetas que crescerem à sombra das suas selvas primitivas" (98). This well-known episode in the young poet's early career undoubtedly provided him with the confidence needed to successfully pursue his chosen vocation. Yet, Herculano's review notwithstanding, *Primeiros cantos* provoked a very different reaction among the growing Portuguese population of immigrants in Rio de Janeiro.

Compelled from Portugal by one crisis or another, including a civil war over regal successions, economic decline, and a failing empire, thousands of young Portuguese, mostly males, were finding their way to Brazil at the time that "Canção do exílio" was published, and for very different reasons than those that had driven Portugal's first explorers. These immigrants came to Brazil out of necessity where they would attempt to make a name for themselves in an emergent petite bourgeoisie. As the most popular destination for immigrants in Brazil, these young men came to the port city of Rio de Janeiro to look for work, often through familial connections, as small-business clerks in the narrow streets of the city's center. Physically filling the shops and, in social terms, the wide gap between the elites and the street-vending slaves, it has been estimated that, in 1846, there were approximately 20,000 to 30,000 Portuguese in Rio de Janeiro, which had a total population of around 200,000 (Nunes 45). Making up at least ten percent of the population, these immigrants inhabited positions of relative privilege and were involved in the cultural happenings and popular events of the city.

Published across the bay in Niterói, the Portuguese immigrants in Rio were some of the first to read and respond to "Canção do exílio." Young males, "cast out" like Gonçalves Dias for one reason or another, certainly sympathized with the poem's youthful longing for home. As we will see, the *saudade* expressed in their own poetry is also for a more innocent age, for home, for family, friends, first loves, and the bucolic villages of their childhood. It is the eventual and inevitable patriotic longing for the "Edens" of youth as these poets, reaching adulthood, unwillingly conformed to the norms and necessities of their time, making the passage across the Atlantic. Yet, as their responses will also show, they vehemently disagreed with Gonçalves Dias on where true paradise could be found.[1] They were not happy with the pitiful shadow of a nameless, almost song-less bird representing their country as they immediately countered Gonçalves Dias's "sabiá" with the European "rouxinol," or nightingale.[1]

In *Utopias, utopias*, Beatriz Berrini compares the role of Gonçalves Dias's "sabiá" with the "rouxinol," providing a summary of the traditional uses of the latter in European literature. Citing the works of Keats, Goethe, and the Greek myth of Philomela, among others, she explains how the song of the nightingale ("rouxinol") and its transnational migratory habits engendered a centuries-old association of the bird with the poetic expression of "saudade" (80–96). The song of the "rouxinol," like Gonçalves Dias's "sabiá," conjures that mystical mix of pain, absence, love, and longing, as it became the symbolic voice of these Portuguese immigrants. When read collectively, the Portuguese responses point to a common desire for a return not only to home, but to a golden age represented throughout the Portuguese Romantic period in narratives and histories about the Reconquista, the Age of Discoveries, and other aspects of Portuguese history and popular culture. But, as a rule, these poets were not so grandiose in design. First and foremost, they sought to reject Gonçalves Dias's proposition that Portugal was somehow inferior.

In 1848, José Ferreira Monteiro published from Rio de Janeiro an anthology entitled *Lisia poética*. Totaling more than 600 pages, the anthology is filled with hundreds of poems, mostly from Portugal, but with many from Portuguese immigrants in Rio. In the introduction, Monteiro describes the contents of the anthology as "uma escolha seleta de todas as poesias que os poetas portugueses modernos têm publicado em vários jornais literários portugueses, que pela sua efêmera não tem chegado ao domínio do público do Rio de Janeiro" ("Introdução iii). Beginning with a discussion of this volume, this chapter explores a handful of early Portuguese responses to "Canção do exílio," then follows the trend from the nineteenth century to more recent times. These texts, while focusing on Portugal, explicitly dialogue with Gonçalves Dias's original as they form the first nodes of an intricate intertextual web.

Far from Portugal, somewhat vulnerable and self-conscious of the poor conditions back home, young Portuguese poets published their writings in Monteiro's anthology to assuage their longing. Of the sixteen Portuguese responses to "Canção do exílio" found among the 500 texts under analysis in this book, the first three are from *Lisia poética*.[2] These three are "A saudade da pátria (imitação)," written by A. J. Ferreira; "Mêz d'Abril em Portugal," written by Lagoa; and "A minha pátria" by Lara e Souza, all from 1847. The other thirteen poems are: "Recordações da pátria," written by an unknown author in 1848; R. Carlos's "Uma resposta" from 1853; "A M.E," published by Antero de Quental in 1861; "À minha terra," from a writer called Alijoense in 1865; "Portugal" by Araújo Pereira Alvim (1873); the song lyrics "Minha terra tem loureiros" from 1875; a similar song from 1876 also called "Minha terra tem loureiros"; the lyrics "Do Tejo-Guanabara," published in a Brazilian newspaper in 1922; "Minha terra" from another newspaper in 1933; "O nôbo sabiá" by Mário Montairo in 1946; Cassiano Ricardo's "Ainda irei a Portugal," from 1947; "Minha terra," written by Armando A. C. Garcia in 1967; and José Paulo Paes's "Lisboa: Aventuras," from 1987.[3]

An early parody of "Canção do exílio" often cited in the criticism is "Recordações da pátria," published on January 5, 1848 in *O correio da tarde*. This poem was identified by Lúcia Miguel Pereira in 1943 in her book *A vida de Gonçalves Dias* (that year was the centennial of the composition of "Canção do exílio"), but it is most certainly not the earliest imitation and the title indicates as much. As printed in *O correio da tarde*, the title reads, "Recordações da pátria—imitação de uma imitação." This admission that the poem is not just an "imitation," but an "imitation of an imitation," not only leads us back to Gonçalves Dias, but also points to an earlier, albeit lesser-known imitation of "Canção do exílio," A. J. Ferreira's poem "A saudade da pátria (imitação)" from 1847. Fittingly, the 1848 poem's dedication, in duly cited quotations, references the commentary from the *Lisia poética* editor's notes to A. J. Ferreira's 1847 poem. The anonymous poet repeats Monteiro's admonition: "Dê-nos mais punhados dessas tulipas, dessas boninas, dessas violetas," etc. ("Recordações" 3).

Chapter Three

Then, the author in compliance with the request, proposes that his poem be considered "mais uma espécie para a coleção de amador" ("Recordações" 3).

As if the dedication were not enough to identify the poem's inspiration, the 1848 "Recordações" also provides a footnote signaled by an asterisk at the end of the twentieth line in reference to A. J. Ferreira's poem which quotes the Gospel of Matthew: "Caesaris Caesari!—Este verso é original da imitação." These lines in question, which read "Minha terra é um paraíso / Onde há benigno Sol" match perfectly with the thirteenth and fourteenth lines from "A saudade da pátria (imitação)." Since many other lines from the poem, including the opening lines, are also lifted from A. J. Ferreira's 1847 imitation, it is not clear why the author feels compelled to make this confession at this particular point in the text.

>Recordações da pátria—
>
>Imitação de uma imitação
>
>Minha terra tem silvados
>Onde canta o rouxinol,
>Onde canta a tutinegra
>E o cuco no pôr do Sol.
>
>Que estrelas que por lá vão!
>Que flores de cor subida!
>Que vida naqueles bosques!
>Que amores naquela vida!
>
>Em cismar sozinho à noite
>Que prazer eu tinha lá!
>Minha terra é um paraíso,
>Que não encontro por cá.
>
>Minha terra tem silvados
>Onde canta o rouxinol,
>Onde o cuco negro e feio
>Descanta no pôr do Sol;
>Minha terra tem silvados
>Onde canta o rouxinol.
>
>Minha terra é um paraíso
>Onde há benigno Sol;
>Minha terra tem belezas,
>Como o ouro do crisol;
>Minha terra produz linho
>Muito bom para lençol.

"Onde canta o rouxinol"

> Permita Deus que ainda veja
> Outra vez aquele Sol!
> E o loureiro e a tutinegra
> E as flores do rouxinol;
> Onde o cuco canta à noite
> De meias com o rouxinol! ("Recordações" 3)

In Lúcia Miguel Pereira's somewhat disparaging critique of the 1848 text, she states that the poem has little literary value: "[E]ssa versalhada ... com uma dedicatória visivelmente destinada a bulir com algum figurão—coisa tão do gosto dos jornais do tempo—só tem o valor de mostrar a repercussão dos versos de Gonçalves Dias" (qtd. in Marques 90). Borrowing directly from Gonçalves Dias's original, there are birds singing in the laurels and brushwoods, beautiful groves filled with flowers and lovers, etc. And, of course, there is the tell-tale closing that articulates the author's hypothetical return to his home in Portugal.

Still, the text is not entirely convincing as a traditional Romantic poem of longing, even though it repeats many of the tropes of the genre. Whether unwittingly or not, the poem also approximates a cultural critique in the vein of O. de Andrade's "Canto de regresso à pátria" (1925). With images of commercial production, symbolized by the linen sheets and the refinement of gold, not to mention the uncharacteristically "ugly" cuckoo, the poem reminds us that nation-making is not a purely Romantic exercise. More importantly, though, in "Recordações da pátria," the traits of a family of Portuguese responses to "Canção do exílio" are affirmed. With "silvados" replacing "loureiros," the poem cites the soon-to-be oft repeated and varied opening lines of A. J. Ferreira's 1847 "A saudade da pátria (imitação)": "Minha terra tem loureiros / Onde canta o rouxinol."

Considering that the existence of an earlier parody is clearly marked in "Recordações da pátria," the reason it has taken critics so long to locate this poem's antecedent must only be that, prior to the creation of the Hemeroteca Digital Brasileira and other digital archives, such as Google Books, the task would have been too daunting and diffuse. However, today, the digital revolution has created an unprecedented opportunity for the critical study of the influence of "Canção do exílio." With the assistance of digital tools, an instantaneous search through millions upon millions of pages for key phrases from "Canção do exílio" (or any other text)

Chapter Three

can be completed with comparable ease. Indeed, most of the texts gathered for this study, including those from the nineteenth century and the early twentieth century, would not have been located without online digital archives. After determining the most repeated phrases from the original in a preliminary study of eighty variations, a search for key phrases, especially "minha terra tem," was carried out in available digitized archives. In this manner, hundreds of unknown variations of "Canção do exílio" were rediscovered, unearthing the textual archeology of its unparalleled popularity.

Written on October 16, 1847 in Rio de Janeiro, less than a year after the publication of "Canção do exílio," "A saudade da pátria (imitação)" makes no qualms about its debt to Gonçalves Dias's original. Its derivative nature is apparent even in the title with Ferreira adding to it the parenthetical qualifier, "imitação."[4] As we know now, variations of "Canção do exílio" would eventually become an unstoppable cultural force, but in 1847 it could not have been so obvious to A. J. Ferreira and others just how popular variations of the poem would be. For this reason, A. J. Ferreira's poem, as the earliest confirmed parody, inhabits a special place among all variations.[5] "A saudade da pátria" was published in *Lisia poética* along with the author's "Recordações de Portugal."[6] In both poems, the theme of longing for Portugal is prominent. Praising A. J. Ferreira for his use of the theme, Monteiro describes him as one possessing "um engenho, e uma propensão tão feliz para a poesia" (*Lisia* 44). He also goes on to request that A. J. Ferreira continue to cultivate his "recordações da terra natal ... para que sobre elas deitemos o orvalho das nossas lágrimas cá pela terra estrangeira" (*Lisia* 44).

> A saudade da pátria (imitação)
>
> Minha terra tem loureiros
> Onde canta o rouxinol,
> Por dias de primavera
> De manhã e ao pôr do sol.
>
> Da minha terra o céu puro
> É mui belo, mui brilhante,
> As flores da minha terra
> Tem um brilho fulgurante.
> Minha terra tem Tulipas;

"Onde canta o rouxinol"

> Tem o lindo Gira-sol;
> Minha terra tem loureiros
> Onde canta o rouxinol.
>
> Minha terra é um paraíso!
> Onde há benigno sol!
> Como o ouro do crizol.
> Minha terra tem loureiros
> Onde canta o rouxinol.
>
> Permita Deus que ainda veja
> Outra vez aquele sol
> Que ainda torne a desfrutar
> O fulgor do Gira-sol
> Que os loureiros inda veja
> Onde canta o rouxinol. (A. J. Ferreira, "A saudade" 43–44)

In form and content, "A saudade da pátria (imitação)" is exactly what one now expects from a classic variation of Gonçalves Dias's poem. As in the majority of the variations to follow, A. J. Ferreira relies heavily on the syntax of the first two lines of "Canção do exílio" as he adapts "Minha terra tem palmeiras / Onde canta o sabiá" to his own frame of reference. Specifically, the binomial pair of Gonçalves Dias's poem, the "palmeiras" and the "sabiá," become the Portuguese "loureiros" and "rouxinol." These two nouns are repeated numerous times throughout A. J. Ferreira's poem within the same syntactical structure as Gonçalves Dias's opening. A. J. Ferreira also uses Gonçalves Dias's first two lines to create other variations so that the bulk of the poem is a further recapitulation of the original's opening, such as "Minha terra tem Tulipas; / Tem o lindo Gira-sol" and "Minha terra é um paraíso! / Onde há benigno sol!" (A. J. Ferreira "A saudade" 43). Another site of strong intertextual activity is in the last stanza employing the line, "Permita Deus que ainda veja" (A. J. Ferreira 43). Here, A. J. Ferreira imitates closely the text of the original while reviewing the previously communicated imagery, emphasizing his desire to return to Portugal.

In order to account for this standard adaptation of the original, so abundant among the variations, this study introduces the notion of *Syntactic Templates*: grammatical structures established in the original from which variations generate related texts. Additionally, the term variation, borrowed from the musical composition method of "variations on a theme," is used to reference any genre of text (and in any length) where borrowing from the original can be found. Among the 500 texts, the most frequently borrowed *syntactic templates* are from the first two lines wherein any noun may be substituted for "palmeiras" or "sabiá," and even at times, "terra," while the rest of the phrase's syntactical structure remains intact. In fact, this type of borrowing takes place even in the original; as a subordinate phrase to the first line, the second line, turning on the adverb "onde," is really only an extension of the first, introducing the noun "sabiá." Likewise, each line of the second stanza as well as the phrase "Minha terra tem primores" is a recapitulation of the first line.

As this study will show, this type of systematic borrowing creates the opportunity for generating lists of token nouns, specifically those that substitute "sabiá" and "palmeiras." These lists form valuable differential readings that morph throughout the generations of texts as perspectives on Brazil and Brazilian identity change in reaction to historical circumstances. In *Foundations of Computational Linguistics*, Roland Hausser writes that a token "explicitly specifies the possible continuations to other *word tokens*, both within its proposition and from its proposition to others" (9). Dependent on Gonçalves Dias's syntax, the determination of what words qualify as tokens is a simple process. For example, when the *syntactic template*, or pattern, of the first two lines of the original text is intact, but in the place of "palmeiras" or "sabiá," the variation introduces new terms, then those latter terms are considered tokens of the original noun types. In order to render a new meaning for the original, variations simply introduce new terms in place of the original ones, based on the appropriate parts of speech. In this way, a basic formula emerges in which one *syntactic template* may be expressed as: "Minha terra tem _____ / Onde canta _____."[7] As mentioned, A. J. Ferreira uses this formula to create the lines, "Minha terra tem loureiros / Onde canta o rouxinol" ("A saudade" 43).

Still, despite its obvious dependency on the original text, what lacks in A. J. Ferreira's poem is perhaps the one element that most galvanized the original in the collective memory of the time. This element is the explicit comparison between Portugal and Brazil, which engendered a competitiveness along former colonial-imperial lines. Through the use of the adverbs "cá" and "lá," Gonçalves Dias categorically states that Brazil is better than Portugal.

Therefore, when A. J. Ferreira and other immigrants respond to "Canção do exílio," stating that they miss the nightingale's song or the rivers and hills from home, the implication is that these features in Brazil are not quite as attractive to them. As discussed in a previous chapter, there are many antecedents in Portuguese poetry that employ these superlative descriptions while inviting comparisons, if not on an international level, at least among the different regions and towns of Portugal. It was within this tradition that "Canção do exílio" emerges transplanted in Brazil and, somewhat ironically, with A. J. Ferreira's response, the first branch of interrelated variations is affirmed, characterized by the "loureiros" and "rouxinol."

Although less textually related, another possible candidate for the first Portuguese response is Lagoa's "Mêz d'Abril em Portugal." This poem was written prior to A. J. Ferreira's, on August 31, 1847, and first published in the *Diário do Rio de Janeiro* on September 7, 1847 (Brazilian Independence Day), a little over one month before A. J. Ferreira's poem was written. The poem appeared again shortly thereafter in *Lisia poética* in 1848. Similar to A. J. Ferreira's poem, "Mêz d'Abril" contains multiple words and phrases in common with the original, especially the repetition of the most repeated three-word phrase found in the original, "Minha terra tem." (The phrase in Lagoa's poem is rendered modified in this manner: "Mêz d'Abril na minha terra tem.") In general, the content of each of Lagoa's stanzas functions as a re-appropriated extension of this potentially borrowed line, listing all the laudable attributes that Portugal claims. The poet repeats the phrase ten times with only slight variation, once in each of the ten stanzas and, apart from the opening line, the third stanza contains other echoes of "Canção do exílio" where Lagoa also introduces the "rouxinol" singing in a tree, among other birds, such as the "tuttinegra" and "rola."

> Mêz d'Abril na minha terra
>
> Tem verdores ... que primor!
> A rocha com seu ardor,
> O salgueiral a falar,
> E sobre um raminho oculto
> O rouxinol a gorgeiar,
> O seu canto a bela, adulto:
> A ovelhinha a saltar;
> E por entre estas belezas
> Que segredos! Que lindezas! (Lagoa 31)

Unlike A. J. Ferreira's text, though, Lagoa's poem is not a true imitation of "Canção do exílio." It lacks the explicit intertextuality and close formal imitation of the original. Nonetheless, among the many images of "Mêz d'Abril," the reader still finds some of the most significant words from "Canção do exílio," such as "Deus," "céus," "amores," and "primores." Additionally, "Mêz d'Abril" communicates the same hypothetical scene of death as Gonçalves Dias's poem, albeit with little textual overlap with the original. In the last stanza, Lagoa desires to fly home to the Douro River, to the mountains, and to his lover named Isbel [sic], and feels that the longing is so painful that he may die: "Mêz d'Abril, na minha terra / Oh Isbel! Ó pátrio Doiro, / Nosso amor ... aquela serra ... / O cabelo que não loiro/ Pobre cantor, voa, corre ... / No desejo, —e ele morre!" (Lagoa 33). Of course, these similarities, instead of pointing only to "Canção do exílio" as a primary source for "Mêz d'Abril," may just as easily point to the milieu of themes and words already associated with saudosistic Portuguese poetry. After being published in *Lisia poética*, "Mêz de Abril" would not have great repercussions, but A. J. Ferreira's "loureiros" and "rouxinol" became a steadfast leitmotiv among Portuguese responses to "Canção do exílio."

With the first clear imitation of A. J. Ferreira's poem being the previously discussed "Recordações da pátria" from 1848, these symbols echo in many other texts throughout the nineteenth century. For example, written in 1847, approximately one month after Ferreira's poem, the indebtedness of Lara e Souza's "A minha pátria" to Gonçalves Dias's original is obvious while the appearance of the "rouxinol" also approximates Ferreira's text. The last stanza reads: "Ah! Permita o meu destino / Que mui cedo torne a ver / Aonde eu brinquei menino, / Nesses campos a perder ... / Aonde eu ao pôr do sol / Escutava o rouxinol" (Lara e Souza 104). A global analysis of the 16 texts included in the group of Portuguese responses shows that Ferreira's opening two-lines are frequently varied and reiterated. Specifically, these lines are repeated verbatim in two popular songs from the 1870s, one from 1875, and another from 1876, both entitled "Minha terra tem loureiros." While the remaining lyrics go on to introduce numerous modifications throughout, the 1875 variation bears the subtitle "Paródia à Canção do exílio," pointing directly to Gonçalves Dias's original while eliding its debt to Ferreira's variation.

"Onde canta o rouxinol"

Regarding this 1875 variation, it was also published unchanged at least two other times (and probably many more), first in *A cantora brazileira* from 1878 and then again in 1893 in *Cancioneiro de músicas populares*. The many *Cancioneiros* published in both Portugal and Brazil throughout the nineteenth century helped promote the original's popularity and its continued variation.

Minha terra tem loureiros: paródia à canção do exílio (1875)

Minha terra tem loureiros
Onde canta o rouxinol,
Canta triste solitário
De manhã e ao pôr do sol.

Quem me dera ouvir de novo,
Nessa terra que eu deixei,
O canto do rouxinol,
Se o seu canto tanto amei!

Minha terra tem campinas
Que tapizam lindas flores,
Trinam lá melhor as aves,
Sabem mais cantar amores.

Quem me dera ouvir de novo
O cantar do rouxinol,
Nessa terra que amo tanto,
Se eu amei tanto o seu sol.

Nem permita Deus que eu morra
Dos anos no arrebol,
Sem que veja o sítio ameno
Em que canta o rouxinol.

Que o prazer que hoje me cerca
É cruel—cruel bem sei.
Quero ver esses loureiros
Que lá na pátria deixei. (60–61)

Minha Terra Tem Loureiros (1876)

Minha terra tem loureiros
Onde canta o rouxinol,
Canto triste o solitário
Que se esconde ao pôr do sol.

Quem me o dera ouvir de novo
Nessa terra que eu deixei!

Chapter Three

> Minha terra tem campinas
> Que tapizam lindas flores,
> Trinam lá melhor as aves,
> Sabem mais cantar amores.
>
> Quem me dera ouvir seu canto,
> Se o seu sol eu sempre amei!
>
> Oh! falsário prazer não me sigas,
> Eu contigo não quero aliança;
> Que ao sepulcro me deve—promete
> Essa ideia da prova—Esperança.
>
> Oh! Quem me dera gozar
> O doce ar que gozei! (71–72)

    Ferreira's first line from "A saudade da pátria (imitação)"—"Minha terra tem loureiros"—is repeated an additional six times among the sixteen poems without any modification to the second line ("Onde canta o rouxinol"), but with the fourth word "loureiros" changed. These six variations occur in three different poems. The earliest of these is "Recordações da pátria" from 1848, wherein "loureiros" is changed to "silvados." In 1873, Araújo Pereira Alvim's poem entitled "Portugal," published in the seventh edition of the periodical *Sexo feminino* (dated October 18), changes A. J. Ferreira's "loureiros" to "colinas" (3). Demonstrating its longevity, Araújo Pereira Alvim's poem is also reproduced as a lyric in 1893 alongside the 1875 variation above in the *Cancioneiro de músicas populares*.

> Portugal
>
> Minha terra tem colinas,
> Onde canta o rouxinol;
> Minha terra é mais amena,
> Mais saudoso o pôr do sol.
> As flores têm mais perfumes
> Nossos frutos mais sabores
> Tem mais mimo a natureza,
> Mais paixão nossos amores.
>
> Mais prazer encontro eu lá
> Em cismar ao pôr do sol;
> Minha terra tem colinas
> Onde canta o rouxinol.

> É mais linda a primavera
> Mais jucundo o nosso estio;
> Mais fértil o nosso outono,
> Mais saudoso o inverno frio:
>
> E assim uma após outra,
> Alternando as estações,
> Há mais viço nas ideias
> Há mais fogo nas paixões.
>
> Não permita Deus que eu morra
> Sem que veja o seu farol,
> Suas tão belas campinas,
> Seu tão doce pôr do sol;
> Sem que pise ainda as colinas
> Onde canta o rouxinol. (179)

The editor of the 1893 *Cancioneiro*, Cesar das Neves, wrote in regards to Araújo Pereira Alvim's variation: "A esta mimosa poesia do celebre poeta brasileiro, respondeu-lhe um português com outra imitativa, não menos repassada de sentimento nostálgico" (179). Then, including a second variation alongside the original, which is identical to the 1875 version above, he concludes enticingly: "Além desta, há muitas outras imitações" (179).

The ethnomusicologist James R. Cowdery, in his article from 1984, "A Fresh Look at the Concept of Tune Family," provides a musical analogy that, when applied to the variations of "Canção do exílio," helps illuminate the process evident in these texts. The concept of tune families is used for organizing folk music into related melodic groups. Cowdery proposes that "certain melodic moves are seen to belong together not as a fixed chain of events, but more as a system of potentialities" (497). He continues, "These motives can recombine in various ways, expanding or contracting, to make new melodies which still conform to the traditional sound" (497). These two lyrical variations above (not coincidentally based on melodies, such as the one prescribed in the 1893 *Cancioneiro*) demonstrate the traits, not of a melodic family, but of a textual one. Adapting Cowdery's theory to the question at hand, the original poem can be understood "not as a fixed chain of events," or words, "but more as a system of potentialities" (497). As the original text functions as a "system," it is modified and "recombine[d] in various ways" (497). Lyrics such as the

Chapter Three

ones from these *Cancioneiros* connote the possibilities for textual variation "as new melodies which still conform to the traditional sound" (497).

In "À minha terra," published in 1865 by an author with the pseudonym Alijoense, A. J. Ferreira's "loureiros" are changed to "salgueiros" while other elements of textual borrowing from both Gonçalves Dias and A. J. Ferreira are also evident, such as a hypothetical return and the singing "sabiá." In general, this poem offers an example of how the phrase "Onde canta o rouxinol" remains unchanged across these sixteen responses, appearing a total of thirteen times while modified versions of it appear a total of eighteen times. Through the use of the template ("Onde canta _____"), birds such as the "cuco negro" and the "melro" in texts like "Uma resposta" and "Recordações de Portugal" appear in place of the "sabiá."

> À minha terra
>
> Minha terra tem salgueiros,
> Onde canta o rouxinol,
> Não há outro como ela
> Debaixo da luz do sol!
>
> Nosso céu de puro anil
> Tem os astros mais brilhantes:
> São mais ternos nossos anjos,
> Nossos amores mais constantes.
>
> Nossos campos no outono
> Tem frutos que aqui não há;
> É mais linda a primavera,
> Que o verão eterno de cá.
>
> Aqui sob o sol ardente
> É sempre a mesma natura;
> Lá os prados sempre belos,
> Variam na formosura.
>
> Nossos ares tem mais pureza,
> É mais brando o nosso sol,
> São lindas as verdes moitas
> Onde canta o rouxinol.
>
> Minha terra tem belezas,
> Belezas que aqui não há;
> Se não tem ricos palmares
> Onde canta o sabiá,

> Tem bosques muito formosos
> Onde cante o rouxinol;
> Não há nada que a exceda
> Debaixo da luz do sol!
>
> Ai! Permita Deus que eu vá
> Meus dias nela acabar;
> Que me não mate a saudade
> Que me faz experimentar:
> Saudade do fundo da alma,
> Daquele lindo torrão,
> Onde o céu, o bosque e o prado,
> Tudo fala ao coração. (Alijoense 2)

Due to its strong semantic relationship with a nation's geography and the process of colonization through a domination of the land, the phrase "Minha terra tem" quickly emerged in the variations of "Canção do exílio" as a significant reference.[8] In fact, already in 1858, this three-word phrase was indicative enough of the original to solicit the need for the anonymous author of "Minha terra tem talentos" to defer to Gonçalves Dias's original in a footnote to his first stanza, even when the rest of the poem bears comparably little resemblance to the original. The poem begins, "Minha terra tem talentos / Que ainda brilham como um sol / Tem um estro mui subido / Que vence o do rouxinol" ("Minha terra tem talentos" 3). The note also references A. J. Ferreira's Portuguese parody from 1847 with these words: "Alusão ao poeta português, que como reclamo, quis responder às melodiosas poesias líricas do sr. Gonçalves Dias" (3). The reference to Ferreira's parody, more than a decade after its publication, further corroborates its lasting impact in the popular poetic imaginary of the period.

As we look more closely at the evolution of Gonçalves Dias's first two lines throughout the whole of the 16 Portuguese responses, some key similarities with the group of 500 texts emerge. In these 16 texts, as in the corpora as a whole, "terra" is the most frequent noun. Appearing a total of 60 times in the group of 16, it is most often appended to the possessive "minha" and to the verb "tem," as in the phrase "minha terra tem." This 3-gram appears a total of 36 times in the 16 texts and the two-gram "minha terra," a statistically weaker link to the original than the three-gram, appears another 17 times. In this way, these

Chapter Three

Portuguese responses attempt to re-appropriate Gonçalves Dias's Romantic assertion of independence by superimposing over the Brazilian poem a Portuguese culture and geography.

There are other nineteenth-century examples of the referential power of Gonçalves Dias's opening phrase. M. A. Pinto de Sampaio's "Minha terra" (not a Portuguese response), published in Maranhão in the *O constitucional* on March 7, 1863, not only gets its title from the phrase in question, it also includes, as many others, the subtitle "Imitação." Pereira de Castro's variation called "Primores da minha terra," published in the *Jaguarary* on December 20, 1860 goes even feven further. This poet feels the need to begin his text with Gonçalves Dias's three-word phrase in quotes as a nod to the original: "'Minha terra tem' florestas, / Tem montanhas, tem colinas; / Cascatas, fontes, regatos, / Ridentes ferteis campinas" (4). Coincidentally, "Minha terra" is by far the most commonly repeated phrase in the titles of the 500 variations. Approximately 1 out of every 8 texts employs it in the title or in the first line when no title is given. Further demonstrating its strength, there is also occasionally some confusion about what the original was called since writers and critics at times name the original not as "Canção do exílio," but as "Minha terra tem palmeiras."

Another useful method of comparing variations to the original is the *Significant Words* category, composed of a list of the most repeated nouns. These nouns outline the general structure of a network, establishing intertextual nodes of contact with the original among the other intertexts. As it turns out, the original poem contains seventeen unique nouns, and the first nine most frequent nouns in the 500 texts come from among these seventeen: "terra," "sabiá," "palmeiras," "deus," "céu," "amores," "vida," "noite," and "flores."[9] For anyone familiar with the poem, the appearance of these most frequent nouns in relative proximity to each other within a single text of comparable size to the original, especially "terra," "palmeiras," and "sabiá," leaves no doubt of its relation to "Canção do exílio," immediately evoking its semantic universe. Specifically, while "terra" represents a broad canvas upon which Gonçalves Dias's utopia is painted, the "palmeiras" and "sabiá" symbolize the specific features of it. Coincidentally, these three most frequent nouns are so important to the symbolism of "Canção do exílio" universe that, in those variations where these three cannot be found in the same felicitous communion as in the original, one often finds a pessimistic vision of Brazil (as discussed in Chapter 5 on the military regime). The other most frequent nouns simply serve as descriptors, reinforcing the utopia evoked by the first three. Tellingly, the tenth most frequent noun among the 500 and the first most frequent noun not found in the original is "Brasil," a word that represents the symbolic sum of all the other most frequent nouns.

From the eight most frequent nouns in the sixteen Portuguese responses, "terra" and "Deus" are the only two nouns that are also found in the list of most frequent nouns among the 500. Serving as common cultural denominators, as mentioned, "terra" appears 60 times in the Portuguese texts. Functioning as a homebase for describing the specific features of Portugal, this noun is constantly modified by the appearance of other nouns and adjectives. On the other hand, the word "Deus" appears only eight times. In all cases evoking a Judeo-Christian God, its presence reminds us of a mainstream religious consonance between Brazil and Portugal established over centuries of colonization. The remaining six most frequent nouns found among the Portuguese responses help us to tease out these texts' differences from the original. Constructing a universe of representative Portuguese symbols, these six words along with their frequencies are: "rouxinol" (24), "sol" (23), "saudade" (9), "pátria" (9), "mês" (9), and "Portugal" (8). These nouns convey the most frequent images and ideas that the Portuguese responses collectively use to describe the singularity of Portugal. In this vein, the inclusion of the word "Portugal" among the most frequent nouns of the Portuguese responses offers an interesting comparison. The word "Brasil" is never mentioned by name in "Canção do exílio," but like "Portugal," it also makes an appearance among the most frequently repeated nouns. Both Portugal and Brazil become, in this sense, entities that, albeit never named in the original, are ever-present in the intertextual universe of variations.

As far as the other most frequent nouns are concerned, in my opinion, "mês," or "mez" (as rendered in the original), can be disregarded for three reasons: it only appears in one of the poems; it adds little to the imagery; and it is often appended by syntax to other frequent words such as "terra" and "Portugal." Likewise, "pátria" adds little novelty to the conversation since, in this case, it is just another way of saying, "Portugal" (or a region

Chapter Three

thereof). Appending "pátria" to "Portugal" and doing away with the anomalous "mês," only three words are left: "rouxinol," "sol," and "saudade." Of these three, "rouxinol" and "saudade" capture the essence of the Portuguese responses, as the first articulates the responses' differences with the original and the second, a similar emotional content. The main role of "sol"—the same sun that shines on every nation—appears almost exclusively as a rhyming companion to "rouxinol," symbolizing the nation as a bright shining beacon to its estranged poets.

In addition to an analysis of the most frequent nouns, the organization of lists of unique terms systematically associated with the verses of the original adjoins the content of the Portuguese variations in non-linear readings, helping to identify other key differences with the original. These lists are composed of the previously described token substitutions for key nouns from the *Syntactic Templates* of the original. Unique nouns from the variations, or *Tokens*, are defined as those words that substitute the most frequently used nouns from the original, called *Types*. In these sixteen responses, the analysis is focused on the tokens associated with "palmeiras." The tokens replacing the term in the sixteen texts are below in alphabetical order. The choice to place the tokens in alphabetical order, as opposed to chronological order (or by some other criterion), encourages a non-linear reading. Without knowledge of when these tokens appear, it is easier to read this list as a single, cohesive unit, describing the Portuguese nation.

Minha terra tem _____.

alegria	carrascos
amendoeiras floridas	castelos
amor	céu puro
árabe	colinas
ardores	dialetos
astros mais brilhantes	escribas
beijo	escura tutinegra
belezas	fadista de raça
belezas mil	flores
bosques	folclore
brilho fulgurante	fontes
cabanas	fragas nuas
campinas	frondosos castanheiros
cantos	frutos

giestas floridas	primor(es)
gira-sol	rios
heróis	rocha
largas ruas	rola
lindas flores	rosas
loureiros	rouxinol
mais pureza	rudes pinhais
mil graças	salgueiral
mil templos do Senhor	salgueiros
minha saudade	santos
mistérios	São João
moitas	silvados
neve	sol
olhares tão ardentes	sopros
ouro do crizol	sorrir de anil
outeiros	toureiros
ovelhinha	tulipas
paixão	vales
palácios	verdores
palmeiras (mais viçosas)	verduras
penedos	vitelos
poetas	zéfiros
praças	zimbros
prantos de um cherubim	

When considering the tokens in this list, it becomes clear that the lexical variety introduced in place of the type "palmeiras" is immense. These tokens represent an attempt to portray a rich and well-established nation, one noticeably different from Brazil, through a litany of Portuguese flora, fauna, geographic features, and human activity. These features are, if not altogether exclusive of, at least specific enough to Portuguese history so that, among the "loureiros," "tulipas," castles, saints, and festivals, a vision of a comparatively distinct nation emerges.

Still, not all sixteen responses employ the use of *syntactic templates*. For example, Carlos's "Uma resposta," published in Rio de Janeiro in the *Periódico dos pobres* in 1853, is a strong response to "Canção do exílio." But, departing somewhat from the still emerging patterns of variation, the author shows less dependency on Gonçalves Dias's original text. To compensate, he is much more direct in his assertions of superiority. Demeaning the Brazilian bird in favor of the "melro" and "rouxinol," the poem begins, "Se aqui vem o negro melro / Não gorjeia como lá; / Pois não gosta das palmeiras / Onde canta o sabiá" (Carlos 5). Then, later in the poem, the author asks directly to Gonçalves Dias, as if he were still in Portugal as a student: "A minha terra é fértil / Sabes por que estás lá / E que em tudo o rouxinol / É superior o sabiá?" (5). Addressing him condescendingly in the informal "tu" form, the poet goes on to ask another direct question: "É tão má a minha terra? / Terra que me viu nascer: / E que tais os habitantes? / Com eles fostes aprender" (5). Then, after having already assured the reader that, "de nada vale o sabiá," he apparently does not feel the need to reject outright the Brazilian "palmeiras" (5). The estranged poet simply proposes that Portuguese palms are better: "Na minha terra tem palmeiras / Mais viçosas do que cá" (5). With his eurocentric worldview, he also asserts that Brazil does not share the same glorious history as Portugal. Whether citing some popular Portuguese myth or simply referring to the whole of the "Old World," the author informs us, "Nessa terra abençoada / Andou Cristo a passear" (5). He closes with a racially charged backhanded compliment, referencing the myth of the sensual "mulata" as the one thing Portugal lacks. After centuries of miscegenation and slavery, the symbol of the "mulata" was already pervasive by this time in Brazilian history. Carlos closes, "Mas lá" in Portugal "não tem mulatinhas / Para meigas te entreter" (5).

Others from the nineteenth century would dialogue with "Canção do exílio" in less offensive and more original ways, including the Azorean poet Quental (for another comparison of this text with Gonçalves Dias's original, see also Berrini, 137–45.) In his poem "A M.E.," written in 1861, evidence of intertextuality, including a re-working of the phrase "Minha terra tem," is undeniable while the text's distinctive take on exile rings clear. Being Portuguese, but from the Azorean archipelago, Quental sympathized with Gonçalves Dias's marginalized perspective. But, different from Gonçalves Dias, Quental's short poem communicates the "primores" to be found in Portugal, not in the Azores. Quental, also a student in Coimbra, writes: "Terra do Exílio! Aqui também as flores / Têm perfume e matiz; também vicejam" (221). He closes with the following messsage: "Eu sou bem como a flor que não descerra / Em clima alheio. Que importam teus encantos? / Não és, terra do exílio, a minha terra" (222). Unwilling to demean the beauties of continental Portugal in favor of his island home, Quental downplayed his origins in an act of deference to the continent. Yet, in the end, the mainland is not his, he tells us, and its beauties do not belong to him, as he indirectly expresses his love for the Azores.

Here, it may be worthwhile to mention another poem with a similar sense of colonial deference. The African José Maia Ferreira's "A minha terra," written on a visit to Rio in 1849 (and published in the very first volume of Angolan poetry), opens with a stanza that, although in the negative, is reminiscent of the Portuguese responses: "Minha terra não tem os cristais / Dessas fontes do só Portugal, / Minha terra não tem salgueiraes, / Só tem ondas de branco areal" (12). J. M. Ferreira's "A minha terra" ironically defines his country not by what it is, but by what it is not (having spent most of his life outside of Africa, this negative declaration is reflective of his personal experience). However, despite his seemingly poor opinion of Angola, his loyalties are made clear near the end of the poem: "Mesmo assim rude, sem primores de arte, / Nem da natura os mimos e belezas, / Que em campos mil a mil vicejam sempre, / É minha pátria! / Minha pátria por quem sinto saudades / Saudades tantas que o peito ralam" (17). Bound to a sense of parochial inferiority, J. M. Ferreira's lengthy poem descants the glories of Portugal (and even Brazil) with almost no mention of his own nation, exposing the complexities of peripheral colonial identities.

When comparing J. M. Ferreira's and Quental's poems with those of Gonçalves Dias, the absence in "Canção do exílio" of any deterministic colonial pessimism becomes important. Different from the Azores and Angola, beginning early in the nineteenth century, Brazil had already experienced the concession of special status of Empire and shortly thereafter continued to independence. In this way, these two other texts, especially J. M. Ferreira's, should not be read as treatises of poorly endowed national geographies that were not worth celebrating, but rather geographic analogies of meagerly articulated political identities vis-à-vis the imperial seat, Portugal. Angola and the Azores, the former a European imposition and the latter uninhabited prior to colonization, would not find their way to independence and autonomy until the last quarter of the twentieth century.

By the end of the nineteenth century, with the exile of Dom Pedro II and the dissolution of the Brazilian Empire, "Canção do exílio" slowly faded from the collective Portuguese memory and responses to the Brazilian poem become fewer and farther between. For this reason, there are only six poems from the twentieth century that can be classified as Portuguese responses. These six poems were published between 1922 and 1987 and, although some common themes do emerge, they are not nearly as related to each other as those from the nineteenth century. The strongest theme to emerge in these is a reformulation of the colonial relationship that deconstructs the hierarchy in favor of difference. Thus, if the nineteenth-century responses were characterized by competition, the poems of the twentieth century propose a truce, extending the proverbial hand of friendship.

As bookends of the subgroup in question, reconciliation is the basis for the anonymous dialogue in "Do Tejo-Guanabara," published in 1922, and of "Lisboa: Aventuras" from 1987. First, the 1922 text is organized as a singing dialogue between two protagonists appropriately named Tejo and Guanabara. In the lyrics, these two geographically bound characters develop a dialogue with the hope of communicating the message that, "Se a distância nos separa / Grande afeito nos enlaça" ("Do Tejo" 2). At the end of the poem, Guanabara quotes Gonçalves Dias's first two lines to which Tejo replies, "Também nossas cantadeiras / Cantam pois como as de lá" (2). In this way, the poem undoes Gonçalves Dias's proposition, stating that the birds in both places actually sing the same. Interestingly, this poem was published at a time when immigration from Europe, to include thousands from Portugal, had once again changed the demographics of Rio de Janeiro and, more especially, São Paulo (Fausto 155–56).

    Do Tejo-Guanabara
Tejo: Belo jardim de Europa
         A beira-mar Plantado
Guanab: A tua gente galopa
         Em um correr alado
Tejo: Pairando em pleno azul
         Buscando o que sonhara
Guanab: Na América do Sul
         Do Tejo à Guanabara
Tejo: Minha bela Guanabara
         Vens trazer-me a tua graça
Guanab: Se a distância nos separa
         Grande afeito nos enlaça
Tejo: Nossos laços de amizade
         Não se desatam jamais

"Onde canta o rouxinol"

Guanab: Também cantam brasileiros
　　　　Do nascer ao pôr do sol
　　　　Minha terra tem palmeiras
　　　　Onde canta o sabiá
Tejo:　　Também nossas cantadeiras
　　　　Cantam pois como as de lá ("Do Tejo" 2)

Similarly, in the diminutive "Lisboa: Aventuras," author José Paulo Paes takes the reader on a short journey through the streets of Lisbon to learn some of the subtle colloquial differences between European and Brazilian Portuguese. During the amusing journey, the poet compares terms, such as "cafézinho" to "bica," the latter a term used for an espresso coffee in Lisbon, and "ó cara" with "ó pá," each country's equivalent to the American "hey, man!" (6). While exhibiting these terms and others, he makes no judgment as to which one is better nor does he hint to which he prefers. Then, he finishes the poem with a reference to "Canção do exílio": "positivamente / as aves que aqui gorjeiam não gorjeiam como lá" (6). This light-hearted ending *prima-facie* appears to convey the opposite message of "Do Tejo-Guanabara," proposing the birds' songs actually differ. But, in reality, the poem sends a similar message to that of the 1922 text. Unlike Gonçalves Dias's original, in Paes's text, the fact that the birds' songs are different does not imply that one is better than the other, only that they should be appreciated equally.

Among the remaining four twentieth-century poems are two traditional responses, Júlio de Castro's "Minha terra" from 1933 and Garcia's poem with the same name from 1967. Both of these rely heavily on the syntax of the first line of the original to delineate a litany of Portuguese flora and fauna. As seen in our list of tokens for "palmeiras," from Castro's poem, one learns that Portugal has "São João" and "santos," including "Pedro, António," and "Luís." And, for the first time, there is mention of "árabe / Na sua origem." In Garcia's poem, Portugal has "giestas floridas," "rudes pinhais," "frondosos castanheiros," "outeiros e castelos," "poetas, toureiros e escribas," "heróis," "santos," and "vitelos." In completing the idea of "Minha terra tem," the second stanza of Garcia's text reads: "Tem o folclore em trajes de cores garridas. / Tem os cantares e a alegria das vindimas. / Os dialetos e as desgarradas em rimas / E, o rubor das moçoilas

51

Chapter Three

atrevidas!" (Garcia). The images continue in this fashion to be unsurprisingly stereotypical of traditional Portuguese culture.

In contrast, Cassiano Ricardo's "Ainda irei a Portugal" from 1947 is not a typical variation by any means. The poem is a self-portrait of a Brazilian man with a Portuguese grandfather who discusses the "saudade" he feels for his grandfather's homeland. But, ironically, Portugal is a place he has never been. The poem opens with these lines: "Nunca fui a Portugal. / Não por falta de querer, / nem por perder meu lugar / que este bem guardado está" (49). In order to justify his seemingly misplaced "saudade," the poet then hypothesizes that in another life he must have been a Portuguese sailor: "Fui marujo, com certeza, / pois tenho alma azul-marinha. / Vim pro Brasil tão futuro / que nunca soube que vinha" (50). In his imagined voyages, Ricardo searches for his roots. While traveling far afield from his grandfather's home, these journeys retrace an Age-of-Discoveries trajectory to which Portuguese identity is so bound, making possible his "future" Brazilian identity while also explaining by proxy his longing for Portugal. He describes his search for roots as a "backwards hope," pointing us to the need for a symbolic return: "Saudade assim por herança / de coisas que não conheço, / chega a ser, quase, esperança ... / Esperança pelo avesso." (51). By the end, the poet has taken us on a strange voyage, rounding the contours of continents in search of his own identity, which he collocates with the Portuguese. Then, affirming the inseparability of Brazil from its colonial roots, the poet ventures far back to the first Portuguese voyage to the "Terra da Vera Cruz," to the foundational narrative of the Brazilian nation: "Condição estranha, a minha. / Sinto que sou quase autor / da carta de Vaz Caminha" (52). In the very next stanza, he alludes to "Canção do exílio": "Esta a saudade que fere / mais do que as outras quiçá. / Sem exílio, nem palmeira / onde cante um sabiá ..." (52).

From a post-colonial perspective, it is no wonder that the Portuguese were the first to respond to Gonçalves Dias's "Canção do exílio." After all, it was the Portuguese through travelogues and other official correspondence who centuries earlier had created the foundations of the Edenic myth on which "Canção do exílio" was based. In the words of Caminha, upon arriving in the New World, "a inocência desta gente é tal, que a de Adão não seria maior." But, in the nineteenth century, finding themselves in a precarious situation, the poem's first respondents, these Portuguese immigrants in Rio de Janeiro, felt threatened and offended by Gonçalves Dias's unflattering comparisons. The emergence of this newly independent Brazilian voice came at the right time in history to fan the flames of Portuguese discontent, especially among a local population, even though their presence in Brazil was only further evidence of Portugal's decline. These young poets, compelled from their native villages along the Douro, Minho, and Tejo, who had gone to the "big city" in a continental way, in order to defend their pride and patrimony, countered Gonçalves Dias's poem with their own nationalistic utopias. Additionally, these responses established many of the traits for future variations, borrowing heavily from the syntax and verbiage of Gonçalves Dias's original. But, as the decades passed, direct Portuguese responses all but faded from existence and, in the few responses that continued, authors attempted to downplay previous assertions of superiority in favor of mutual respect.

Chapter Four

"Onde canta o periquito"
The First Republic to the Vargas Era (1889–1945)

From 1889 to 1945, Brazil passed through multiple regime changes, transitioning first from a nineteenth-century empire (1822–89) to a democratic state, known as the First Republic (1889–1930), and then to two authoritarian regimes, both under Getúlio Vargas (1930-1937; 1937-1945). In hindsight, the rise of authoritarianism in Brazil, a country already accustomed to imperial rule, seems almost inevitable. Vargas, a retired colonel and the Governor of Rio Grande do Sul, after failing to win the presidential elections of 1930, seized power with the support of a coalition of state-run militias. Re-asserting his rule in 1937, he stayed in control of the country continuously until 1945. Under the premise of a possible communist takeover, Vargas preempted the open elections planned for 1938, proclaiming Brazil's Estado Novo in 1937, and the period between 1937 and 1945 is not just considered authoritarian, but dictatorial. Eventually, Vargas allowed for open elections, which saw the victory of former General Eurico Gaspar Dutra. Then, in 1950, Vargas regained power, this time elected democratically, only to commit suicide in 1954.

Authoritarianism was not unique to Brazil at the time. In fact, dictatorships were quite common throughout Latin America in the mid-twentieth century, a predictable regional response to a complex set of internal and external factors. Namely, in Brazil, there was the propensity for strong-arm military intervention in domestic affairs, a precedent set by the coup that ousted Dom Pedro II in 1889. But, even after the military handed over power to Prudente de Morais in 1894, Brazil's first elected civilian president, the nation failed to establish a strong democracy due to the prevailing interests of oligarchs, their influence in rigged elections, and the large economic disparities among the regions (Skidmore 102–16). Then came the Great War, the Great Depression, and

Chapter Four

the perceived failure of Western capitalism, along with the rise of alternative ideologies, especially communism, to further erode an already weak democratic state (Skidmore 102–16).

The political turmoil notwithstanding, modern-day Brazil, in terms of culture, identity, and demography, has its roots in this important post-imperial era. Accompanied by the mass adoption of the radio and intense migration to Rio de Janeiro and São Paulo, especially from the Northeast and abroad, one of the key questions facing Brazilian intellectuals at the time was the articulation of a national identity that could take into account Brazil's diversity. Unlike in years past, intellectuals in the early twentieth century sought to celebrate the nation's cultural milieu as a strength. Most famously formalized in the 20s and 30s by the anthropologist Gilberto Freyre and the Modernist poet Oswald de Andrade through their theories of luso-tropicalism and cultural anthropophagy respectively, the dominant idea was that Brazil was a stronger nation because of, and not despite, syncretism and miscegenation.[1] During the 30s and 40s, this trend in identity politics would be normalized by Vargas through official state-sponsored cultural programs "designed to," not only homogenize the culture, but to "help soften the dictatorship's image of repression and censorship" (Skidmore 119).

The texts under consideration in this chapter shed further light on this crucial time in national history as they adapt Gonçalves Dias's poem to a variety of contexts and forms. Played on the radio as popular song and published in periodicals across the country, the poem's intertexts from the period evince a vibrant dialogue through which Brazilians become ever more mindful of their role in constructing an identity as a single nation. Gonçalves Dias's poem is evoked to exalt the nation in sambas during Carnaval. It is used to promote consumerist culture through newspaper advertisements and for suggesting potential plays for the popular "jogo do bicho," a gambling game begun in Rio which quickly spread across the country, while the trend of parodying the original as political satire also continued in earnest. Commentators of the burgeoning soccer culture, a national pastime with origins in the period, borrowed too from the poem to tell news of victories and defeats, especially for São Paulo's Palmeiras team. "Canção do exílio" even found itself translated into other languages (Esperanto, Tupi, et al), and parodied in "caipira" and the satirical pseudo-Italian "português macarrônico." The Modernists, following O. de Andrade's lead, also articulated a number of canonical responses, guaranteeing the poem's continued presence in literature throughout the twentieth century.

Among the variations from the 1889–1945 period, there is possibly no better example with which to begin than the national anthem. With lyrics written by the poet Joaquim Osório Duque Estrada in 1909, and music composed almost a century earlier in the 1820s by Francisco Manoel da Silva, the national anthem was officially adopted by the Brazilian government in 1922 on the eve of the centennial of independence (Decreto No. 15.671). One of only four national symbols ratified by federal law (Lei No. 5.700), including the flag, the presidential seal, and the Brazilian coat of arms, the anthem begins by narrating the "Grito do Ipiranga," the speech-act that symbolically separated Brazil from Portugal on September 7, 1822. Along the banks of the Ipiranga River, Dom Pedro I of Brazil (born Dom Pedro IV of Portugal), son of Portuguese Emperor Dom João VI, surrounded by high-ranking state officials, ushered in a new era for his country, defiantly declaring, "Independência ou morte!" In the national anthem, Duque Estrada paints the scene: "Ouviram do Ipiranga as margens plácidas, / De um povo heróico o brado retumbante, / E o sol da Liberdade, em raios fúlgidos, / Brilhou no céu da Pátria nesse instante." Praising the nation and all things in it, the anthem goes on to describe Brazil's incomparable natural beauty, its brave people, and its destiny to be counted among the greatest nations of the world: "Gigante pela própria natureza, / És belo, és forte, impávido colosso, / E o teu futuro espelha essa grandeza / Terra adorada, / Entre outras mil, / És tu, Brasil, / Ó Pátria amada."

The anthem also reiterates the central position of "Canção do exílio" within the national imaginary, seamlessly dovetailing its lines into the second stanza of the second verse: "Do que a terra, mais garrida, / Teus risonhos, lindos campos têm mais flores; / 'Nossos bosques têm mais vida' / 'Nossa vida' no teu seio 'mais amores.'"[2] Borrowing from the only verse in "Canção do exílio" that employs the first person, plural possessive ("nossos bosques," "nossa vida"), these lines remind Brazilians not only of the beauty of their land, but also of their collective responsibility for it. In contrast to the original, however, Duque Estrada goes beyond the "cá" / "lá" binary, claiming that Brazil is not only more beautiful than Portugal, but the most beautiful of all nations: "Do que a terra, mais garrida / Teus risonhos, lindos campos têm mais flores." The anthem also personifies the nation throughout, using possessive adjectives based on the informal "tu": "*Teus* risonhos, lindos campos," "no *teu* seio" (emphasis added). In this way, Gonçalves Dias's individual lament is transformed into a communal experience, turning the eyes of Brazilians of all backgrounds toward the nation which calls them to the singular task of bringing about its grand prefigured destiny.

The inclusion of these lines from "Canção do exílio" in the national anthem further entrenched Gonçalves Dias's already immensely popular poem in the culture, and at a time when that same culture was becoming more homogenous. Today, it is law that children ages 6–14 sing the anthem in unison once a week in school (Lei No. 12.301). But, in the 30s and 40s, not many years after Duque Estrada's lyrics had become official, there was already an educational program that had children singing its lyrics in unison by the thousands along with other patriotic and folkloric tunes (Ferraz 164). Appointed as Getúlio Vargas's director of music education, the modernist composer Heitor Villa-Lobos developed and implemented a nationwide program that gathered well-rehearsed schoolchildren in "concentrações orfeônicas" to sing the praises of their nation to the public (Ferraz 164). According to Villa-Lobos, these events served an important role in the education of young Brazilians during the populist and hyper-nationalist Vargas regime (1930–45): "Entoando as canções e os hinos comemorativos da Pátria ... a infância brasileira vai se *impregnando* aos poucos desse espírito de brasilidade que no futuro deverá marcar todas as suas ações e todos os seus pensamentos" (qtd. in Ferraz 177). Through the success of this program and others during the Vargas period related to the "Reforma Campos" and the subsequent "Reforma Capanema," Brazil's educational program became highly standardized across its expansive regions, reinforcing uniformity in the national culture (Ferraz 167). In the words of Gabriel Ferraz, "Vargas fomentou, por meio de uma política nacionalista e populista, que promovia 'brasilidade' e os sentidos de dever cívico e disciplina, a ideia de uma sociedade homogênea, onde todos eram importantes para a edificação da nação" (163).

Among other Vargas initiatives to unify the culture was an effort to promote samba and Carnaval. By 1930, when Vargas took power, the popular Brazilian musical genre and pre-Lenten festival already stood center stage in Rio's cultural scene. Today, the Carnaval industry employs thousands year-round in response to the demands of the "foliões," or party-goers, and many other Brazilian capitals, such as São Paulo and Salvador da Bahia, also host millions of tourists and locals alike during the celebration. But, the Vargas regime "was the first federal government to promote samba schools and the Rio parades," seeking to fortify "the nation's new sense of its identity as at least partly Afro-Brazilian" (Skidmore 119).

Regarding samba, the official genre of Carnaval, decades before assuming the role of director of musical education under Vargas, Heitor Villa-Lobos was already interested in its rise as a purely Brazilian art form. In the 1910s, in contrast to the elites of previous generations, such as Rui Barbosa, who had disparaged its popular rhythms, modernists like Villa-Lobos, Mario de Andrade, O. de Andrade, and Raul Bopp were witnesses to samba's evolution as it made its way from the shantytowns to the main thoroughfares of Rio (Fernandes 40). These modernists and others focused on rearticulating a Brazilian identity for the twentieth century obsessed less with the nation's lack of European-ness, or whiteness, recognizing the important role that samba, with African, indigenous, and European roots, could play in a hybrid American nation in search of its post-slavery, post-colonial identity.

One location in Rio particularly important to the popularization of samba was the home of Hilaria de Almeida, or Tia Ciata, "a gathering point for the musical talent that had migrated from Northern Brazil. At [her] parties, there was dancing in the sitting room, samba at the back of the house, and batuque in the yard" (Gilman 69). One of the many collaborations to result from these gatherings was "Pelo telefone," which "tells a story of stolen love and a telephone conversation with the chief of police" (Gilman 70). This song, widely regarded as Brazil's first recorded "samba," was registered in 1916 by Donga, who was a mainstay at Tia Ciata's parties along with Sinhô, João da Baiana, and Pixinguinha, and was a huge hit at Rio's Carnaval the following year in 1917 (Gilman 70). Although "Pelo telefone" contains no traces of "Canção do exílio," it serves as a key point of historical reference in Rio de Janeiro's early twentieth-century music scene. Samba, through recordings and radio, would go on to deeply influence national culture.

In those early years of samba, a musical variation of Gonçalves Dias's poem also made its debut at Rio's Carnaval. Published in the *Correio da manhã* on January 30, 1910, an article describing the groups to be seen at that year's festival, their floats, costumes, and songs, includes the playful lyrics of "As sete palmeiras." The lyrics were an ode to the purported mystical powers of its colorful author Múcio Teixeira, poet-diplomat turned prophet, who would spend his time fortune telling and miracle working beneath the shade of "the seven palms" of the Mangue canal: "'Minha terra tem palmeiras, / Onde canta o sabiá,' / Algumas são verdadeiras / Mas, outras, quá ... quá ... quá ... quá ... / Por isso eu só quero as sete / Do Mangue, ó lá lá, lá lá ... / Muita gente há que promete, / Mas não dá, não dá, não dá, não dá ..." ("As sete" 8). In an article from 2017, Paulo Henrique Pergher writes that the prolific Teixeira, largely forgotten by literary critics today, using the pseudonym Barão Ergonte, eventually "transformed himself into ... a prophet, hierophant ... mainly active between 1911 and 1915" when he predicted numerous "national calamities ... in editions of his almanac, the *Almanaque do Barão Ergonte*, which he sold alongside other texts and poems" (Pergher par. 10).[3] A divisive figure in Rio's popular culture, the newspapers from the time boast several references to the author for good and bad.[4]

In 1937, "Canção do exílio" appears again at Carnaval through a popular samba refrain heard echoing in the streets of Rio. In his article, "Minha terra tem palmeiras," published in *A noite* on January 7, 1937, the young poet Raimundo Magalhães Júnior provides the lyrics, but first he describes the general delirium of Rio during the festival. According to him, even though there were those who disapproved of the excesses of Carnaval, resistance was futile: "O carnaval tem a força das avalanches e das inundações. É inútil tentar opor-lhe obstáculos, em artigos sentenciosos ou discursos cheios de virtude. Ele esmaga tudo, sobrepõe-se a tudo" (1). Not taking a personal position on the moral propriety of Carnaval ("não sou nem contra, nem a favor"), Magalhães Júnior still opines of the music presented during the festival. Complaining tongue-in-cheek that some "sambistas" should be jailed for their unoriginality, he calls their music "plagiary," "falsely Brazilian," and repetitive. He then ends the article by including the refrain of a variation of "Canção do exílio," which he describes in contrast as "uma coisa notável, genial mesmo ... entre todo

"Onda canta o periquito" (1889–1945)

o imenso acervo de músicas carnavalescas" (1). Considering that Magalhães Júnior was a poet, it is easy to understand his infatuation with the catchy refrain: "Minha terra tem palmeiras, / Onde canta o sabiá, / Oi, terra boa, / P'ra se farrear" (1). Showing his excitement for this lyric, he closes the article with instructions on how to sing it: "Cantem-na assim, com música de samba ... e não haverá brasileiro que se aguente lá por fora." He then suggests that this verse represents the first time that Gonçalves Dias had "touched" Brazil's "popular soul," seemingly unaware of the poem's already long tradition of responses (1). Possibly more important is the fact that Magalhães Júnior does not recognize in this quatrain João de Barro's lyrics recorded the previous year.

Carmen Miranda, the Brazilian singer and actress who would become famous for donning the tutti-frutti hat in Hollywood productions, was an active participant in the festival in 1937, being elected as Rainha do Carnaval Inter-clubs ("Um quinteto"). Singing João de Barro's lyrics, her song "Minha terra tem palmeiras" was also popular that year. Between the choral refrains of "Oh, que terra boa para se farrear!" (slightly misquoted by Magalhães Júnior), Miranda sings variations of Gonçalves Dias's first two lines: "Minha terra tem lourinhas, moreninhas 'chocolat,'" "Minha terra tem Bahia, tem Ioiô e tem Iaiá," "Minha terra tem pitanga, cajá, manga e cambucá" (Miranda). Praising the nation's ethnic and biological diversity, the mention of "lourinhas" is a reference to the "blondies" of Southern Brazil; the "moreninhas 'chocolat,'" a reference to the chocolate-brown skin of the sexualized mulata, most readily associated with Rio; and "Ioiô" and "Iaiá," colloquial terms for "senhor" and "senhora," or "sir" and "ma'am," not only point to the deferent dialect of the Northeast, but also to the nation's African roots (and legacy of slavery). Then, referring to a variety of fruits found in Brazil, the song like the national anthem and "Canção do exílio" represents the greatness of the nation's people by its flora, where the exuberance of life in Brazil's forests is only matched by the Brazilians' love of life.

By the mid-1930s, a general sense of the purpose of Carnaval and samba, one that continues today in themes of samba school parades, was understood to be the exaltation of national culture. In fact, around the same time as the recording of Carmen Miranda's "Minha terra tem palmeiras," Ari Barroso composed his famous "Aquarela do Brasil," considered the official beginning

Chapter Four

of the "samba exaltação" subgenre. As the name implies, this type of samba places the nation above all else and its nationalist focus not only brought "samba exaltação" closer to "Canção do exílio," but also conveniently matched with Vargas's efforts to build "a new model of national identity ... in which distinct cultural elements were selected from the already-existing regional models and recombined to form an official national culture" (Gilman 71). In the words of Lisa Shaw, "samba-exaltação," "characterized by its patriotic lyrics which extolled the virtues of Brazil and its people, to a large extent endorse[d] the Vargas regime's construction of populist mythology" (163).

Another variation from the period which hints at an additional role for Carnaval in Brazilian culture is a poem entitled "Divagando," written by the "Bloco dos Acadêmicos Poetas," described as "Um grupo de acadêmicos [que] não se canta e só se recita" ("Divagando"). Their humorous poem, published in the *Jornal das moças* for the 1917 Carnaval, opens with a complaint of economic woes, comparing the nation's troubles to those of Senegal (possibly only because the latter rhymes loosely with "sabiá"): "Eu sei que a minha terra tem palmeiras / Onde canta o famoso sabiá, / E sei também, que aqui fazem-se asneiras / Que nem no Senegal ninguém fará" ("Divagando"). Then, instead of proposing a solution to the nation's ills, this group of poets, led by "Marquez Humorista," recommends that the "foliões" should simply forget their troubles and have fun at Carnaval: "Se nós só vemos grandes quebradeiras, / Desde os pampas do sul ao Grã-Pará ... Deixemos todos, os males endenicos [sic] / E divirtamo-nos no Carnaval!" ("Divagando"). The group's position on Carnaval as a time to forget troubles aligns perfectly with the celebration's popular mythology. In a society exacerbated by economic disparity and inequality, the festival has historically offered a short reprieve from troubles of all types, whether personal or societal, and the overarching myth of Carnaval is that for three days, from Sunday until dawn on Ash Wednesday, all Brazilians are empowered equally to be happy and to partake of the festivities regardless of race, gender, or social class.

In the words of Robert Moser, in his Bakhtinian analysis of the figure of the dead in Brazilian literature, "During carnival, the social order is turned momentarily on its head, a reversal symbolized by the ritual decrowning of the king and the subsequent crowning of the pauper. It is, in short, the ritual trading of social places" (136). This same Carnaval myth can be found in works of literature from the period, such as João do Rio's short story "O bebê de tarlatana rosa" or Marques Rebelo's "Uma senhora." Dona Quinota, the protagonist of Rebelo's story, after penny pinching all year long just to enjoy a few days of Carnaval, explains, "A vida era aquilo mesmo: três dias—falava. Mas pensava: por ano" (102). In the denouement of João do Rio's story, as the dawn of Ash Wednesday shines into the alleyways of downtown Rio, the affair between a masked "bebê" of humble origins and the upper-class Heitor ends tragically when he forcefully removes the girl's mask, exposing a horrendous physical defect, "uma cabeça sem nariz, com dois buracos sangrentos" (32). In response, the "bebê" exclaims, "Não me batas. A culpa não é minha! Só no Carnaval é que eu posso gozar. Então, aproveito, ouviste? Foste tu que quiseste" (Rio 32). Afterwards, Heitor returns to his comfortable life and parlor friends to recount his elitist cautionary tale while the "bebê," her mask undone and Carnaval over, fades into the common masses of Rio.

The music of carnaval was not the only place where "Canção do exílio" would find a foothold during the period in question. Among the 74 texts from the period (1889–1945) a multitude of themes and genres abound. Broken down by decade, there are 6 from the 1890s, 15 from the 1900s, 8 from the 1910s, 12 from the 1920s, 24 from the 1930s, and 9 published between 1940 and 1945, this final year seeing not only the end of Vargas's Estado Novo, but also the end of World War II. On average these 74 texts demonstrate a textual similarity of 35% to the original, which is also the running average among the entire body of 500 (this calculation is based on a *String Similarity Test*, a computational operation discussed in greater detail in Chapter 6) and the most similar text was written by an author from Recife using the clever pseudonym K. Mões. His 1904 parody "Minha terra" (discussed below) was calculated at 67% similarity to the original.

In terms of narrative modes, of the 74 texts, thirty are classified in the positive, 28 in the negative, and 16 as other. As will be shown, the simultaneous reliance on the text of the original and the refutation of its central message are at the heart of the negative mode and negative variations have appeared in almost every decade since the 1840s. Critical of Brazil, negative texts play an

Chapter Four

important role in the intertextual universe of "Canção do exílio." Promoting an open dialogue about the country's problems, they counter Gonçalves Dias's mythical construction with a dose of reality while tracing the contours of the ideas, ideologies, controversies, and practices that have defined the nation over the decades since the original's publication. All variations in the negative mode fall under the category of parody, described by Linda Hutcheon as "a double process of installing and ironizing" which "signals how present representations come from past ones and what ideological consequences derive from both continuity and difference" (93).

By way of definition, a variation in the negative mode parodies the original text while maintaining the principal referent, Brazil. Employing Gonçalves Dias's poem against itself, texts in the negative mode emphasize that Brazil is not the utopia described in "Canção do exílio." Importantly, however, not all parodies are in the negative mode. There are parodies among the 500 that qualify as being in the positive mode; for example, A.J. Ferreira's 1847 Portuguese response discussed in the previous chapter. Specifically, this response reverses what was originally "there" (Brazil) and "here" (Portugal) so that the Brazilian paradise is transplanted to Portugal. The main purpose of a text in the positive mode, as parody or pastiche, is to convey the same romantic ideal as found in the original, whether for Brazil or some other nation. On the other hand, the purpose of the negative mode is not to replace Gonçalves Dias's paradise with another, but to empty it and refill it with varying degrees of pessimism. Like the original, texts in the negative mode are about Brazil, but not the same Brazil found in "Canção do exílio." This other Brazil is a nation instilled with attributes textually mutated from the original so that only shades of Gonçalves Dias's paradise remain.

K. Môes's parody from 1904, "Minha terra," while more textually similar than any other text from the period, is a classic example of the negative mode. Dedicating his variation to the citizens of Rio and Recife, K. Môes writes: "Minha terra não tem nada, / Nem cantos nem sabiá … / Eu nunca vi tanto lixo / Como se encontra por cá. / Nossas praças têm estrelas, / Nossos becos belas flores, / Nossas ruas têm mais gatos / E cães podres que doutores!" In 1907, from Maceió, the capital of Alagoas, another author writes on issues of personal hygiene and municipal sanitation, attesting to the wide attention that the topics received in

"Onda canta o periquito" (1889–1945)

Brazil at the time: "Minha terra tem palmeiras / Onde nascem caranguejo / Minha cama tem colchãos [sic] / Onde mato persevejos" (Fute). Many Brazilian capitals, most famously Rio de Janeiro, suffered from similar public health problems and carried out sanitation and remodeling initiatives that would provoke their own variations. Teresa Meade writes that, in the first decade of the 1900s, "a far-reaching and innovative government sanitation, public health and urban renewal program ... was the cornerstone of the Brazilian urban elite's plan to transform Rio de Janeiro" (302). This initiative was an effort "to create a Rio compatible with the needs of merchants, planters, and British traders, at the expense of the city's laboring poor" (302).

Alcino del Sino in "Charada antiga," also published in 1904, writes about the extensive and seemingly unending renovations of downtown Rio: "Minha terra tem palmas, / Nem palmeiras há por lá ... Minha terra tem apenas / Obras do porto, mais nada / Por outra, tem uma rua / Larga mas não preparada." In November 1904, the same year that del Sino's variation was published, Rio's working class revolted upon learning that smallpox vaccinations would be made mandatory. Thousands marched in the streets and ransacked businesses. One week later, "the capital lay in shambles" (Meade 301). As Meade argues, these citizens had grown tired of the systematic marginalization they suffered for the elite's economic progress (302). By the time Avenida Rio Branco was complete, the locals who had once inhabited the downtown area would be relocated to the hills of the periphery, populating the city's nascent favelas, the realities of which, by the end of the twentieth century, would earn their own branch of negative variations discussed in Chapters 6 and 7.

Although negative responses were prominent in the 1900s, looking back even earlier, the first text to position "Canção do exílio" against itself is "Minha terra natal," a text about Bahia published in 1853. Approximating Sérgio Buarque de Holanda's treatise on "ociosidade" and "cordialidade," propounded decades later, this poem considers the dysfunction of Bahia and those responsible.[5] The nobles, the church officials, the government and its deputies, and even the stereotyped women with their gossip as well as the shopkeepers with their greed are spared no quarter in the poet's eyes for the sad state of Bahian affairs. According to the text, because of neglect and egoism, the nation is unable

Chapter Four

to develop adequately. This idea is one of the most prevalent recurring themes in the negative variations, if not in all Brazilian history. Similar to many other variations, "Minha terra natal" can easily be read as a prolonged extension of Gonçalves Dias's first line: "Minha terra sendo rica / Tanto deu, que ficou pobre; / Tem terrenos sem cultura / E tem muita gente nobre. / Tem bachareis, como areia, / Uns letrados, e outros não" ("Minha terra natal" 2). The poem continues: "Tem Governos, que não tratam / De nos tirar da ruína. / [...] Minha terra tem empresas, / Infieis aos seus contratos [...] Minha terra tem uns padres, / Que se chamam formigões, / E mal o Bispo os ordena, / Vão meter-se em eleições; [...] Minha terra tem seu berço / Muito ao pé da sepultura; / De todas as profecias / Esta é a mais segura" (2).

Another poem to let us know that all is not "palmeiras" and "sabiás" in nineteenth-century Bahia is João Nepomuceno da Silva's "Belezas de minha terra." The poem appears in Belém do Pará's *Gazeta oficial* on April 21, 1860. Written for Dom Pedro II on the occasion of his official visit to Salvador, the text spends most of its time praising Bahia in typical fashion, but the reader is told from the beginning that some problems will be exposed as well: "Se narro, senhor defeitos, / Que a minha província tem, / Em seus primores me cumpre / Elogiá-la também" (J. Silva 3). At the end of the poem, he makes his appeal to the emperor with Gonçalves Dias's "lá" pointing an accusatory finger at the administration: "Minha terra não floresce, / E num paradeiro está, / É porque a proteção / Falta das gentes de lá" (4). The footnote to this last line reads: "Refiro-me às más administrações, que tem tido esta infeliz província, pelo que ela jaz abatida" (4).

The words of S. B. de Holanda contextualize these variations with broad strokes as he contemplates the nature of Portuguese colonization: "Essa exploração dos trópicos não se processou, em verdade, por um empreendimento metódico e racional, não emanou de uma vontade construtora e enérgica: fez-se antes com desleixo e certo abandono. Dir-se-ia mesmo que se fez apesar de seus autores" (*Raízes* 43). Although a far cry from the defiant desperation of negative texts from later generations, especially from the dictatorship period (1964–85), these two poems about Bahia, the first published only seven years after the original, contain the beginnings of the negative mode, explicitly countering the original with a pessimistic evaluation of a nation with a history of haphazard and uneven development.[6]

"Onda canta o periquito" (1889–1945)

In 1862, an author by the name of Muribeca published, supposedly from St. Petersburg, Russia, a variation about Fortaleza entitled, "Gente dos cajuais alerta!!!: Canção popular." After opening with the lines, "Minha terra tem um foro, / Onde gira um cajuá / Animal tão bruto assim / Não tem aqui como lá" (3), his poem, complaining of a corrupt judge in the Northeastern capital, also follows closely the wording of Gonçalves Dias's second stanza to convey the message: "Nosso país é mui quente / Nossa praça faz calor; / Nosso foro todo clama / Contra um juíz oppressor [sic]" (3). Similar poems complain of a general ineptitude among the ruling class in Fortaleza during the final decades of the nineteenth century. Scevalo wrote his "Canção do exílio" in 1873 which directly insults a certain Nogueira family: "Minha terra tem Nogueiras / Onde canta o Manquitó / Tem caninanas (sem rabo) / Das bandas do Cabrobó. / Nosso céu está nublado / Nossas várzeas ressequidas / Por causa dos persevejos / As carnaúbas … roídas" (3). One year later, in 1874, criticisms of the wealthy nobility continue in Recife with João Francisco's "Canção do exílio," which contains the line: "Minha terra tem fidalgos / Que mal sabem o B-a Bá" (5). Published in Bahia's *Binóculo: Jornal satírico, chistoso e literário* in 1877, Pimpolho's "Lá vai obra" riffs negatively on Casimiro de Abreu's "Minha terra" (an 1856 response to Gonçalves Dias's original): "Todos pintam a sua terra, / Também vou pintar a minha" (2). Afterwards, the author calls a certain unnamed viscount a thief and womanizer: "Das Marinhas da cidade / É o Visconde o primeiro; / Quem quiser apreciá-lo / Venha à terra do dinheiro. / Esse ladrão, esse ínfame, / Que faz tudo quanto quer, / Não respeita a virgindade / Da mais incauta mulher" (2). He then closes with a warning to all nobles who abuse their power: "Mosquitas, Condes, Viscondes, / Barões, Mureiras também, / Todos eles reunidos / Em forcas acabar vêm" (2). The century then ends with Lúcio's "O Bezouro." Published in 1892 in Rio, already after the abolishment of the Empire, the playful poem directed at the governor of the state of Alagoas, Gabino Suzano de Araújo Besouro, repeats the phrase "Minha terra tem coqueiros / Onde canta o bezourinho" various times (Lúcio 8). In the fourth stanza, Lúcio offers his opinion of the governor: "É Bezouro e é Suzano / Pequenino, zunidor, / É jeitoso para tudo / Menos para Governador" (8).

These nineteenth-century parodies, complaining of bad faith governance and other imperial abuses, remind us of the general

Chapter Four

resistance to the Empire that played out in the Northeast through numerous nineteenth-century revolts. And even though the reign of Dom Pedro II, a generally beloved figure, brought positives to Brazil, especially in terms of intellectual institutions, political discontent grew as the century progressed, eventually leading the nation's elite to oust the emperor and tentatively embrace an American-style democracy. The Republican Party, established in Brazil in 1871, expressed this sentiment in their manifesto: "National sovereignty can only exist, can only be recognized and practiced in a nation whose parliament has the supreme direction and pronounces the final word in public business ... We are from America and we want to be Americans" (qtd. in Skidmore 72).[7] Two decades later, on November 15, 1889, a group of military officers led by Deodoro Fonseca would exile the Emperor Dom Pedro II and establish Brazil's First Republic, originally called The United States of Brazil. Five years later, in 1894, the military delivered the government to Prudente de Morais, Brazil's first democratically elected president.

During the First Republic, a major shift in demographics from rural to urban took hold while at the same time the economy, especially in the Southeast, moved toward greater industrialization. Industrial development had been generally stymied during the nineteenth century by the continuation of colonial policies favoring agricultural exports in exchange for manufactured goods, especially from Great Britain. But in the First Republic, greater economic liberalization and positive legislation quickly incentivized national industry (Hanley 253–58). "It was innovation in corporate law after the fall of the Empire and the declaration of the Republic (1889) that opened up capital markets to industrialists and allowed Brazil's hallmark large-scale industrialization to develop" (252). Coincidentally, this was the beginning of a century of intense demographic change and economic development that, in a few short decades, would transform Brazil's population from majority rural to majority urban (Théry 6). Prompted not only by the abolition of slavery in 1888, but also by unemployment and cyclical droughts, migrants, or "retiradas," from the agricultural Northeast began moving to the Southeast in search of new beginnings while immigrants from Asia, Europe, and the Middle East also flocked to São Paulo and Rio by the thousands.

A survey of the newspapers and periodicals of the period attest to how "Canção do exílio" accompanied this transition as

"Onda canta o periquito" (1889–1945)

variations of its simple and highly imitable phrases expand into a variety of new contexts, industrial and otherwise, reflecting the societal changes afoot. Indeed, in the early twentieth century, "Canção do exílio" makes its way into the day-to-day life of Brazilians, touching on subjects of popular culture and mass consumption. By the early 1900s "Canção do exílio" was recognizable by most readers and, in a pre-radio and pre-television culture where print still served as the primary outlet for disseminating information, the poem was easily adaptable. We find instances of its use in advertising, in the "jogo do bicho," in "futebol," didactic translations in Tupi, and even performances in Esperanto.

In terms of advertising, usage of "Canção do exílio" does not expand much beyond the period in question, or even constitute a robust trend during it, but the examples found are still noteworthy, showing evidence of a growing consumerist culture and of a new focus on national products. An advertisement published in the Estado de São Paulo on May 13, 1923, entitled "O 13 de maio atual!" in reference to the 25th anniversary of the abolition of slavery, suggests that no Brazilian is truly free until accompanied by a glass of "Guaraná Espumante." Complementing the text is a cartoon showing two Afro-Brazilian men dressed in suits, sitting at a table, smoking cigarettes, both sweating profusely and in obvious need of refreshment. Soliciting their order from the white waiter, the ad reads: "O freguês ao garçom: / 'Venha, venha o Guaraná!' / Porque a velhíssima história / Da liberdade, por cá, / É uma burla ilusória, / Desque não regada / Com esse refrigerante ... Nossa terra tem palmeiras / Onde canta o sabiá, / Mas só fulge entre as primeiras / Porque tem—o 'Guraná'! [sic]" ("O 13" 8). Calling "guaraná" the "national drink," the advertisement's accompanying testimonials from three doctors all confirm its goodness and its viability as an alternative to alcohol. To wit, the testimony of Dr. A. de Paula Santos claims: "Não tenho dúvidas em declarar que o 'Guaraná Espumante' de par com seu sabor agradável, apresenta a vantagem de substituir bebidas alcoólicas, sempre prejudiciais à saúde" (8).

There are at least two other cases of the use of "Canção do exílio" in advertising during the period. The Casa Muniz, a variety store located in the bustling Rua do Ouvidor in Rio, published the following rhyme in the *Correio da manhã* on May 4, 1919. Between advertisements for bank services and a perfume shop, we read: "Minha terra tem mangueiras / Onde cantam bem-te-vis / A primeira entre as primeiras / —A antiga CASA MUNIZ" ("Casa" 2). More than a decade earlier, in Pernambuco, a candle shop embarked on an ad campaign, publishing dozens of quatrains, some with literary references, to sell its product. With advertisements scattered throughout various issues of the *Província*, one from January 29, 1904 reads: "Minha terra tem palmeira / Onde canta o sabiá, / Mas coisa melhor tem lá, / Que é a VELA BRASILEIRA!" ("Vela" 1). In all of these advertisements, "Canção do exílio," the most Brazilian of poems, was not only meant to convince readers that they should consume the products advertised, but that doing so also made them better Brazilians, a clear sign of the developing twentieth-century relationship between consumerism and modern nationalism.

"Canção do exílio" can also be found a few times in reference to the "jogo do bicho," or the animal game, a popular lottery that "began as a legal raffle intended to fund Rio de Janeiro's privately-owned zoo, but soon slipped irretrievably from state control" (Chazkel 536). "At the beginning of Brazil's First Republic (1889–1930), the clandestine lottery ... gained enormous popularity in Rio de Janeiro, the city of its origin, and soon in the whole of Brazil" (535). Machado de Assis's short story "Jogo do bicho" (1904), which follows the "carioca" protagonist Camilo's manic experience with the game, explains how to play: "O jogador escolhe um número, que convencionalmente representa um bicho, e se tal número acerta de ser o final da sorte grande, todos os que arriscaram nele os seus vinténs ganham, e todos os que fiaram dos outros perdem" ("Jogo" par. 13). The same story mentions that contributors to local periodicals would offer suggestions, or "palpites," for the day's winning animals. Camilo "[n]ão queria ir pelos palpites dos jornais, como faziam alguns amigos" ("Jogo" par. 15). It is in this context that the following two variations were both published in the satirical weekly *O malho*. The first from October 14, 1916 suggested that the best plays for the eighteenth of that month were the monkey and the butterfly: "'Minha terra tem palmeiras, / Onde canta o sabiá,' / Tem Borboletas faceiras / Tem Macacos d'alto lá!" ("Bis-charada"). Years later, Dr. Zootechnico suggested the ostrich and the rabbit as plays for the twenty-fifth of May in the May 19, 1923 edition: "Minha terra tem palmeiras / Onde canta o meu conselho, / Um Avestruz de perneiras / E um ligeiríssimo Coelho."

"Onda canta o periquito" (1889–1945)

"Canção do exílio" adaptations also follow the early rise of Brazil's most popular sport, "futebol." Soccer was introduced in Brazil in 1894 by Charles Miller, son of a Scottish father and Brazilian mother, who famously returned to São Paulo from his studies in England with "two soccer balls, two uniforms, one book of rules, one pair of cleats, one air pump and one needle" (Murad 118). The first Brazilian soccer league was established in that city in 1901 and the second in Rio in 1905. During this early period, which lasted until about 1920, participation by blacks, mulattoes, and poor whites was extremely limited (120). But, due to the immense popularity of the sport, the working classes began to put together teams and eventually win the leagues. Vasco da Gama, "champions in the second division in 1922," won Rio's first division in 1923, by "recruit[ing] the best players from the working-class suburbs, whether they were white, black, or mulatto" (J. S. L. Lopes 247). In São Paulo, "Palestra Itália," later known as Palmeiras, "and Corinthians Paulista, both of which had more popular origins than the elite clubs that had created the football league, were admitted to the first division of the city's league after some of the elite clubs had left" (253).

In the 1940s, a time when the sport had already gained universal popularity in Brazil, especially with the help of Vargas's cultural policies, the fortuitous coincidence of the Palmeiras name with the poem began to inspire variations. Published in the sports section of Curitiba's *O dia* on May 11, 1941, this quip from Di Pino is found among others on the subject of soccer: "Minha terra tem Palmeira, / onde canta o sabiá, / No Palastra tem Palmeira / mais quem canta é ... 'periquito.'" The "Palastra," or Estádio Palestra Itália, is the name of the stadium where Palmeiras played until the 2000s and the "parakeet" that sings there in place of Gonçalves Dias's "sabiá" is the mascot for the team. A similar rhyme appears when Palmeiras defeated the famed Italian club Juventus in the Copa Rio in 1951. In a short text entitled, "Fim de festa," published in São Paulo's *O governador* on August 2, 1951, a certain Castro Barbosa[8] shows his national pride, providing this response regarding the "vitória brasileira": "Minha terra tem PALMEIRAS / onde cantam os PERIQUITOS" ("Fim" 12). On March 4, 1943, in the *Jornal dos sports*, an author going by the pseudonym Keeper published "Off-side poemas." This text includes the prediction of another Palmeiras victory by a player nicknamed "Fish": "'Peixe,'

71

Chapter Four

do Palmeiras, declarou / Estar 'certo de poder cantar vitória …' / E eis aí, meus amigos, meus leitores, / Como o Diabo tece o fio de uma história … / Amanhã um paulista escreverá / Este poema, e que ninguém se queixe: / 'Minha terra tem Palmeiras, / Onde canta o Peixe …"(Keeper).

After the Vargas era, the variations continue with texts such as "O que o locutor não disse," published on May 19, 1955 in the *Jornal das moças*, in reference to Palmeiras' dominance over Rio's Flamengo: "Minha terra tem palmeira / Onde canta o sabiá / Em S. Paulo tem o 'Palmeira' / Que faz o Flamengo 'pará'" ("O que" 70). A satire published in *O governador* on August 30, 1951 and written in the "caipira" dialect associated with rural São Paulo's less educated agricultural population begins by also making reference to the famed club: "Minha terra tem Parmêra / Onde canta o periquito" (Taquara 10). The text goes on to complain of politics among other troubles: "E tem muita ladroêra / E na Assembréia tem conflito" (Taquara 10). However, the first time the parakeet is associated with the poem is not in relation to soccer, but in a "caipira" variation preceding the creation of the Palmeiras Club by a few years.

Published in Curitiba's *O olho da rua* on June 8, 1907, and signed by Dominguinho Trancoso, the first two stanzas of "Cartas de um caipira" read: "Minha terra tem Parmera / Nas Quar canta o periquito / Cuando vejo Moças feia / Sempre tenho faniquito. / Noço séu tem mais Estrela / Noças Mata mais Pavão / Não hai nada neste mundo / Como um prato de Fejão." The figure of the "caipira" in Brazilian culture is a longstanding trope associated with rural backwardness, bad manners, ignorance, and an inability or unwillingness to change. Most famously represented in the early twentieth century as the character Jeca Tatu in the works of the pre-Modernist Monteiro Lobato, and later in the films of Mazzaropi, in opposition to the state and its institutions, the anti-heroic "caipira" serves as a dialectical counterpoint to the discourses of national progress and modernization. In the words of Eva P. Bueno, commenting on Jeca as he is portrayed in the works of Mazzaropi, "even though he is ugly, awkward and speaks a most undistinguished version of Brazilian Portuguese, [he] weaves his way through Brazilian history, Brazilian problems, Brazilian religion, and especially Brazilian popular culture" (56).

"Canção do exílio" variations appear not only in "caipira," but in other languages and dialects too during the period. There are didactic translations in Tupi, performances in Esperanto, and even a variation in Juó Bananère's pseudo-Italian "português macarrônico." An article on the Tupi language, published on February 1, 1930 in the *Jornal do Recife*, proposes the following translation, interspersing the indigenous language with the original: "Minha terra tem palameiras / 'Ce retama orecô pindóctá' / Onde canta o sabiá / 'Mámé çabiá onheen' / As aves que aqui gorgeiam / 'Guirá onheengare iké uaá' / Não gorjeiam como lá / 'Inti aetá onheen aépe ianê' (Sampaio 2). The newspapers of the time also mention numerous performances of the song "Minha terra tem palmeiras" in Esperanto: in the *Gazeta de notícias* on September 19, 1910, in the *Gutenberg* on August 14, 1910, and again in *O imparcial* on June 1, 1926. Both Tupi and Esperanto were popular linguistic subjects of the time, the former due to a renewed interest in folk and indigenous culture and the latter as a novel language invented by Ludwig Lazarus Zamenhof with hopes to one day unite the world.[9]

In the 1910s, "Canção do exílio" was parodied in another "invented" language commonly referred to as "português macarrônico," a pseudo-Italian dialect used in the satire of Alexandre Marcondes Machado and O. de Andrade. These authors' creation of this dialect was intended to humorously chronicle the politics, culture, and daily life of São Paulo through the eyes of the many first-generation Italian immigrants of the city who, while still learning the nuances of the nation's language, culture, and history, were transforming its social landscape. According to Vera Maria Chalmers, the Italian-Portuguese dialect first appeared in *O pirralho* in 1911 with O. de Andrade's "As cartas d'abax'o pigues," published under the pseudonym Annibale Scipione (33). In 1912, when O. de Andrade left for Europe, Marcondes Machado, using the pseudonym Juó Bananère, took over the dialect from O. de Andrade, publishing numerous texts in the *O rigalegio* section of *O pirralho* and creating an entire lexicon to accompany the pseudonym's personality (Chalmers 33). Bananère's parody of "Canção do exílio," entitled "Migna terra," appeared in *O rigalegio* on May 3, 1913. This poem, jokingly called a "sunetto do Camonhes" (soneto do Camões), supplements a satirical recounting of the "discovery" of Brazil by "Pietro Caporale" ("Pedro Cabral") called "A invençó do Brasile" ("A invenção do Brasil"):

Chapter Four

> Migna Terra
>
> Migna terra tê parmeras,
> Che ganta inzima o sabiá;
> As aveses che stó aqui,
> Tambê tudos sabi gorgeá.
>
> A abobora celestia tambê,
> Che stá lá na mia terra,
> Tê muitos maise strella
> Che o céu da Ingraterra.
>
> Os rios lá sô maise grande,
> Dos rio di tudas naçó;
> I os matto si perdi di vista
> Nu meio da imensidó.
>
> Na migna terra tê parmeras
> Dove ganta a gallinha d'angolla;
> Na minha terra tê o Vap'relli,
> Chi só anda di gartolla. (Bananère)

Conflating numerous currents and historical timeframes to include modern-day São Paulo with Portugal's Age of Discoveries, Bananère's article, and accompanying poem capture the festive and chaotic optimism of a catachrestic São Paulo.

Fifteen years later, in 1925, O. de Andrade would follow the lead of Bananère by writing his own variation, a Modernist ode to the city entitled "Canto de regresso à pátria." This variation would eventually become one of the most recognizable parodies of Gonçalves Dias's original. In 1973, commenting on Caetano Veloso and the Tropicália movement, the poet Affonso Romano Sant'anna considers the role of O. de Andrade's parody: "A paródia retoma a linguagem comum de maneira assimétrica e invertida denunciando aí a ideologia subjacente" (2). In "Canto de regresso à pátria," O. de Andrade reworks the original, questioning the monolithic imperial designs hidden in its subtext. It begins in this manner: "Minha terra tem palmares / Onde gorjeia o mar / Os passarinhos daqui / Não cantam como os de lá" (144). As often is the case, O. de Andrade's first line of the poem is borrowed verbatim from the original, but with an important token modification: the fourth word is changed from "palmeiras" to "palmares," a different although similar sounding noun. This subtle substitution constitutes a postcolonial critique, alluding to an early historical conflict between the colonial army and a community of freed and runaway slaves in northeastern Brazil called Palmares. In the second stanza, the poem further exposes the economic motivations and geopolitics of positioning behind the "invention" of Brazil. As a counter-reading to Gonçalves Dias's paradisiacal paradigm, O. de Andrade reminds us of the materialistic underpinnings of Caminha's letter to the king. The possible existence of gold in Brazil was, as previously mentioned, one of the first issues considered in Caminha's letter. In O. de Andrade's parody, Brazil does not have more life, loves, or stars, but more land and gold: "Minha terra tem mais rosas / E quase que mais amores / Minha terra tem mais ouro / Minha terra tem mais terra" ("Canto" 144). Still, in the closing lines of "Canto de regresso," the poet somewhat ironically embraces the industrial milieu of progress of the early Republic by wanting to return to São Paulo's financial center, Rua 15 de novembro, instead of Gonçalves Dias's garden paradise. Rua 15 de novembro, in this case, becomes an ambiguous symbol for either modernization and progress or for the reformulation of the oppressive project of colonization under a capitalist banner.

João Accioly's "Pauliceia" from 1937 is an equally tumultuous anthem of early twentieth-century São Paulo. In futurist fashion, the poem conveys the madness of a city in constant motion: "São Paulo é São Paulo! / Ou aqui ou no inferno / São Paulo é São Paulo! / —Cale a boca doido. / Deixe o povo trabalhar" (121). The poem then touches on themes such as mass immigration, unhinged economic development, and unwieldy urbanization: "Automóveis, Bondes. Caminhões, Carroças e o diabo. / Gente. Italiano. Judeu. Banqueiro. Tudo!" (121). In his closing lines, Accioly replaces the tokens "palmeiras" and "sabiá" with "arranha-céus" and "Zeppelin" as symbols of modern technology: "Minha terra tem arranha-céus / Por onde voa o Zeppelin: / As fábricas que aqui gorgeiam / São muito diferentes dos sabiás de Gonçalves Dias!" (123).[10]

Carlos Drummond de Andrade, who may have written more variations than any other canonical poet,[11] expresses a similarly critical view of romanticized national narratives. In a line from his unpublished "Eu protesto" from 1926, he observes: "A literatura em minha terra é oficial como as palmeiras" (qtd. in T. I. Castro 266). He would return to Gonçalves Dias's text many times during the course of his career, most notably in 1930 in "Europa, França e Bahia." In this poem, C. D. de Andrade surveys the whole of Europe before directing his thoughts to his home nation. After more than a century of independence, the poet considers that Brazil has lost the innocence and promise of its youth. The fact that the author is unable to remember "Canção do exílio" is tantamount to questioning the reality of its message: "Meus olhos brasileiros se fecham saudosos. / Minha boca procura a 'Canção do exílio.' / Como era mesmo a 'Canção do exílio'?" (C. D. de Andrade 19).

Modernist variations from the 1930s would continue to question the existence of any Romantic national essence. Bringing into relief Brazil's foreign dependencies, Murilo Mendes begins his "Canção do exílio" with the following two lines: "Minha terra tem macieiras da Califórnia / onde cantam gaturamos de Veneza" (M. Mendes 33). In a lesser known variation from the same year, an author going by the name of Guy writes: "São Paulo tem ainda uma pequena alma brasileira ... entre a trama nervosa destes fios elétricos canadenses, destes explosivos automóveis "yankees," desta mercantil ópera-lírica fascista ... Minha terra tem palm ... Tem cedros, lindos e tristes cedros, onde canta o sabiá" ("A sociedade" 2).

Faced with tremendous cultural shifts, Brazil emerged from the nineteenth-century, the abolition of slavery, and the end of the Segundo Império to embrace industrialization, consumer capitalism, and a new urban immigrant reality. In the 1920s and 30s, Modernists like O. de Andrade and others led the way in re-articulating national identity in light of these changes, questioning the dependencies of the present as much as the relevance of a colonial past. In the 1920s, as the nation celebrated its centennial of independence from Portugal, its relationship with the US emerged for the first time among the variations. In the short "Trovas" section of *O careta* published on July 2, 1921, an unknown author hints at the dependency of the economy on the US dollar: "Minha terra tem palmeiras, / Onde canta o sabiá: / Pois até onde ele canta / O tal dólar subirá" ("Trovas"). The Modernists eventually found a way to understand how Brazil could leverage both the realities of its syncretic past and the inevitability of foreign influence as strengths.

In 1928, O. de Andrade's *Manifesto antropófago* famously employed a cannibalistic cultural metaphor grounded in the history of the indigenous warrior who devoured vanquished foes in order to assume their powers and attributes. The syncretic ideal behind this metaphor, which famously begins, "Só a antropofagia nos une: socialmente, filosoficamente, economicamente," would influence Brazilian intellectuals for generations to come. Demonstrating its incredible versatility and adaptability, variations of "Canção do exílio" from the period also embody this syncretic ideal, assuming a multitude of forms and in varied contexts to consolidate its continued presence in the ongoing discourses of national identity, its keywords and phrases serving as the connective tissue to conjoin Brazil's past and present. Subsequent generations, especially the counterculture Tropicália movement of the 60s and 70s, would take up both O. de Andrade's *Manifesto* and Gonçalves Dias's poem to successfully oppose the military regime despite an atmosphere of censorship and oppression (the subject of the next chapter).

Chapter Five

"Minha terra só tem tanques"
The Military Regime
(1964–1985)

On April 1, 1964, in the midst of the Cold War, a group of Brazilian military elites mobilized a well-designed large-scale coup that ousted from office President João Goulart. On the following day, in what turned out to be a grossly premature statement, US President Lyndon B. Johnson, whose administration had been supportive of the military coup, extended to the civilian Ranieri Mazilli, the "warmest good wishes on your installation as President of the United States of Brazil" (qtd. in Leacock 215). Mazilli, a political pawn, was only president for a few days as the military had other plans. Two weeks later, on April 15, General Castelo Branco assumed control of the government, ushering in an authoritarian regime that would endure more than two decades.

In the period leading up to the military coup, beginning with its participation in World War II, Brazil had as a general rule aligned itself with the US. But, in the 1960s, under the administrations of Jânio Quadros (1961) and João Goulart (1961–64), the country began to make significant changes to its foreign policy. This new approach, appropriately termed an "Independent Foreign Policy," "reviewed all aspects of Brazilian foreign affairs with the aims of expanding the country's autonomy within the international arena and reducing the constraints imposed by the bipolar international order" (Parker 7). For US-trained Brazilian general officers, this new foreign policy, coupled with friendly diplomatic visits to China and Russia by Quadros and Goulart respectively, began to take on more of a communist feel than an independent one. Eventually, the military became convinced that Goulart planned to subvert democracy, establish himself as a dictator, and seize control of the country. Four days before the Brazilian military forcefully took charge of the country, Lincoln Gordon, the US Ambassador to Brazil, sent a top secret message to the State Department in which

Chapter Five

he reported that Goulart intended to "seize dictatorial powers" and that Brazil would soon come "under full communist control" (qtd. in Parker 69). Subsequent evidence would support the position that the military, by installing its own authoritarian regime, had acted against a president who had made "no apparent preparations to stage a coup or to fend one off" (196).

Throughout the dictatorship and up until the "abertura" in the mid-80s, control of the country exchanged hands between a close-knit group of generals who quelled any public resistance to the regime, communist or otherwise. From Castelo Branco to Figueiredo, these generals unilaterally decided the political and economic fate of the country and its citizens for decades. Between 1968 and 1974, under Costa e Silva and then Medici, Brazilian citizens faced the most repressive years of the heavy-handed regime. The period was defined by the implementation of the Ato Institucional 5 (AI-5), unequivocally granting the regime power to supersede the constitution at will, as the military exerted total control over the government, making local courts irrelevant. In the nation's streets, censorship and curfews became commonplace and imprisonment the standard punishment for those who opposed the regime's power. During the *anos de chumbo* ("years of lead") in reference to the heavy-handedness of the regime, as these most repressive years are called, hundreds of journalists, students, artists, and left-wing militants were corralled, tortured, killed, and "disappeared," leaving a dark legacy that still plagues the collective memory of Brazilians today.

On the day AI-5 was implemented, during a musical performance in Lisbon, the poet and diplomat Vinícius de Moraes made the following statement: "No meu país foi instaurado, hoje, o ato institucional n° 5. Pessoas estão sendo perseguidas, assassinadas, torturadas. Por isso, quero ler um poema" (qtd. in Castello 282). The poem Moraes defiantly read that night in Lisbon was "Pátria minha." Written almost two decades prior, in 1948, it presages many of the themes to be associated with the "Canção do exílio" variations published during the dictatorship period. Specifically, "Pátria minha" laments the vulnerability of a nation hedged in internationally by a bipolar world order and oppressed locally by authoritarian leaders (Enslen, "Vinícius" 419–23). In the opening lines of the poem, he describes Brazil as if it did not exist: "A minha pátria é como se não fosse" (Moraes, "Pátria" 383). This

"Minha terra só tem tanques" (1964–1985)

same desperate reality of a nation lost to forces out of its control reverberates throughout the "Canção do exílio" variations of the dictatorship period.

From the twentieth century, there are 169 texts among the 500 total variations, making the average number of variations published per decade slightly under 17. With 50 variations total, the running average during the 60s, 70s, and 80s stays basically unchanged from the other decades and, from the specific years comprising the dictatorship (1964–85), there are 36 texts. Still, the 1960s saw less than average output with only 13 texts, and only six of these being written after the coup of 1964. From the 1970s, the only full decade of the dictatorship, there are a typical 18 texts. Owing to the influence of the rising Tropicália movement, almost half of these 18 variations are song lyrics.[1] To balance the sparsity of the 1960s, there are a total of 19 texts from the 1980s with 12 of them published between the years of 1980 and 1985. Thus, it seems that neither the general oppressiveness of the dictatorship nor the censorship of AI-5 significantly slowed the publishing of "Canção do exílio" variations. Still, the dictatorship influenced the variations in other, more significant ways, as the preponderance of a negative national narrative weighs heavily.

During the dictatorship, themes of international duress and state-sponsored oppression played key roles in the "Canção do exílio" variations. Of the 50 texts published in the decades of the dictatorship, 31 bear the marks of a dystopic nation, silenced and tortured.[2] And, of the 36 published between 1964 and 1985, 21 are in what this study has termed the *negative mode* (see Chapter 4).[3] The consolidated core of negative variations demonstrates the unmistakable influence that the realities of the Cold War and the dictatorship exerted during this dark period. These texts' distorted reflections of Gonçalves Dias's paradise point in varying degrees to the impossible reality of its "foundational fictions" (Sommer) while delimiting various reasons for its frustration.

An important feature that clearly emerges among the dictatorship period texts in relation to the negative mode is the disruption of the felicitous union between the "sabiá" and "palmeiras." The first two lines of "Canção do exílio" establish the "sabiá" singing in the "palmeiras" as a powerful binomial pair. This pair, when found happily together as in the original, serves as a symbol for an idealized Brazil: the thrush, joyfully alight in the palms, sings the

Chapter Five

incomparable wonders of its nation. Emphasizing the importance of this motif through repetition, of the 24 lines in the original poem, four pairs (or eight lines total) end with "palmeiras" followed by a "sabiá." A *Frequency Analysis* of the 500 texts also confirms the importance of the pair. These two words constitute two of the three most repeated nouns and appear in relatively equal numbers. With "palmeiras" being repeated 417 times while "sabiá" repeats a closely correlated 372 times, the pair benefits from stability throughout the 500 texts. Additionally, many other birds and trees often stand in for the pair as token substitutions while maintaining the meaning of the original, such as the "rouxinol" and the "loureiros" in the Portuguese variations. Yet, in the dictatorship texts, this partnership is frustrated. "Sabiá" appears 58 times while "palmeiras" appears only 25 times and, whenever the "sabiá" has no palm tree in which to sing, or when he sings defectively or not at all, the negative mode has typically been evoked, communicating the frustration of Gonçalves Dias's Brazilian paradise.

The union of this binomial pair represents hope in a Brazil that, having been invented in narrative, may one day be in reality. This is the subtext of all "Canção do exílio" variations. Unfortunately, though, the sabiá-laranjeira, which is commonly accepted as the exact species to which the original refers, does not typically rest in palmeiras. Fully aware of this fact, Rubem Braga famously attempts a hopeful reunion of the mythical communion between the two in a "crônica" from the late 1950s, even as the Cold War divided the nation's politics:

> Se eu dissesse que cantava, mentiria. Não cantava. Estava quieto; demorou-se algum tempo, depois partiu.
> Mas eu presto meu depoimento perante a História. Eu vi. Era um sabiá, e pousou no alto da palmeira. "Minha terra tem palmeiras onde canta o sabiá." Não cantou. Ouviu o canto de outro sabiá que cantava longe, e partiu. [...]
> Mas ele estava pousado na palmeira. Descansa em paz nas ondas do mar, meu velho Antônio Gonçalves Dias; dorme no seio azul de Iemanjá, Antônio. Ainda há sabiás nas palmeiras, ainda há esperança no Brasil. (28–29)

During the Cold War, Brazil was gripped in the vice of the bipolar system, torn between opposing ideologies that would lead shortly to the military regime. Even so, in this short episode, Braga was unwilling to relinquish the hope symbolized by the binomial pair. While he admits that the "sabiá" he saw never actually sang, he bears witness of it resting for a few fleeting moments in a "palmeira." Then, at the very same moment, some other "sabiá" nearby, calling out its tune, gave the bird a voice, if only by ventriloquism. For Braga, this is evidence enough to inform the defunct Gonçalves Dias, now part of the syncretic pantheon of Brazilian gods alongside Iemanjá and others, that "ainda há esperança no Brasil" (29). Thus, Braga's "crônica" reinforces the continued belief in the romantic national myth of the original and the binomial pair remains even today deeply connected to the elemental narrative of a nation greater than its present struggles, a nation unwilling to give up hope in its future despite the circumstances.

Braga was not the first to comment on the inconvenient truth that "sabiás" do not actually sing in "palmeiras." J. Rego Costa had already communicated as much in 1948. In an anonymous verse quoted as part of an article in the *Diário de São Luiz*, a newspaper from the capital of Maranhão, Gonçalves Dias's home state, the author observed that the "sabiá": "Na mata virgem canta que se espoca, / Mas na palmeira nem um pio dá" (Costa, "Em meio" 3). In the first stanza of another poem in the same article by an unnamed, but apparently well-known author, the theme is elaborated further: "Minha terra tem palmeiras, / Onde canta o sabiá. / Mentira grossa, eu garanto! / Sabiá não canta lá!" ("Em meio" 3). Relatedly, a journalist by the name of Majoy in 1939, after admitting that the "sabiá" does not sing in palm trees, still urged young children not to shoot the symbolic bird with slingshots since, "se não canta em palmeiras, canta nos jardins" (2).

Sidnei J. Munhoz, in his essay "At the Onset of the Cold War," writes that "anti-communist practices and policies were implemented" across Latin America generally at the end of World War II (131). In Brazil, in 1945, the newly elected Dutra and his administration "started an intensive process of socio-political repression in the first months of power" against institutions and individuals with demonstrated communist sympathies and affiliations (139). Specifically, police forces around the country were ordered to violently repress protests organized by communist-affiliated political parties and workers' unions (143). Coincidentally, in 1947 and 1948, two poems by Camarada Lorotoff, a communist-inspired pseudonym for the journalist

Chapter Five

Eduardo Palmério (Fonseca 67), appeared in the *Diário da noite* in Rio de Janeiro, not only describing what was happening at the time, but also foreshadowing what was to come in the miltary regime. These poems entitled "Minha terra tem palmeiras" and "Quadra de onze" both deal with the topic of state-sponsored violence. In the northeastern state of Alagoas, instead of the "sabiá," the "pau" or stick "sings" as it smacks against flesh and bone: "Na Alagoas, canta o pau, / Canta fino e canta grosso, / Canta na carne e no osso. / Minha terra tem palmeiras / onde canta o sabiá. / Na minha terra o pau canta, / Mas não canta como lá" (Palmério 2). In 1948, "Quadra de onze" continues in like fashion: "Minha terra tem palmeiras / Onde canta o sabiá! / Eu nasci nas Alagoas, / Mas não volto mais pra lá! / O Sabiá já não canta, / O coitadinho só chora, / Lá quem canta é o pau ... agora!" (4). The image in Palmério's second poem of a "sabiá" that no longer sings typifies a motif that gained momentum throughout the first half of the twentieth century. In "Quadra de onze," the "pau" sings violently, but the "sabiá" does not sing at all, instead he cries, signaling the destabilization of the bird's mythical union with the "palmeiras."

In 1953, Jânio Quadros, the president whose resignation in 1961 signaled the beginning of the end for democracy, received an honorable mention in a variation. In the April 9 issue of *Gazeta de Paraopeba*, Jair Silva wrote: "Minha terra tem mendigos, que tais não encontro eu cá. Paraopeba será uma boa cidade para os comícios de Jânio Quadros. O mendigo de hoje escolherá o presidente da República de amanhã" (J. Silva). Throughout the 1950s, even with the optimism and prosperity of the Kubitschek presidency, to include the construction of Brasília, signs of trouble can still be found in the variations. In 1957, in a section entitled "Farpas políticas," an unknown author writes of the political climate: "Minha terra tem pinheiros / Onde choram os saudosistas / Nela faltam bons obreiros / Mas sobram 'intervencionistas'" ("Farpas" 1). In a chant registered in a December 1958 issue of *O semanário*, students protest against Roberto Campos, director of the BNDE (National Bank for Economic Development) and eventual member of General Castelo Branco's cabinet, shouting in the streets of Rio: "Minha terra tem petróleo, que o Roberto quer levar; mas também tem estudante, que não deixa entregar" ("Minha terra tem petróleo" 7). In 1958, there are other variations that complain about the shape of Brazilian democracy. For example, a journalist

"Minha terra só tem tanques" (1964–1985)

in Rio's *Jornal do Brasil* writes: "Minha terra tem palmeiras / Onde canta o sabiá / Mas tem uma democracia / que também é de amargar" ("Votos pitorescos" 5).

The texts from the early 1960s grow even more desperate about the political climate. Evoking Pedro Álvares Cabral's "discovery" alongside "Canção do exílio," among other points of historical importance, a "crônica"[4] from 1960 entitled "Minha terra" (possibly authored by C. D. de Andrade, who commonly contributed to the journal where the text was published) provides a satirical commentary on the country:

> Minha terra tem palmeiras onde canta o sabiá (turdus leucomelas). Minha terra tem poetas. Minha terra é um Jardim Botânico. Pedro Álvares Cabral, que está perto do coração de todos nós, por causa da inflação, nas notas de mil, nas carteiras, nos bolsos de todos os paletós, foi o nosso Cristóvão Colombo. Descobriu o Pau-Brasil. Brasil menos pau = brasil. Primeiro, Ilha, depois terra, da vera, da Santa Cruz. [. . .] Quanto ao povo, é muito ordeiro e, nas revoluções, não corre sangue. Essas revoluções são periódicas e se chamam pororocas. Ocorrem no Amazonas, por ocasião das cheias, e são considerados verdadeiros fenômenos. ("Minha terra" 21)

Relating the nation's political climate to the "pororocas," a violent tidal bore phenomenon in the Amazon, this text suggests that periodic revolutions are an inevitable characteristic of the Brazilian nation. This logic lumps together the historical conflicts of colonial times, the struggle for independence, and the regional conflicts of the nineteenth century with the continued disruptions of the twentieth century, all of which hearken back to Brazil's foundational moment, the arrival of Cabral, at the heart of Brazilian identity.

In Quintana's 1962 "Uma canção," as the coup knocks at the door, the erasure of Gonçalves Dias's binomial pair is total and complete. In the first stanza, he categorically states that there are no palm trees nor thrushes, and the birds that sing are invisible. In the second stanza, the clock seems to represent the countdown to some impending doom. In the last stanza, the poet in desperation does not only struggle to find the "sabiá," but cannot even find where "onde" is, an interrogative pronoun strongly connected with the syntax of the phrase "onde canta o sabiá." Then, in the last two lines, the negative mode is reiterated as the site of exile is located in the author's very own Brazil.

Chapter Five

> Uma canção
>
> Minha terra não tem palmeiras...
> E em vez de um mero sabiá,
> Cantam aves invisíveis
> Nas palmeiras que não há.
>
> Minha terra tem relógios,
> Cada qual com sua hora
> Nos mais diversos instantes...
> Mas onde o instante de agora?
>
> Mas onde a palavra "onde"?
> Terra ingrata, ingrato filho,
> Sob os céus da minha terra
> Eu canto a Canção do Exílio! (443)

In Candango Forçado's 1960 "Canção do brasílio," printed in Rio's *Correio da manhã*, the poetic protagonist also feels exiled in his own country or more appropriately in Brasília. The opening stanza provides a classic stance in the negative mode by simply inserting the word "não" into the text of the original at the opportune moments: "Brasília não tem palmeiras, / onde canta o sabiá; / aves aqui não gorjeiam [sic], / pois aqui aves não há" (1). Here, the author idealizes Rio while complaining of life in Brasília. If "Brasília's history is the history of a utopia" (Almino), then in "Canção do brasílio" this constructed utopia, erected out of nothing in the 1950s upon the plains of the nation's interior, is questioned. Candango Forçado continues, "nada de 'mais amores'/ que mulher não há por cá. / 'Mais flores' também não temos, / Porque nem grama aqui dá" (Candango 1). "Canção do brasílio" does not contemplate the larger political landscape that would shortly give way to the military coup of 1964, but its negation of "palmeiras" and of the bird's song finalizes the point that, based on a long tradition of variations that begins almost as soon as the original is published, variations in the negative mode have played an important role in opposing the utopia proposed by Gonçalves Dias's original.

In the 39 texts from the dictatorship period, the eight most frequent nouns (along with how many times they appear in the plural or singular) are as follows: "terra" (71), "sabiá" (58), "palmeiras" (25), "mundo" (25), "vida" (18), "banana" (17), "deus" (16), and "povo" (16). The words "Piauí" and "tanque," tying for ninth place, appear 13 times each. The term "Brasil" lags just behind these other less significant non-original nouns with

"Minha terra só tem tanques" (1964–1985)

only 11 appearances. Of the 11 words listed above, only five can be found in the original poem, representing an important departure from the main group of 500 texts wherein the first nine most frequent nouns are all from the original. As previously mentioned, "Brasil," as the tenth most frequent noun in the 500 texts and the first non-original noun, symbolizes the silent yet ever-present sum of the other nine. But, in the 39 dictatorship texts, "Brasil" does not configure so closely to the nouns of the original. In fact, it does not even manage to crack the top ten, surpassed in frequency by other somewhat indeterminate non-original nouns, such as "mundo," "banana," "povo," and "tanque." The odd rise of the terms "banana" and "tanque" during the period is not arbitrary.

"Minha terra só tem tanques" by F. Lopes repeats the latter term many times, foreboding the military coup. Published in Rio de Janeiro's *Tribuna da imprensa* in October 1963, only a few months prior to the Army's takeover of the country, it paints a dichotomy by comparing the military parading threateningly in the streets with the parades of carnaval. "De uns tempos para cá / minha terra só tem tanques / que ameaçam atirar," the poem begins (F. Lopes, "Minha terra" 8). It goes on to desire a return to happier, if stereotypical, scenes of Brazilian culture: "A verdade que se encerra / em toda essa confusão / é que o povo desta terra / só briga para ter feijão / futebol e carnaval" (8). According to Lopes, Brazil has done itself no favors by exchanging its paradise for "tanques / revólver, fuzil, canhão" (8).

Similarly, the term "banana," appearing in four different texts, portrays a general fear that Brazil had become yet another US puppet state, or "Banana Republic." The term "Banana Republic" originally referenced Honduras and Guatemala, where the United States had extended its influence, changing the local political landscapes to protect the interests of American businesses. In "Marginalia II" from 1968, Gilberto Gil hints at a similar reality in Brazil; singing, "Yes: nós temos banana / até pra dar / e vender" (a reference to a song by João de Barro), he suggests that the nation is easily sold out to foreign interests. Similarly, in an effort to convey the helplessness felt by many at the time, Fernando Leite Mendes's "Ladainha da Implosão" (1975) ridiculously proposes a revolution carried out with bananas: "Vamos implodir o mundo, senhora. / O mundo da fome, com bananas de banana, senhora. / O mundo da guerra, senhora, com bananas de paz. / Vamos

Chapter Five

implodir a pose dos fariseus com milhares de bananas de mão no ângulo do antebraço" (9). The other two variations in which the word appears are Chaves's "Take me Back to Piauí" and C. D. de Andrade's "Fazendeiros de cana."

Appearing 71 times in the corpora, the most frequent noun "terra" makes up more than one percent of the total number of words of the 39 texts with the second most frequent, "sabiá," appearing 58 times.[5] But, even if the two most frequent nouns remain the same as in the main body of 500 texts, the difference with these 39 texts is that the ratio between "sabiá" and the third most frequent noun, "palmeiras," has changed drastically. Typically, the ratio between "sabiá" and "palmeiras" keeps the binomial pair tightly bound. In the 500 texts, for every nine "palmeiras," there are approximately ten "sabiás" and, in the original, the ratio is exactly one to one. But, within these 39 texts, there are only 4.3 "palmeiras" for every ten "sabiás" so that more than half the national birds have lost their mythical homes. This new reconfiguration, as demonstrated in the texts, connotes the deep divisions taking place in Brazil during this period.

In the 39 texts, in place of the "sabiás" and "palmeiras," there stand a broad range of tokens with both negative and positive connotations.[6] This eclectic list underscores the confusion of the period, capturing a multiplicity of tokens in both modes. As in other chapters, the terms have been listed in alphabetical order in an effort to read them as a single cohesive unit.

Minha terra tem _____

abricó	cana crioula
açúcar marrom	cana rajada
aquela preta velha	cana-do-governo
bagaço	cana-pitu
banana	canhão
banho	castanhas
bate-bate	chacrinha
beleza	cheiro de parati
borboletas	Corinthians
buchada	desejos
bumba-meu-boi	dívidas
buriti	dona Hebe
buriti perdido	encantos
caboclo	engenhocas
cachaça	espelhos
cana caiana	farol de Alcântara

"Minha terra só tem tanques" (1964–1985)

figo
fio de esperança
Fla[mengo]
foguete
frevo bom
fuzil
gaiolas
garapas
heliporto
Inter[nacional]
juca
juçara
lagos
laranja
maçã
manga
mangaba
maracatu
medo
morcego
morena formosa
novidades
outras canas
outras relíquia[s]
palmares
Palmeiras (the soccer club)
paredes
pauleira
pé de juazeiro
peixada
pereira
piaçabais
pinheiros
pipira morena
ponta da areia
português dos "molhados"
português dos "secos"
praias
pranetas [sic]
recantos
rede
revólver
Rio Negro
riquezas
rolete de cana
sabores
Sacavém
santinho
São João de Ribamar
sapoti
sorvais
subsolos minerais
tanja
tanques
tanto carro
teixeirinha
tiquinho
turco dos "atacados"
turco dos "retalhos"
voodoo

Onde _____

brilha o neon
canta o bem-te-vi
canta o FMI (the IMF)
canta o tico-tico
cantam os rouxinóis
dormia cotia
existia briga…a cavalo
existia tanque … puxado na mão
sopra o vento da fome
[sopra o vento] da morte
[sopra o vento] do medo
tinham danças
tinham lindas meninas
vejo e revejo a face oculta da fome
vejo e revejo o rosto negro da morte

Taken together, there is no clear theme that emerges from these tokens associated with "palmeiras" and "sabiás." This is its own message, denoting the confusion of a time when the future of the country was in question. Texts in the positive mode from the period, such as the marginally related and innocuous "Boiadeiro," published in 1984 near the end of the dictatorship, carry on with the paradisiacal longing of the original with bucolic images of cattle, fruit trees, singing cowboys, and afternoons in the hammock ("Boiadeiro" 84). Other texts, such as Antonio Peticov's delightful quip from 1986, "Minha terra tem palmeiras, / Onde brilha o neon," are related textually, but remain ambiguous in message (qtd. in "Palmeiras imperiais"). Still, 23 of the 39 texts are clearly in the negative mode and within this mode there are still innumerous ways of representing Brazil. For example, Lee's carnivalesque ode to the Cold War, "Pirarucu," one of only four female-authored texts in the twentieth century, contemplates a nation caught "entre o russo e americano." This text further parodies the original by introducing ridiculous tokens such as voodoo, bats, and butterflies, among other things, in place of "palmeiras" and the "sabiá." "Minha terra tem 'pranetas' / Onde canta o uirapuru / Tem morcego, borboletas / Tem santinho, tem voodoo!" she sings (Lee). Different from the tokens of the Portuguese responses, which represented a clear and positive transposition of the original, these texts, like Marília Barbosa's 1978 song "Coração de candango" (written by José Carlos Pádua and Egberto Gismonti) present Brazil as a house of mirrors where nothing is as it seems and no one can be trusted. The lyrics begin, "Minha terra tem espelhos / Onde vejo e revejo / O rosto negro da morte / A face oculta da fome. / Minha terra tem paredes que encerram, que devoram" (Pádua).

A continued look at the changing relationship of the binomial pair among the dictatorship texts better reveals the dissatisfaction apparent in the majority. The first text in the negative mode that employs the word "palmeiras" is Gil and Torquato Neto's "Marginália II" from 1968. Portraying the desperation felt by the Brazilian people at this time in history, the lyrics open with the following declaration, "eu, brasileiro, confesso / minha culpa meu pecado." The song continues in like fashion to expose the "negra solidão" felt by many Brazilians at the time. In the lyrics, the word "palmeiras" is mentioned only twice and, although there is no mention of the "sabiá," there is the mention of the metonymous "canto do juriti." In place of the "sabiá," the lyrics evoke the tokens of hunger, fear, and death: "Minha terra tem palmeiras / onde sopra o vento forte / da fome do medo / e muito principalmente da morte."

In the same year, Chico Buarque de Holanda (referred to as Chico) and Antonio Carlos (Tom) Jobim would protest the dictatorship in a much milder tone. In the song "Sabiá," winner of the III Festival Internacional da Canção (competing alongside Geraldo Vandré's, "Pra não dizer que não falei das flores"), the soothing lyrics of this bossa nova tell of a protagonist that longs to return home, to lie beneath the "palmeiras," and to listen to the song of "uma sabiá" (curiously articulated in the feminine). The Brazilian referent "lá" from Gonçalves Dias echoes in the first stanza: "Vou voltar / Sei que ainda vou voltar / para o meu lugar / Foi lá e é ainda lá / Que eu hei de ouvir cantar / Uma sabiá" (C. B. de Holanda, "Sabiá"). But, he is unable to have his wish since the palm trees are gone. Still, Chico hopes that one day he will make it back to that Brazil symbolized by the "sabiá" and "palmeiras": "Vou voltar / Sei que ainda vou voltar / Vou deitar à sombra / De uma palmeira que já não há / Colher a flor / Que já não dá / E algum amor / Talvez possa espantar / As noites que eu não queria / E anunciar o dia" ("Sabiá"). In this verse, in addition to evoking the binomial pair, the lyrics also echo three of the most prominent nouns in the original: "flor," "amor," and "noite." In the article "A volta de Gonçalves Dias," published in the *Jornal do Maranhão* on December 8, 1968, José Brasil compares Chico and Jobim's song with the original: "A comovedora mensagem de esperança que nos transmite a letra de 'Sabiá,' afirmando outra volta, certamente ao planeta das palmeiras e dos sabiás, que [Gonçalves Dias] tão bem soube cantar em sua 'Canção do exílio'" (5).

In his short essay written in 1968, "Tropicalismo por uma nova canção do exílio," José Carlos Oliveira philosophizes about the exile of Brazil's artists during this period, such as Chico: "o exílio é o problema político fundamental dos nossos dias … Por que chora o exilado senão por aquilo que perdeu e que é a sua terra" ("Tropicalismo" 3). Written two years later, in the same year he went into exile in Europe, Chico's song "Agora falando sério" is not as optimistic as "Sabiá." Instead, he expresses misgivings about the possibility of a return to Gonçalves Dias's romanticized national ideal. In a world where everything seems upside down, Chico wants to shoot the "sabiá" and run away: "Agora falando sério / Eu queria não cantar / A cantiga bonita … Dou um chute no lirismo / Um pega no cachorro / E um tiro no sabiá / Dou um fora no violino / Faço a mala e corro / Pra não ver banda passar" ("Agora"). Then, hinting again at the "flores" and "amores" of the original, Chico sings: "Quer saber o que está havendo / Com as flores do meu quintal? / O amor-perfeito traindo / A sempre-viva, morrendo / E a rosa, cheirando mal."

Gil's song "Show de me esqueci" is another lyric from the Tropicalia Movement that hints at an escape from the oppressive military regime. Included in the soundtrack for the 1969 film *Brasil Ano 2000*, the song's dialogue with the original is clear, containing the parodic refrain: "Minha terra tem foguete / Onde canta o sabiá." The lyrics begin with the following request, "Ah, foguete / Com teu cone / Teu atômico / Combustível … Quando for a uma estrela / Me leve daqui / Quando for a uma estrela / Me leve de Me Esqueci" ("Show"). These lyrics, instead of expressing a desire for a paradisiacal return to the author's homeland, demonstrate a desire to escape a land that, no longer called Brazil, but "Me Esqueci," has "forgotten itself" in the decades since 1846.

A few years later, when the nation was experiencing the "economic miracle" of the 1970s, Antônio Carlos de (Cacaso) Brito's "Jogos florais I" makes a playful reference to the popular melody, "Tico-tico no fubá," and another to Christ's first miracle and crucifixion. In this poem, a gluttonous "sabiá," representative of the booming economy, gorges itself on the author's "fubá" while the "tico-tico" sings as if nothing were wrong. In the end, the text proposes that progress has come at too high a cost. Just as these two birds have mixed up their roles, so has Brazil confused vinegar for wine. In a sly comparison to the Roman soldiers who offered Christ vinegar instead of water while he hung on the cross, the false promises of the dictatorship have done the same, crucifying the people and their rights in the process: "Minha terra tem palmeiras / onde canta o tico-tico / Enquanto isso o sabiá / vive comendo o meu fubá. / Ficou moderno o Brasil / ficou moderno o milagre / a água já não vira vinho / vira direto vinagre" (Cacaso, "Jogos I" 110).

The "crônica" entitled "Nova canção do exílio" authored by the cryptic L.M. (assumedly to protect the author's identity from the government censors) offered an equally scathing review of the period. Following closely the text of the original, the "crônica" uses a cannibalistic metaphor and others of environmental destruction to explain Brazil's situation in 1974: "Minha terra é tão faminta / Que até come o sabiá … Nosso céu é mais poluído / Mais poluído é o nosso mar; / Nossos bosques arrasados, / Nossa vida amargar"

(8). Later, in a phrase reminsicent of Chico's "Sabiá," the author laments what can no longer be found: "Pensando nessa falseta / Que se faz com o sabiá. / Minha terra tem saudades / De coisas que já não há ... Minha terra tem gaiolas / Onde morre o sabiá" (8). At the end of the poem, the author recapitulates the two ideas above: "Não permita Deus que eu coma / Por lebre, gato ou gambá, / Muito menos que devore / Por faisão o sabiá / —Que cantava nas palmeiras / Que havia, mas já não há" (8).

In the song "Terra das palmeiras," recorded one year later (1975), an exiled Taiguara ruminates from the safety of London over a missing national bird, "Sonhada terra das palmeiras / Onde andará teu sabiá? / Terá ferido alguma asa? / Terá parado de cantar?" In the next verse, censorship looms large in the words: "Sonhada terra das palmeiras / como me dói meu coração / como me mata o teu silêncio / como estás só na escuridão." The musical works of Taiguara, like those of many other musicians from the period, were often denied distribution by the government. Recording and writing in Europe was a way to circumvent the censors, but Europe was not without its challenges. Contemplating the precariousness of his exilic experience in London, Taiguara states: "Cheguei em Inglaterra em meados de 1973 ... Logo percebi que os sul-americanos são para os ingleses, uma coisa pitoresca, um ser de outro planeta ... um pobre coitado que não alcança a grandiosidade da cultura inglesa" (Confete 2). Like Taiguara, many other artists fled to Europe in exile, most notably Caetano Veloso, Gil, Chico, all from the countercultural Tropicália movement.

The comedian Chaves was another exiled artist in Europe who, in 1970, recorded the playful song, "Take Me Back to Piauí." In his satire, much more upbeat than Taiguara's song, Chaves simultaneously parodies the ufanistic tendencies of both Simonal's then-popular "País tropical" and Gonçalves Dias's original. In the first verse, he makes light of a Brazilian exile's predicament, ironically complaining about Paris and the caviar, "Adeus Paris tropical, adeus Brigite Bardot / O champanhe me fez mal, caviar já me enjoou / Simonal que estava certo, na razão do Patropi / Eu também que sou esperto vou viver no Piauí!" (Chaves). Then, in the second verse, he possibly alludes to "Canção do exílio," employing its most powerful three-word phrase, while also referencing a celebrity love affair gone awry between Carlos Manga and Hebe Camargo, the later attempting suicide in despair (Reipert). "Na minha terra tem chacrinha que é louco como ninguém / Tem Juca, tem Teixeirinha, tem dona Hebe também / Tem maçã, laranja e figo / Banana quem não comeu / Manga não, manga é um perigo / Quem provou quase morreu!" Chaves then closes with another allusion to "Canção do exílio." Reminding us of the original's closing stanza ("Não permita Deus que eu morra / Sem que volte para lá"), Chaves evokes with praise the hypothetical scene of his death on the modern highways of his homeland: "Aleluia, aleluia vou morrer na BR-3!"

In C. D. de Andrade's "Fazendeiros de cana" from 1977, the poem starts with a question: "Minha terra tem palmeiras?"(6). Afterwards, the poet answers in the negative while replacing "palmeiras" with the dictatorship's robust production of sugarcane as a nod to the "milagre econômico." Yet, whilst listing all the types of sugarcane in production, another narrative emerges from the subtext: C. D. de Andrade employs the ambiguous term "cana-do-governo," alongside "cana-pitu" and "cana rajada," and it is possible to interpret the former as not only "government sugarcane," but also as "government prison" since stalks of cane are a colloquial term for the bars of a jail cell (6). The rest of the poem supports this alternate reading as the "porcos em assembleia grunhidora diante da moenda" stand in for the power-hungry military and the "junta de bois de sólida tristeza e resignação" represent the masses toiling away under their control (6).

In Veríssimo's "Nova canção do exílio," written in 1978, the criticism is even less veiled. Satirizing the regime's politics of "panis et circensis," Veríssimo substitutes soccer, samba, and telenovelas for Gonçalves Dias's "palmeiras" and "sabiás." The poem begins with a double meaning for the word "palmeiras" wherein it signifies both "palm trees" and the popular soccer team from São Paulo by the same name: "Minha terra tem Palmeiras / Coríntians [sic], Inter e Fla" ("Nova"). This list of local teams reminds us of Brazil's grand culture of soccer as Veríssimo hints at the hopes of a victory in the World Cup taking place that same year, represented by a potential fourth star on the national uniform. But, in the same stanza, he also complains that his nation still continues in darkness: "Nosso céu tem mais estrelas, / mas no chão continua no assombro / a melhor conjunção do horóscopo / é a de quatro estrelas no ombro" ("Nova"). In reference to the soap opera "Dancin' Days," Veríssimo asks: "Minha terra tem palmeiras / onde cantava o sabiá. / Grande questão só há uma: / a Júlia fica com o Cacá?" ("Nova"). The rest of the poem protests Brazil's pollution, deforestation, and urban violence while poking fun at other elements of popular culture. Yet, the poem is about much more than just football and soaps. It is a satire of the tactics of distraction employed by the authoritarian regime who hoped that Brazilians would not notice that the "sabiá" no longer sang: "O sabiá, eu sei, já não canta … Mas ninguém sentiu muita falta, / agora existem as Frenéticas. / Descobriram um sabiá renitente / que insistia em cantar, por mania. / Seu número não passou na Censura: / ele insistia em cantar: 'Anistia!'" ("Nova").

The dissolution of the union between the mythical binomial pair, signaling the estrangement of Brazil from its Romantic origins, continues into the late 70s and early 80s. In 1983, Assisão's "Sabiá na seca" pleads for the return of a lost love represented by the "sabiá." The bird has left the "sertão" which, in its absence, is nothing but a wasteland: "Foi um tempo traiçoeiro, sabiá / Veio a seca e carregou." Geraldo's "Sabiá" from the same year can also be read as an appeal for the end of censorship and violence. Having the same title as Jobim and Chico's tune, the lyrics seem to request the return of Brazil's preeminent artists from exile: "Sabiá pousava nas palmeiras / E cantava a vida do seu povo / Há de esperar a vida inteira / Pra ver sabiá cantar de novo / Quem viveu com ele aquele dia / Guardou na lembrança uma canção / Que se fez em toda cantoria / Que pousou em todo coração" (Geraldo). In Gal Costa's 1984 "Ave nossa" (written by Antônio Carlos Moreira Pires, better known as Moraes Moreira, and Béu Machado), the tragicomic message is that, in times of censorship and oppression, artists must be creative to get their message across. G. Costa's "sabiás" do not sing, but craftily convey their message with whistling. To understand the bird's song, you must be initiated in the tongue-twisted subtleties of the times: "Será que o sábio sabia / Que só aqui assobia o sabiá?" (Moraes Moreira).

Similar to the poems of Eduardo Palmério (better known as Camarada Lorotoff) from the late 1940s, G. Costa's "Ave nossa" also makes reference to state-sponsored violence in its opening lines. By changing Gonçalves Dias's "palmeiras" to "pauleira," "Ave nossa" turns the branches of the palms into sticks for beatings and torture: "Minha terra tem pauleira / Desencanta e faz chorar" (Moraes Moreira). The statistics on torture and death in the dictatorship are condemnatory. Although not as staggering as the numbers of deaths and disappearances in Argentina and Chile, thousands were imprisoned and tortured during Brazil's military dictatorship and, in 1995, "o governo brasileiro reconheceu oficialmente a responsabilidade do Estado em 356 casos de pessoas mortas ou desaparecidas enquanto os militares estiveram no poder" with "outros 113 casos apontados" ("O acerto").

Dalton Trevisan, best known for the macabre and predatory stories of *O vampiro de Curitiba*, wrote his own "Canção do exílio" in 1984. In his poem, while flippantly proposing that "a morte não é séria," he repeats the dystopic leitmotiv of the time with the phrases: "já não canta o sabiá" and "o sabiá não canta mais" (Trevisan 2). E. A. da Costa's "Outra canção do exílio," written one year later in 1985, holds a similarly dismissal view, even as the nation swears in its first civilian president since the coup. Reeling from the dark days of the dictatorship, the "sabiás" are silent, and in their place, Edgar Allen Poe's ravens: "Minha terra tem Palmeiras, / Corinthians e outros times de copas exuberantes / que ocultam muitos crimes. / As aves que aqui revoam / são corvos do nunca mais, / a povoar nossa noite / com duros olhos de açoite / que os anos esquecem jamais" (E. A. da Costa "Outra" online).

Leaving an indelible mark on the history of its nation, one must only browse the headlines in Brazil today to understand that E. A. da Costa's thirty-year-old assertion that Brazilians will not forget still rings true today. Time has not diminished the memories of the nightmares of the dictatorship. The popular slogan, "Não vai ter golpe," that reverberated throughout the anxious streets of the metropolises in 2016 is only one of many contemporary examples which remind us of the deep scars left on the collective conscious by the regime and the important role that "Canção do exílio" has played in articulating this popular mistrust.

As one last late example, Andrey TNT's "Canção do exílio à milícia" from 1997, twelve years after the "abertura," sums up in hindsight the damage inflicted by the decades-long authoritarian regime while still hinting at an enduring hope:

"Minha terra só tem tanques" (1964–1985)

Canção do exílio à milícia

Minha terra tem palmadas
Que se espanta o sabiá.
E os gritos sufocados
Já viajam pelo ar.

No céu ainda há estrelas,
Mas no chão, sangue e morte.
Estão matando nossas vidas
Com madeiras, facas e cortes

A madeira da palmeira
É o caminho para lá.
E apesar de todo o sofrimento
Prefiro ficar eu cá.

Minha terra tem horrores
Que eu não encontrarei por lá,
Mas na tortura dos piores
Mais prazer encontro eu cá.
E a coruja procura atenta
Onde canta o sabiá.

Não permita Deus que eu morra,
Não desejo ir para lá.
Na presença dos piores
Vou me encontrar por cá.
Quero ainda a esperança
Para ver cantar o sabiá... (56)

As the texts in this chapter demonstrate, the disruption of the binomial pair of "palmeiras" and "sabiás" characterizes a fundamental disillusionment with Brazil concretized during the military dictatorship. In the variations published during the period, Brazil's "sabiás" no longer sing as they once did, if they sing at all, and the "palmeiras" have all but disappeared, victims of a slash-and-burn campaign perpetrated by repressive forces. Yet, poems in the negative mode began in the nineteenth century, almost as soon as the fiction of the original was created. In fact, when Gonçalves Dias placed his singing "sabiá" in a "palmeira," he had already unknowingly pointed out the impossibility of his Brazilian utopia within the original, reinforcing the fictitious qualities of his foundational myth. From 1964 to 1985, this doppelgänger rears its Hydra-like head, as the utopia of Gonçalves Dias's childhood is all but lost,

Chapter Five

in its place, tanks, torture, and death. If the negative mode was a periodic occurrence in the variations prior to the dictatorship, after the dictatorship it becomes entrenched. In the texts of later generations, this mode will dominate even as the nation's focus shifts from the oppression, censorship, and violence of the military regime to the trafficking of drugs, guns, and poverty of the late twentieth and early twenty-first centuries.

Chapter Six

"As sirenes que aqui apitam"
Twenty-First-Century Songs of Exile (1999–2015)

Afonso Celso de Assis Figueiredo's *Porque me ufano de meu país*, published in 1900, is a superlative national apologetic loosely focused on eleven specific reasons why Brazil should be considered the greatest nation in the world. Equal parts fact and fantasy, the text describes the nation's many natural wonders as symbols of its greatness, such as the immensity of the Amazon, the magnitude of the Paulo Afonso waterfall, and the dynamic beauty of the Guanabara Bay. At the end of the fifth chapter, after quoting the second verse from "Canção do exílio," Afonso Celso makes the following claim about the nation's natural beauty:

> Impossível seria descrever minuciosamente os primores do Brasil, que tais o poeta não encontrava na Europa, e cuja magnificência impressiona os estrangeiros mais que os nacionais, por estarem estes habituados a gozá-la.
>
> No meio de muitas maravilhas que, em grau menor, existem em outras zonas, possui o Brasil, sem êmulas, quatro grandes curiosidades naturais.
>
> São: o Amazonas, a cachoeira de Paulo Afonso, a floresta virgem e a baía do Rio de Janeiro.
>
> Cada uma bastaria, por si só, a notabilizar um país. ("Porque" 21)

Through this turn-of-the-century text and others like it, such as Euclides da Cunha's *À Margem da história* (1909), one comes to understand how Brazil's physical features have been used as national symbols. To be more precise, its natural grandeur is a perduring metaphor for the nation's vast untapped potential. However, by the end of the twentieth century, Afonso Celo's *ufanismo*

Chapter Six

would be turned on its head and the realization of the nation's promise increasingly more doubtful.

In 1999, the prominent historian José Murilo de Carvalho put Brazil's twentieth century under review in a "crônica" published in the *Folha de São Paulo*. After revisiting the exaggerated claims of *Porque me ufano*, he makes the following observation: "Ao final do quinto século, é preciso admitir que nossos melhores sonhos têm sido sistematicamente frustrados por nossa incapacidade de torná-los realidade. A retórica do ufanismo só serve para encobrir nossa frustração como povo e como nação." Affected by numerous setbacks originating from both internal and external factors, some of the predominant themes of the twentieth century were inefficient government, uneven economic development, inequality, authoritarian regimes, state violence, torture, censorship, rampant inflation, and poorly maintained infrastructure, all problems that still impact the nation today to one degree or another. Despite some progress over the course of the century, Brazil is still considered a "sleeping giant," its success always seemingly just beyond the horizon. Or, as Brazilians wryly joke, Brazil *is* the land of the future, and always will be. Referencing the author of *Brazil: Land of the Future*, published in the 1940s, Carvalho closes his critique with this thought: "Nesse distante futuro talvez deixemos de ser o país do futuro que hoje desapontaria Stefan Zweig." Thus, if in 1900 the Amazon was a metaphor of Brazil's immense potential and imminent glorious future, today the region's labyrinthine rivers and streams, dramatic flooding, and impenetrable forests have come to signify the complicated path to making that potential a reality.

Evidence of this same widespread frustration expressed in Carvalho's "crônica" from 1999 is abundant in the "Canção do exílio" variations from the twenty-first century. Many of the 244 texts comprising the years 1999–2015 offer visions of a corrupt class of elites that exploits a polluted and crime-ridden country filled with a colossal population of marginalized citizens deprived of basic privileges and opportunities for social advancement. Divided into three separate, yet non-exclusive categories, 61 of these 244 texts have been chosen as a representative sample for discussion. The first category, comprised of 31 texts, focuses on a concern for the mismanagement and destruction of the nation's environment synonymous with a squandering of its future. These environmentally oriented

"As sirenes que aqui apitam" (1999–2015)

texts draw on Brazil's long-lasting love affair with its biodiversity and natural beauty at the heart of Gonçalves Dias's and Afonso Celso's texts. The second category, termed "literatura marginal," deals with a multiplicity of themes related to the urban periphery and earns this name for its affinity with an already significant and well-known body of contemporary works under the same moniker. Characterized by disillusion and contempt with modern Brazil, "literatura marginal," through verse and prose, takes on serious socio-political issues from the perspectives of the historically less privileged. There are 29 representative texts for analysis in this category. The third category, comprised of only 13 poems, deals primarily with political corruption, focusing on scandals of recent decades, such as the Mensalão and the divisive and monumental Lava-Jato Investigation, the latter giving way to the impeachment of President Dilma Rousseff.

Of the 500 texts in the main corpora, 242 were published in the year 2000 or later. Even though the period is made up of only 16 years (2000-2015), it averages 15 texts per year, a number that is ten times higher than the average number of texts published in previous years, and epresents roughly half of the corpora. The with the most texts in the study was 2012 with 66 texts. The other 15 years average about 12 poems per year with five years of only five texts each (see Appendix). Based on thematic similarity and chronological proximity, texts from 1999 have also been included in this group. These are Fernando Bonassi's "Cena 9" (in "15 cenas") and Luís Antônio Cajazeira Ramos's "Canção do exílio," bringing the total number of texts for analysis to 244.[1]

Due to the large amount of texts produced in this period, close readings will be supplemented by more distant readings of the group and with the 500 texts as a whole. With the explosion of variations online, many other texts in addition to these 244 texts could have been included in this chapter. In fact, hundreds of other texts from the current century have already been located.[2] Notwithstanding, the analysis herein has been limited to the numbers described above in an effort to create a body of texts which would be both robust enough to render quantitative analysis interesting, but not so large that the texts could not all be read closely by a single reader in a reasonable amount of time. In this way, close and distant readings have been joined together in a critical method approximating what Marti A. Hearst has termed reading at the "middle distance."

Chapter Six

According to Hearst, "Midway between close read[ing] and distant statistics," reading at the middle distance is designed to "help with hypothesis formulation, refinement, and verification." Specifically, a middle-distance reading of the 244 texts from 1999 to 2015 reveals an unexpected, but noteworthy paradox. Based on the results of a *String Similarity Test*, these 244 variations are more similar in word choice to the original than those that precede them, but close readings of the 244 texts reveal that, despite this textual similarity, these latter variations are more distant in message. In fact, in the twenty-first century, as compared to the other two centuries together, more than 50% of the texts are articulated in the negative mode for the first time and the paradox emerges that, while time has not diminished direct borrowing from the utopic original, the trend of texts in the negative mode, which materialized in earnest during the dictatorship, has only grown stronger. Teasing out the features of this paradox, this chapter will present the results of a *String Similarity Test*, a *Significant Words Analysis*, a *Modal Analysis*, and a *Types and Tokens Analysis*, along with close readings based on the three categories described above.

String Similarity Tests have broad applications in different disciplines, including DNA studies, linguistics, and computer science. Developed primarily for use in computer science, these tests measure the relatedness of one string of text or code to another. Envisioning each text as a sequence of characters, independent of its semantic meaning, this measurement can produce a coefficient of similarity based solely on the sequences shared between two texts. For our purposes, this test measured how a variation looked in comparison to the original and not necessarily how much meaning the two shared in common. An added benefit to the *String Similarity Test* is that, based on the comparison of characters, it also implicitly considers formal concerns through the measurement of elements such as spaces and line breaks. For this reason, while the project remains open to other possibilities, it is assumed that the granularity achieved through the application of this test was far superior (and founded upon much more robust science) than what could have been achieved by devising an idiosyncratic formula specific to the texts at hand.

In a word, a *String Similarity Test* functions as a counterpoint to close readings. With the use of an online tool founded in peer-reviewed research, each of the 499 variations was individually com-

"As sirenes que aqui apitam" (1999–2015)

pared to the original and, without regard to meaning (except that which is implied by textual similarity), the application calculated a percentage of relatedness for each.[3] In general, the results demonstrated that the 242 texts published after 1999 had a greater than average relation to the original. The average for the 499 variations was 35.7% relatedness. When broken down by century, the averages only vary slightly. The 88 texts from the 1800s and the 169 texts from the 1900s were together 33.4% related to the original while the texts from the 2000s were at 38.25%. These numbers attest to a great consistency in word choice among the entire corpora while slightly favoring the more recent texts. As demonstrated throughout our study, this consistency is owed to the fact that the original has been adapted in predictable ways through the use of *syntactic templates* and token substitutions. The 4.85% greater similarity of the 2000s texts becomes more significant when one considers that 40 of the 242 of these texts were calculated at 50% similarity or more.[4] By comparison, in the 1800s only 8 of the 88 texts and in the 1900s only 6 of the 169 were equal to or greater than 50% related to the original. Additionally, of the top ten most similar texts to the original, nine of them were written in the 2000s, confirming that the text of the original as stabilized in print does not pass through secondary and tertiary channels before being reproduced in a variation. It is accessed directly even today by each author, drawing an uninterrupted line from each variation to the original, no matter when, where, or how a variation is written and published. In other words, unlike the discombobulated results which often accompany the children's game of "telephone," variations in general do not represent vague recollections of the original, but rather direct and deliberate dialogue; a trait that has not diminished despite the passage of time.

Achieving a 73% similarity coefficient, the poem most like the original among the 499 texts perfectly encapsulates the twenty-first century paradox of being textually similar while semantically different. Robertson Frizero Barros's creative variation "Uma canção do exílio" from 2009 employs words that, although reordered in each line, are almost identical to the original, while also managing to propose a contradictory meaning.

> Uma canção do exílio
>
> Terra tem palmeiras. Minha?
> Canta o sabiá. Onde?

Chapter Six

> Que aqui gorjeiam? Aves?
> Gorjeiam como lá? Não.
> O céu tem mais estrelas. Nosso?
> A várzea tem mais flores. Nossa?
> Os bosques têm mais vida. Nossos?
> Vida, nossa, mais amores? ...
> Sozinho, à noite, cismo em cismar:
> prazer encontro eu lá? Mais
> palmeiras ... Minha terra tem
> sabiá. Onde? Canta?
> Primores, minha terra tem,
> e tais não encontro; eu, cá,
> em cismar—à sozinha noite—
> mais me encontro lá. Prazer,
> minha terra tem. Palmeiras,
> onde? Canta o Sabiá.
> Permita Deus que eu morra; não
> sem que eu volte para lá.
> Primores, que os desfrute por cá.
> Que ainda aviste as palmeiras sem
> o sabiá—que canta onde?

With the addition of only a few words different from the original, one can see how Barros' poem achieved such a high similarity coefficient, but the changes the author employed are important. The words in each line have been introduced in a new order and, with the addition of question marks, among other novel punctuation choices, this reordering unhinges its meaning from the original. Reminding us of texts from the dictatorship period, Barros's perfect deconstruction negates G. Dias' assertions as he questions quite literally the utopia that Brazil symbolized. From the beginning, the reader is made aware of the relativization of the original's assertions. The text accomplishes this by adding the indefinite article "uma" to the title. Barros's is not the only Song of Exile, but one among many. Then, in a reformulation of the first two lines, he sets the stage for his negation: "Terra tem palmeiras. Minha? / Canta o sabiá. Onde?" (Barros). The rest of the poem follows suit until the end where the author requests to die not after returning to Brazil, but before. He accomplishes this with the reordering of the first line of the last stanza and with the insertion of a semicolon: "Permita Deus que eu morra; não / sem que eu volte para lá."

A frequency analysis adds additional support to the conclusion that the texts from the 2000s are more closely related to the original while more distant in meaning. Specifically, the 2000s (and the two texts from 1999) use more nouns from the original and at a more frequent rate than the other 255 poems. In the texts from 1846 to 1998, there are a total of 40,887 words and 8139 unique words. In the texts from 1999 to 2015, there are a total of only 22,309 words with 4837 being unique. The average length for texts between 1846 and 1998 is 160 words while the average text length from 1999 to 2015 is 91 words. This reduction in average text size, representative of the new media culture within which many of these later texts were published, does not diminish their relation to the original, which contains 116 words including the title. One reason for this is that the use of nouns from the original is more pronounced.

While the list of most frequent nouns from 1999 to 2015 is at 12, the list of most frequent nouns from the previous group is made up of only seven (these lists have been capped at the appearance of the first most frequent noun not from the original poem). The twelve most frequent nouns from the 2000s are as follows: "terra" (485), "sabiá" (174), "palmeiras" (161), "noite" (103), "vida" (100), "deus" (90), "céu" (74), "amores" (67), "canção" (66), "exílio" (57), "estrelas" (52), and "aves" (50). The seven most frequent nouns from 1846–1998 are "terra" (743), "sabiá" (220), "palmeiras" (199), "amor" (122), "céu" (116), "deus" (113), and "flores" (101). While the two groups share the top three most frequent nouns in common—"terra," "palmeiras," and "sabiá"— these three words are much more common in the 2000s than in the texts from the previous two centuries. Additionally, there are 1479 appearances of the most frequent nouns from the 2000s, representing 6.54% of all words in that group and there are only 1613 appearances of the most frequent nouns from 1846 to 1998, despite the higher word count.

Another interesting observation to be made concerning the lists of most frequent nouns is the difference in location of the word "Brasil." Appearing 45 times, the first non-original noun to make the list in the 2000s is "lugar," which is generally indicative of the poet-protagonists' quests for a sense of place and identity. Yet, this generic term is not nearly as descriptive or specific as "Brasil," the most frequent non-original noun from the 1846–1998 group. In the 1846–1998 group, this term appears 100 times and places just before the metonymically related "pátria," which appears 89 times.

In contrast, the word "Brasil" appears only 21 times in the 2000s, making it the twenty-second most frequent noun in that group and, like the dictatorship texts, is beat out by other non-descript nouns, such as "mundo" and "tempo." This distancing of the word "Brasil" from the most frequent nouns of the original points to an important change in perspectives on the country, already discussed in the dictatorship chapter. Just as "Brasil" is no longer closely associated in frequency with nouns from the original, the texts from the 2000s far from reproduce the Romantic ideal represented by the original poem. To the contrary, these texts, dominated by the negative mode, lament the misplacement of Gonçalves Dias's utopic Brazil brought on by centuries of misguided governance.

A *Modal Analysis* further quantifies the trend toward the negative in the 2000s. Each of the 499 variations was assessed through close readings and then placed in one of three modal categories: positive, negative or other. As discussed elsewhere, texts in the positive mode maintain the utopic perspectives of the original in relation to the referent nation (typically Brazil) while texts in the negative mode adopt a dystopic view in varying degrees. Texts placed in the other category, whether utopic, dystopic, or neither, do not explicitly employ Brazil or any other country as the referent and therefore occupy an entirely different paradigm than that established by the Romantic nationalism of the original.

The process for determining the mode of each poem was simple. Each poem was read individually and then sorted based on the following criteria. First, it was determined whether the referent or subject of the poem was Brazil, including its regions (or some other nation by exception). Those few poems that failed to pass this first checkpoint, not being explicitly focused on the nationalist enterprise at the heart of the original, were immediately placed in the category of "other." If the answer was in the affirmative, then it was determined whether the perspectives on the referent in question were generally positive or negative. Admittedly, this was a judgment call made through multiple close readings of each of the poems.

Written in 1850, Hipóllito Pereira Garcez's "Gôa" is an interesting non-Brazilian example of a text in the positive mode. Published only a few years after the original, this text not only provides a classically Romantic variation, it demonstrates the original's influence across the Portuguese empire. In this variation, Garcez continues with the original's colonial dynamic, comparing the beauty of his own Portuguese enclave to the European capital.

> Gôa
>
> Minha terra tem palmeiras,
> Tem mais densos arvoredos,
> Onde avesinhas canóras
> Trinam de amor os segredos.
>
> É mais claro o nosso céu.
> Nossos jardins tem mais flores,
> Há frutas mais saborosas,
> Mais constância nos amores.
>
> A minha terra é mais fértil,
> Tem mais fontes cristalinas,
> Lindos rios, várzeas, prados,
> Mil verdejantes campinas.
>
> Não permita Deus que eu morra
> Sem ver a terra natal;
> Sem que disfrute os prazeres,
> Que não gozo em Portugal;
> Sem que me sinta extasiado
> À sombra do arecal. (356)

In Garcez's "Gôa," "Canção do exílio" reappears as a template to convey a similar message about the author's homeland. The text's *string similarity* is 52.65% related to the original. With the repetition of phrases like the opening line "Minha terra tem" and the borrowing of singular words in the comparative mode, such as "flores," "céu," "amores," and "avesinhas" (the diminutive of "aves"), all in relative proximity to their same formal location in the original, its significant textual relatedness to the original is confirmed as the poem transplants Gonçalves Dias's paradise to the west coast of the Indian subcontinent.

The negative mode, in contrast to the positive, while still maintaining Brazil (or at times some other nation) as the referent, conveys a dystopic, satirical or parodic inversion of the original's paradise. Among the three centuries in question, the 2000s contain the greatest number of texts in the negative mode. With a Brazilian reality seemingly distancing itself even more from Gonçalves Dias's ideal, negative variations demonstrate

Chapter Six

a growing frustration with the nation's inability to guarantee basic rights and an acceptable standard of living for many of its inhabitants.

Texts falling under the category of "other," in a surprising departure from the nationalistic paradigms of the other two modes, do not have Brazil (or any other nation) as an explicit referent. Due to this double disjuncture with the original, these "other" texts can vary widely in subject matter and often entertainingly so. A clear example of the "other" mode would be Rosa Pena's text from 2012. This short poem's content is as unexpected as it is suggestive as a male "sabiá" and a female "palmeira," corresponding with their grammatical gender, consummate their symbolic relationship in heteronormative union.

> Em sonhar, sozinha, à noite,
> teimo em contigo estar.
> Entre minhas coxas uma palmeira,
> que adora teu sabiá!

Opening with a slightly modified line from the original that changes "Em cismar" to "Em sonhar," Pena's poem is only a mere 20% related as the nocturnal desires of the poet-protagonist differ enormously from those of Gonçalves Dias. Still, with the appearance of the binomial pair "palmeiras-sabiá," the text manages to exhibit clear signs of a variation.

There are other interesting textual anomalies that emerge in the "other" category and merit mention. Among them is a "crônica" from 1914 written by an anonymous author and published in Juíz de Fora in the magazine *Pharol*. Entitled "Minha terra tem palmeiras...," this text tells of a spat of jealousy and a subsequent physical altercation between two prostitutes, all based on the textual premise of "Canção do exílio."

> "Minha terra tem palmeiras ..."
>
> "Sabiá," já muito conhecido nesta cidade, é uma destas pobres raparigas que por aí vivem vendendo amores ...
>
> Ontem, cerca de oito horas da noite, saiu a passeio em companhia de uma sua "colega," e isto com o fim de tirar uma desforra.
>
> Chegadas que foram, à ponte da rua Halfeld, "Sabiá" interrogou sua amiga sobre certos ciumesinhos, derivando daí engalfinharem-se.

> "Sabiá," que é mais forte, arrumou um murro em sua companheira, ferindo a bastante em uma das vistas.
>
> E bateu asas ... ("Minha terra tem palmeiras" *Pharol* 2)

As can be seen by the title and the name of the protagonist, this "crônica" is easily associated with the original, but its content is only marginally related. If Gonçalves Dias's "sabiá" symbolizes Brazil's exuberant Romantic hopes, then perhaps the "Sabiá" of this "crônica" infers all the nation's conflicts, ironies, and disparities. And it does so, tellingly, in an urban setting where the drama of human society most readily plays out, not in some mythical tropical paradise.

Posted in 2008, Galdriel'ves Dias's "Canção do exílio" shows another unexpected possibility for the adaptation of the original poem. The closing stanza reads, "Não permita Eru que eu morra, / E que não volte para lá; / Que atravesse os mares / E Silmarils não leve de cá; / Sem qu'inda aviste Mandos gritando / E os sabiás em Valmar cantando." If this poem hints at the fictional qualities of the original by substituting characters and toponyms from the *Lord of the Rings* saga, then it also demonstrates the pervasiveness of the original's rhetoric in Brazilian popular culture. Likewise, Breno Lobato and Samara Cristina's positive adaptation "Minha terra tem o brega," posted on their teacher's blog in 2013, entertainingly describes a technobrega band from Belém do Pará: "Minha terra tem o brega / Que faz o povo dançar / Super pop, o Águia de fogo / Faz a galera endoidar" (Cristina).

According to the results of the *Modal Analysis*, only for a brief shining Romantic moment in the nineteenth century did Brazilians view their nation in a primarily utopic light. In the 1800s, when the Romanticism of the original reigned, 52% of the 89 texts were classified as positive (including the original), 25% were classified as negative, and 23% were classified as other.[5] Since then, however, with the exception of a few decades like the 1930s, perspectives have soured toward a generally negative vision of Brazil.[6] In the last century, the trend toward the negative mode increased drastically, especially in the 1960s. In the 1900s, only 29% of texts were positive, 54% percent were negative, and only 17% were considered as other. And in the 2000s, with 21% of the texts classified as "other" and 29% as positive, the negative mode also roundly eclipses the other two categories. Of the 242 poems published in 2000 or later, slightly more than 50% (122) were negative.

Chapter Six

Expressing the main concerns and complaints of Brazilians today, the texts making up the three categories emerging from the 2000s are replete with examples of negative perspectives on contemporary Brazil. Discounting the small number of texts shared among the three categories, there are a total of 61 unique texts, representing 25% of the 244 from the period (1999-2015) and exactly half of the texts in the negative mode. There are other texts in the negative mode from this period that could have been included in this analysis, such as Barros's previously cited "Uma canção do exílio," but those texts manage to be in the negative mode without discussing, or only marginally discussing, the main themes of the three categories: environmentalism, "literatura marginal," and corruption. A *Types and Tokens analysis* of these 61 texts provides a general overview of the imagery associated with this set of variations. Specifically, two separate lists of terms show token substitutions for the two types "palmeiras" and "sabiá" with other images from the contemporary landscape.

By way of introduction to the lists at hand, "Terra minha," written by Simões, is a creative variation from 2005 that touches on all three categories. The poem begins: "Minha terra tem palmeiras … mas também tem bandalheiras, privatizadas ou não, onde meteram e metem a mão, levando os anéis sem deixarem os dedos." In this case, the negative token "bandalheiras" is placed on the list as a substitution for "palmeiras" while the equally negative "mão [metida]," by following the adverb "onde," replaces the "sabiá" (this poems is discussed in greater detail later in the chapter) Instead, all the tokens from the 61 texts have been conflated so that this reading will convey the totality of the images associated with the period. With 438 tokens substituting "palmeiras" and 38 substituting "sabiás," the picture painted of present-day Brazil is of a largely nightmarish hue and of extreme complexity, even though some Romantic images, whether refuted or not in context, continue to echo throughout.

The first list is of tokens that completes the phrase "Minha terra tem _____" or an obvious variation thereof. At times, this list includes tokens substituting the nouns from the related second verse of the original, "Nosso céu tem mais estrelas," etc. This expansion of the list is justified since the four lines of this second verse of the original are themselves variations of the first line. The second list is made up of tokens completing the phrase,

"Onde canta _____." From the original's second line, variations also often substitute the verb "canta" while still being reliant on the syntax of the original, as in the phrase "onde amanhecem cadáveres emborcados," from Bonassi's "Cena 9" (607). In the list below, these verb tokens have been listed parenthetically alongside the nouns that they accompany.

As in previous chapters, all tokens have been listed in alphabetical order as opposed to chronologically or by some other organizing principle. This alphabetical approach further detaches the tokens from their original context, helping the results to read as a single cohesive unit with its own internal organization. In this way, each list constitutes something of a meta-variation, a new text made up of the other texts. Also, when a term appears with a line drawn through it, this signifies that the absence of said token has been explicitly mentioned in the text. There are numerous examples of this narrative tactic throughout the texts, employed to simultaneously evoke and erase the existence of the original Edenic paradise. As an example, the context of the tokens "madeira" and "sabiá" refute their own existence, as we read in the first two lines of the 2009 variation, "Canção do exílio moderno": "Nessa terra sem madeira, / Onde tinha Sabiá, / As aves, que aqui ficavam, / Foram levadas para lá" (Sostisso).

Minha terra tem _____

300 deputados
.32 [arma]
.38 [arma]
.45 [arma]
acarajé
água
altares de ouro
alvarás saindo à farsa
ambição
amores
analfabetos
AR15 [arma]
arara azul
arvoredos
árvores
asfalto
assassinos
assentamentos irregulares
Atlético [futebol]
aves
bala a passar
bambu
bandalheiras
bandido
belezas
bosques mortos
buracos
caça
caçadores
cadeia (para pobre, preto, e puta)

Chapter Six

camarão
campos de futebol
campos de soja
canalha
canto emudecido
cantores do rock
carência
carro da polícia
cartões postais
casas (sem rebocar)
~~catedrais~~
celulares
cemitério
chagas na alma
cheiro de queimada
chimarrão
churrasco
~~cipó pendurado~~
coisas feias
coisas verdadeiras
cola pra cheirar
concreto
consciência
consciência pesada
contrastes
Corinthians [futebol]
corrupção (deslavada)
corruptos (roubando adoidado)
corvos
criança de rua
crianças (massacradas, desprovidas de direitos)
crianças [com] fome
Cruzeiro [futebol]
damas da noite
dengue
derrubados
desamores
desmatamentos
desrespeito

dinheiro [para rico]
doenças
dores
droga
droga (de árbitro, de deputado, de governador, de prefeito, de presidente, de senador, de síndico, de técnico, de vereador)
eletrônico da China
empreiteiras
encantos mil
ervas
escolas
escolas (sucateadas, ignoradas)
escravos
escritores (ótimos)
esgoto a céu aberto
especiarias
estádios
estrelas
excrescência
explorador de viúva
falta de vida
favelas
fé
feijoada
feridas nas montanhas
filas
flores
fogo
fogueiras
~~fronteiras~~
fumaça
gana
ganância
~~gavião de pescoço branco~~
gente (astuta, bonita, alegre)
gente [com] fome
gente morrendo

"As sirenes que aqui apitam" (1999–2015)

golpes [na terra]
governo enganador
grades
gralha
grama
grileiro
helicópteros
hipócrita
HK [arma]
horrores
IBAMA (perdido, desorientado)
~~índio~~
injustiças
inquérito
instrução
Internacional [futebol]
ladrão
latifúndio
língua
língua envenenada
lixo
M21 [arma]
madeira
madeireiras
madeireiros
maior carente
mal
malária
maldade
mandato cassado
mansão [para rico]
mãos (sujas)
maus odores
mendigos
menino (de rua, na lixeira)
menor abandonado
menos cores
menos flores
menos vida
mensalão

milhões de quilómetros quadrados
milhões sem eira nem beira
miséria
mistérios
motosserras
muros de bloco
músicas religiosas
~~mutum-de-alagoas~~
nome
ódio
óleo
olho
órfãos
ouro
Palmeiras [futebol]
pânicas
pantanal
papas na língua
pardais
pavores
pedras
pedrinha cor-de-bile
pessoas
pica pau do parnaíba
piolho
plantas
pobreza
poeira
poeta (incompetente e inconformado)
políticos (que roubam)
poluição
ponto g ignorado
ponto (por debaixo dos panos)
porqueira
povo ("que é forte, impávido, colosso")
pragas no pomar
praias (lindas, maravilhosas)

Chapter Six

prédios
problemas
professores
professores (desvalorizados, deprimidos, frustrados)
profusão de asfaltos
promessas de políticos
puteiro
queimadas
queimados
rasgos nos pés
recursos
rio
riso masturbado
roubalheira solta
~~sabiá~~
sacrilégio à verdade
saída
salvação
sangue
São Caetano
~~saúde~~
segurança
seringueiras sangradas

serras ... de ferro
~~Severino~~
sol
soldadinho do araripe
soldado na favela
sujeira brasileira
tapetes na porta à espera
temores
tietê de coroa
tiro (na testa)
tudo [para rico]
valas [para mosquito]
vantagem [para rico]
varejeira
Vasco
verme
verso, frente, rosto, fundo
viciados
~~vida~~
violência
vítimas inocentes
vozes (da ética, da família, em nome da honra, em patética encenação)

Onde _____

cacos de vidro (pousam)
cadáveres emborcados (amanhecem)
crianças (mendigam)
desorientados (há)
dinheiro (reina)
droga (manda)
esperto (prevalece)
estuprados (há)
favelados (moram)
lixo [se joga]
mão (se mete)
medo (impera)

miséria (há)
muitos perdidos (há)
nação (deve e não cresce)
natureza [escuta]
o que há (roubam)
o social (morre)
o tiroteio (canta)
os que vivem bem (há)
outros que passam frio (há)
poucos sabiás (cantam)
primores (se via)
urubu (voa)
viciados (fumam)

"As sirenes que aqui apitam" (1999–2015)

When Pandora of Greek lore opened her box, all the ills of the world escaped never to be captured again. The only thing that remained in the container was hope, resting alone in the half-light of the bottom. Gonçalves Dias's "Canção do exílio," representing the nation in an original (if fictional) state of grace, finds itself in a similar position as did Pandora's hope. Beaten, battered, and buried by the negative palimpsestic onslaught of the tokens listed above, the Edenic paradise of the original has been overwhelmed with the defining evils of twenty-first century Brazil. In counterpoint to the long-established urban equivalents of the original's stereotypes, such as the beautiful sunsets and tanned bodies of Ipanema, these tokens emerge from the dark streets and alleyways of a wasted cityscape to paint a hellish picture of violence, poverty, corruption, addiction, and destruction.

Composed of more than 650 words, Simões's poem "Terra minha," published in 2005, is responsible for more than a dozen of the tokens represented in the two lists above. Standing in for "palmeiras," these authors propose the tokens "hipócrita," "canalha," "bandalheiras," "desmatamentos," and "corruptos" (Simões). In the place of "sabiá," one finds the politician's furtive hand and a stagnant and indebted nation. Of the sixteen free-form verses that make up the body of the poem, fourteen begin with the words, "Minha terra tem palmeiras." The first verse sets the stage with a cast of questionable characters: "Minha terra tem palmeiras..... mas também tem muito hipócrita, e, olhe, quanto canalha, e quantos corvos, e quanta gralha, quanta gralha, 'que nos palácios se assoalha, em úberes mananciais de tetas sufragam a sugação do comum.'"[7] Establishing a pattern in this opening verse, the remaining lines typically borrow the first line from the original and follow it with an outright refutation of its message. Concerning the environment, the authors write: "Minha terra tem..... tantas queimadas, desmatamentos..... derrubados, e um Ibama perdido e desorientado." Writing of both the poverty associated with the periphery and the political corruption that has given way to social neglect of the poor, the poem reads: "Minha terra tem palmeiras..... e tem milhões sem eira nem beira que vivem a tomar rasteira de discursos, de decretos, de verbas tantas desviadas..... onde o esperto prevalece, a nação deve e não cresce, e o social morre sem prece" (non-standard elipses in original).

Chapter Six

This negative narrative is met with only a few exceptions in the text. In the last four verses of the poem, a counter to Simões's pessimistic picture is given. These verses propose a few of Brazil's redemptive qualities, such as "amigos que fazem questão de ... beber um copinho de pinga no final da tarde, enquanto falamos de poesia e enrolamos um cigarrinho de rolo." After this partial redemption, "Terra minha" ends by proposing the re-discovery of Brazil as a *tabula rasa* in a future where what has gone awry has not yet been. Collocating itself alongside the original "Canção do exílio" and other texts in a descriptive tradition dating back to Caminha's letter, the poem evokes Cabral's voice as the catalyst for a revamped Brazilian universe exploding on the scene: "Ah! Minha Terra, tão longe e tão perto, quando foi que desisti de ti e me mudei para dentro de mim? Quando será que um outro Cabral gritará deslumbrado: 'Terra à Vista'?" (Simões).

Bonassi's "Cena 9," as one of the episodes in "15 cenas de descobrimento de brasis," also rediscovers the nation in a contemporary light, but without any redemptive qualities. Bonassi's fifteen scenes offer multiple perspectives on the darkest and most egotistical sides of human nature couched in the context of Brazilian history. With socially marginalized characters, such as drunk indigenous husbands and fathers who prostitute their subaltern wives and daughters, and others in social positions of power who perpetrate acts of violence and exploitation, such as murderers, drug dealers, and dictators, Bonassi's "15 cenas" examine up close and personal the varied stories of those strewn along the roadside of national progress. Together, these scenes suggest an impersonal process of nation building that inevitably requires the exploitation of those in positions of inferiority. Specifically, in "Cena 9," Bonassi adapts Gonçalves Dias's original to provide a portrait *en masse* of those stranded in the urban periphery. Impoverished, unemployed, and corralled by violence, these marginalized Brazilians are trapped in the favelas with no prospect for escape and, in the place of "palmeiras" and "sabiás," one finds "cadáveres," "muros de bloco," "cacos de vidro," "sirenes," and a litany of handguns and assault weapons (607). Borrowing the syntax from the third and fourth lines of the original, the poem closes with this dismal vision: "As sirenes que aqui apitam, apitam de repente e sem hora marcada. Elas não são mais as das fábricas, que fecharam. São mesmo é dos camburões, que vêm fazer aleijados, trazer tranquilidade e aflição" (607).[8]

"As sirenes que aqui apitam" (1999–2015)

There are many other texts from the 1999–2015 group expressing pessimistic views of a marginalized periphery. Iosif Landau's "Exilado" from 2003 recounts a story in poetic form of a male protagonist who finds himself unemployed and embroiled in a violent dispute with his neighbor. The poem begins with the phrase: "Minha terra tem palmeiras, onde canta o tiroteio." After ten years in prison for killing his boss, the poet-protagonist contemplates moving to Vietnam to escape his problems while lamenting the "tristeza do que eu tenho sido." "Expropriados," from 2010, one of two texts by Liria Porto, is more straightforward in its critique of race and class relations in Brazil. The short poem spends three verses of four lines each condensing the nation's social ills before closing with the question, "minha terra?" The last verse that draws attention to the well-documented and longstanding gap between the haves and have-nots while hinting at a lamentable correlation between poverty and African descent, "minha terra tem cadeia / para preto pobre puta / para rico tem dinheiro / tem mansão vantagem / tudo."

In Éder Vieira's "Onde eu moro," from 2012, the author dialogues with the eurocentric angst of Gonçalves Dias's original by refocusing the polarity of "cá" (Europe) versus "lá" (Brazil) on the streets of urban Brazil. Here is the creative four-line quip in its entirety: "Onde eu moro / tem bala a passar / tem o carro da / polícia passando / pra lá e pra cá." In this narrowly focused text, any concern with national identity and international status is swallowed up by the worry of dodging bullets and avoiding confrontation with a heavy-handed police force. Other poems, such as Beatriz Lourenço's 2015 "Minha terra,"[9] focused on prostitution, and Gustavo Silva's untitled poem from 2012, concerned with drug abuse, further delineate the problems associated with Brazilians who find themselves in harm's way on the periphery of mainstream society.

In recent years, Brazil has been called the most dangerous country for environmentalists. Scientists and activists are currently being murdered at an alarming rate there.[10] This tragic surge in murders is only one of the latest symptoms of decades upon decades of environmental exploitation and mismanagement. While the Amazon's verdant canopies and untamed rivers teeming with incalculable life have long represented the promise of Gonçalves Dias's Brazil, in these twenty-first century variations, the polluted rivers of the nation's urban centers and the embroiled reality of illegal logging, farming, and mining elsewhere heatedly rebuke this Romantic portrayal. The texts in the environmental category strike at the heart of the nation as they demonstrate that, with the destruction of its environment, not only are Brazil's forests and rivers at risk, but also its identity.

To wit, in Eloí Elisabete Bocheco's 2015 poem, "Minha terra tem chagas na alma e chora," (visually represented on this book's cover), the author personifies a self-sacrificial land which suffers under the abuse of unchecked and illegal exploitation:"Espumas ácidas lhe saem das entranhas feridas / Minha terra leva golpes em seus poros todos os dias / As palmeiras de minha terra balançam pânicas diante / de motosserras, poluição, queimadas." Published on the same blog as Bocheco's text, along with a group of other variations, Helena da Rosa's "Exílio é para quem fica" holds a similar view: "Ah, nossa terra! Tantos bosques / tanta vida e naturais belezas / extinguindo-se pelas mãos da ignorância / do filho cruel a esmagar a harmonia da Natureza." Another poem entitled "A terra que há," written by Elzimara Souza in 2012, changes the verb "tem" in the first line to "tinha," summing up the general sentiment of this category of texts: "Minha terra tinha palmeiras / mas o homem começou a cortar."

As in the other two categories, the main message of the texts in the corruption category is that Brazilians themselves are to blame for the failure of the utopia once envisioned for their country. It is important to note, however, that such failure to some degree or another is written in the cards for every nation-state; no nation has ever nor ever will completely live up to the ideals of its myths. Even the word itself, *utopia*, a term invented by Thomas More soon after the discovery of the Americas, can be translated as either "no place" or "happy place." The point in these texts regarding corruption in Brazil is that those citizens specifically designated as elected officials with a mandate to implement change that could bring the utopia to fruition are not only failing to do so but making things worse. While themes of corruption and abuse of the public trust have been present in the "Canção do exílio" variations since the nineteenth century, in the twenty-first century, these abuses present themselves in more pervasive ways vis-à-vis contemporary scandals, such as the "Mensalão" and "Lava-Jato."

"As sirenes que aqui apitam" (1999–2015)

The Lava-Jato Operation, begun in 2014, was a monumental investigation that uncovered widespread money laundering within the state-owned Petrobrás Company, implicating not without controversy many high-profile public officials, such as the former President Luiz Inácio Lula da Silva, among many others. The investigation eventually led to a problematic impeachment process that controversially ousted President Dilma Rousseff, Brazil's first democratically-elected female head of state. Further confirming the continued adaptability of Gonçalves Dias's original to current events, the Lava-Jato Operation makes at least two appearances in the texts from 2015. With a unique title that manages to be consonant with the original, the poem "Extinção do empecilho," by Tere Tavares, longs for a Brazil freed from corruption as he places his faith in the results of the Lava-Jato. Littered throughout with terms from the original, such as "sabiá," "estrelas," and "céus," the first few lines pick up where the title leaves off, which, if translated, would read as the "extinction of [our] empediment": "Se isso ocorrer de fato / Haverá menos Gato e Rato / Orfanato e Cão / Toda fé na Lava Jato / A fatal Operação."

In 2006, a group of high school students published a variation online amid the Mensalão, a scandal where Brazil's ruling party had been exposed for buying votes in congress. This variation, called "Canção da revolta," levels the following complaints against Brazil's politicians: "Minha terra tem políticos / Que só sabem roubar / Enquanto muitos trabalham / Outros só sabem desviar" (Elysa et al.). Then, the poem closes by expressing a desire to see those responsible for the "mensalão" in jail: "Não permita Deus que eu morra / Sem ver o mensalão acabar / Sem que possa ter a felicidade / De os políticos na cadeia colocar."

In an article entitled "You Had Me at Hello: How Phrasing Affects Memorability," Danescu-Niculescu-Mizil and others analyzed 1000 movie scripts to determine what makes some movie lines more memorable than others. The two main observations made from the results of the study showed that "memorable quotes often involve a distinctive turn of phrase" and that they "tend to invoke general themes that aren't tied to the specific setting they came from, and hence can be more easily invoked for future (out of context) uses" (Danescu-Niculescu-Mizil et al.). Demonstrated by their continued popularity and constant re-invention, the lines of "Canção do exílio," especially the first two, function in a similar

Chapter Six

manner, easily satisfying both conditions. They are highly memorable yet generalized enough to re-invent themselves constantly in new contexts and at the hands of newer generations. As the word "terra" takes on different characteristics depending on, among other factors, narrative mode and historical context, the discursive space created by its presence is constantly re-populated by an ever-evolving cast of nouns representing the Brazilian nation. Like the texts written during the military dictatorship, the original's most recent variations have adopted a generally negative outlook for Brazil. Constituting a virtual list of societal ills, these variations present some of the more troubling issues in Brazilian society today, namely destruction of the environment, political corruption, and inequality, all discussed in further detail in the next chapter on female-authored texts.

Chapter Seven

"Sou ali"
Variations by Female Authors
(1867–2015)

Published in 1991 in *Simians, Cyborgs and Women*, Donna Haraway described "A Cyborg Manifesto" as an "effort to contribute to socialist-feminist culture and theory ... in the utopian tradition of imagining a world without gender" (150). In the manifesto, Haraway employed the idea of the cyborg as a transcendent "hybrid of machine and organism" capable of overcoming the dualisms of Western society (149). Her specific argument states that "high-tech culture challenges dualisms," such as manwoman and human-machine, as she proposes that women, using technology, may augment their powers and presence, intellectual, physical, and otherwise, while obscuring gender differences (177). This technological transformation would allow women to no longer be bound by the category of "other" historically imposed upon them by the patriarchy; a move that would help women more easily overcome long-established barriers to equality and opportunity. As controversial as it was influential, Haraway's "A Cyborg Manifesto" not only imagined, for a pre-internet public, important theoretical stances for feminism, but it also anticipated many of the profound changes that the spread of technology would provoke in the decades to follow.

In the study at hand, there is an example of the almost literal fulfillment of the cyborg proposition as the advent of the internet and social media have given unprecedented numbers of Brazilian women the opportunity to contribute publicly to the nation-making dialectics bound to the intertextual universe of "Canção do exílio." This drastic increase in female authorship reflects positively on the current Western "shift of all culture to computer-mediated forms of production, distribution, and communication," demonstrating one of the many ways that technology can be used as a grand equalizer (Manovich, *Language* 19). Grossly underrepresented in the "Canção do exílio" variations published prior to the year 2000, female authors now have an almost equal share in authorship. The significance of this increase in female voices in the new millennium in contrast to historical absence makes this chapter a welcome and necessary operation specifically intended to recognize female authors' contributions to the ever-expanding narrative tradition.

Considering the year 2000 as a convenient dividing point (although the internet came to Brazil a few years prior), there are drastic differences in the pre- and post-millennial numbers of female authors. Between 1846 and 1999, only 5 of the 258 texts were of female authorship.[1] On the other hand, in the first 16 years of the twenty-first century (2000–15), 98 of the 242 texts, or 40%, were written or co-written by at least one female author with most of these texts published electronically. Indeed, if the current authorship trend continues, the last variation by a sole male author will be published in just a few short years with female-authored and collaboratively mixed-gender authored texts completely dominating the scene. More likely, however, is that the ratio of male-to-female authors will stabilize as women gain parity and reflect more accurately Brazil's balanced population dynamics.[2]

Importantly, these 103 texts are not the only female-authored variations ever written. There are certainly other pre- and post-millennial female-authored texts beyond these 103 texts. The assumption, though, is that the statistics presented about these texts are representative enough so that, even if the hurdle of large amounts of dark data[3] were overcome, every variation ever written were located, and the gender of the author known, the ratio of female-to-male authored texts among all variations would continue to be basically the same. The pre–2000 variations would be vastly dominated by male authors (although I would not mind being proven wrong in this case) and the post-internet texts would evince an obvious surge to the contrary.

This chapter presents distant and close readings of these 103 female-authored variations as it reveals the important narratives that emerge vis-à-vis the nation. In general, our readings will show that most of these 103 poems challenge the homogenizing and heteronormative paradigms of the original through a post-structural and intersectional questioning of Brazilian identity. Refuting the utopic narrative of the original in favor of more sobering views of Brazil, these poems discuss themes such as pollution, poverty, racism, corruption, machismo, and violence, often conflating the struggle of women with those of other historically excluded groups.

An analysis of the most frequent nouns among the 103 female-authored texts helps to trace their general word-choice contours. Quantifying the number and frequency of nouns borrowed from the original delineates the most obvious textual similarities shared by the group with the original. These repeated nouns serve as nodes of semiotic convergence connecting texts across time while providing glimpses into the breadth of intertextuality existent in the corpora. The results of a frequency analysis of the 103 female-authored texts were compared with the same analysis of the 244 texts from 1999–2015 and then again with the entire group of 500 texts.[4] In the 103 female-authored texts, the first eleven most frequent nouns from the original poem closely approximate those of the 2000s as a whole. The list is as follows (from the greatest to the least number of occurrences): "terra" (204), "sabiá" (60), "palmeiras" (56), "noite" (54), "deus" (42), "céu" (30), "canção" (23), "estrelas" (20), "exílio" (19), and "flor" (19).[5] The overlap in the two groups coupled with the fact that they both share "lugar" as the first most frequent non-original noun corroborates the observation that these female-authored texts—all authored in the 2000s with the exception of 5—differ little from contemporaneous texts by male authors.

The three most frequent nouns of the female-authored texts—"terra," "sabiá," and "palmeiras"—are also the same as the three most frequent nouns (and in the same order) as those of the entire corpora of 500. As the study at large shows, the prominence of the binomial pair, "sabiá" (60), and "palmeiras" (56), along with the frequency of "terra," especially in the phrase "minha terra tem" ("terra" appears 204, "minha" 205, and "tem" 265 times in the female-authored texts), are the tell-tale traits of most variations. Thus, these female-authored texts, by containing most of the 17 unique nouns appearing in the original, and the same three most frequent nouns, evince great textual similarity not only with the 2000s text, but also with the rest of the corpora. In this aspect, there is little difference across the texts from 1846 to today.

Despite this consistency, the paradox found among the texts from the 2000s remains intact in the female-authored texts. While being 4% more textually related to the original than those written prior to the new millennium, the female-authored texts are less like the original in message. Specifically, these 103 female-authored texts are mostly pessimistic about Brazil, with only 32 in the positive mode, 21 in the other mode, and 50 in the negative mode. Themes involving the defining social ills of Brazil today dominate the thematic content. As already demonstrated, however, this is not a new occurrence; sadly, since the dictatorship, the negative mode has controlled the discourse. The sense is that, as the texts continue to be more textually related to the original, but contrary in meaning, Brazil could be potentially approaching a paradigmatic shift in identity wherein the original is entirely subverted, becoming a shell of its former self. On the other hand, as indicated by the 32 texts in the positive mode, all is not lost. Many Brazilians are still not prepared to give up completely on Stefan Zweig's "land of the future" and Brazil's reality most certainly rests somewhere in between. The cataloguing of tokens that replace "palmeiras" within the fifty negative texts further details the generally dark vision of Brazil that characterizes the 2000s. A precursory reading of the titles of these texts in the negative mode sorted by year of publication already begins to demonstrate what we might expect to see in a *Types and Tokens Analysis*.[6] Nouns such as "pobreza," "grito," "expropriados," "revoltas," "martírio," "corruptos," and "contrários" stand out among the titles. The *Types and Tokens Analysis* below focuses on the first line of the original. Of note is the tendency among these texts to negate the assertion of the original as in "Minha terra não tem palmeiras" or "Minha terra tinha palmeiras." In such cases, as before, the noun disclosed has been struck through to indicate its negative (i.e.: ~~palmeiras~~)

Minha terra tem _____

acarajé   ~~asfalto~~
algumas árvores   atlético
altares de ouro   ~~aves~~
analfabetos   bananeiras
antas   bandidos
araras de safira   beleza
arroios de diamantes   ~~belezas~~

"Sou ali" (1867–2015)

borboletas
buracos
buzinas
cadeia (para preto pobre puta)
cadeias (mal assombradas)
calvário
canto emudecido
carência
casas (sem rebocar)
~~chão verde~~
cheiro de queimada
chimarrão
churrasco
cidades sepultadas
cobras grandes
coisas feias
colibris de opalas
contrastes (agudos)
corrupção
corruptos
criança de rua
crianças (a mendigar)
crianças (desprovidas de direitos)
crianças (massacradas)
cruzeiro
damas da noite
desamores
dinheiro (para rico)
doenças
drogas
encantos mil
engana-tico no fubá
~~escolas~~
escolas (ignoradas)
professores (desvalorizados)
professores (deprimidos)
escolas (sucateadas)
esgoto (a céu aberto)
especiarias
estádios
~~estradas~~
~~estrelas~~
exílio
favelas
feijoada
flores
~~flores~~
fome
fomes
frutas com coroas e cravos
~~frutíferas árvores~~
fumaça
gado de corte
gente alegre
gente astuta
gente bonita
granadas
grileiro
grutas que faíscam no escuro
heitores
horrores
~~hospitais~~
igrejas
~~índio~~
infância do exílio
injustiças
~~inquérito~~
Internacional [futebol]
janela
ladrões
lagos
latifúndio
lírios mosqueados
lixo
macacos
madeireiras
maior carente
mais fumaça
mangueiras (mais)

Chapter Seven

mansão (para rico)
mar
maravilhas (encomendadas)
marginais
mendigos
menino (sem camisa)
menino na lixeira
menor abandonado
~~mico-leão-dourado~~
misérias
morcego
muralhas
nuvens de poluição
o efeito estufa
ódio
~~onça~~
órfãos
os fortes
~~os fracos~~
Palmeiras [futebol]
~~palmeiras~~
palmérios
pântanos (que choram lágrimas de óleo em vez de água estagnada)
papagaios
~~papas na língua~~
pássaros
pedras
pés que nascem fugindo
piolho
pobreza
poeira
poema concreto
poema sujo
políticos
~~políticos modelo~~
ponto g ignorado
ponto por debaixo dos panos
povo ("forte, impávido, colosso")
pragas

praia
praias maravilhosas
pranetas
~~prazeres~~
preto no branco
primores
~~primores~~
problemas
professores (frustrados)
profusão de asfaltos
promessas de políticos
prostituição
puta
puteiro
queimadas
quilômetros de sede
~~recursos~~
relíquias de amantes fantasmas
~~rio~~
rolas de âmbar
rosas
~~sabiá~~
~~salvação~~
sangue
santinho
~~saúde~~
seringueiras sangradas
serra de ouro
sol
soldado na favela
dificuldades (tantas)
tapetes na porta à espera
~~terra~~
tudo que há de bom
varejeira
Vasco
verde (mais)
verme (explorador de viúva)
violência
voodoo

The above list of tokens clearly demonstrates that the female-authored texts in the negative mode are concerned with an abundance of issues pertaining to modern-day Brazil. This systematic reading presents a mosaic of the nation's problems in counterpoint to the original's unifying narrative. In its place, these varied images portray critical perspectives of Brazil bound closely to feminist political strategies; the texts question and subvert the hierarchies and discourses that, over the course of the nation's history, have led to the exploitation and exclusion of some in favor of the privilege of others. The messages of these texts are multitudinous and, applying the theories of Joan W. Scott, the feminist political strategies that these texts embody form an "exposure of the kinds of exclusions and inclusions—the hierarchies—it [in our case, Brazilian identity] constructs, and a refusal of their ultimate 'truth.'" (48). These narratives, thus, constitute perspectives that promote "an equality that rests on differences ... that confound, disrupt, and render ambiguous the meaning of any fixed binary position" (Scott 48). Subsequently, the superlative position of Brazil is disrupted as the binary of "cá" / "lá" has also burst into a constellation, replacing a capitalized singular National History with not just numerous small (his)stories, but more especially (her)stories.

In 1867, H. de Mendonça from Goiás published "Saudades da minha terra" in the *Jornal das famílias*. Written in the positive mode, the content of H. de Mendonça's early variation is not especially unique, but the text is still historically significant since it is, for now, the earliest known female-authored variation. The text assumes the narrative voice of the author's sister, assumedly in the court of Emperor Dom Pedro II in Rio de Janeiro.

Saudades da minha terra:

paródia por uma goiana à sua irmã na corte
Minha terra tem palmeiras,
Que mais belas nunca vi,
As campinas verdes cores;
Lá viceja o Buriti.

Nossas flores tem perfumes
Que na infância eu colhi,
Nossas brenhas mais negrumes;
Lá descanta a Juriti.

Chapter Seven

Puros ares sem neblina
Foi só lá que eu fruí!
Que país mais rico de ouro,
Haverá no mundo assim?

Nossas aves têm endeixas! ...
Mais saudosas nunca ouvi.
Aqui ... são tristes as queixas.
Melodias?! ... só ali.

Negros olhos buliçosos
Mais formosos que eu já vi;
Róseos lábios são viçosos
Sem carmim como os daqui.

Nesses lagos cor de prata
Quantas vezes eu me vi?!
Os rios formam cascata;
Junto deles eu nasci ...

As florestas são gigantes,

Lá sibila a sucuri;
Nesses campos verdejantes
É que cresce o muricy.

Nossas redes são macias,
Mais macias que as de cá;
Nas bebidas, todas frias,
Prima o doce guaraná!

Os rios todos piscosos ...
As frutas todas sabor ...
Quem nos fez assim ditosos?!
Foi o mágico Criador.

Tudo lá indica a Deus,
Almo rei da criação:
Esse azul puro dos céus
Não te inspira à oração?!

A alma toda pudor
De magia transcendente,
Foi só lá que eu vi-a crente,
Alvo ninho do amor! ...

Eu não sei se é saudade

De tudo o que lá eu vi ...
Dizei-me pois a verdade:
Nossa terra não é assim? ...

"Sou ali" (1867–2015)

> Dizei-me, ó alma crente,
> Se acaso eu me iludi?!
> A Goiana nunca mente,
> Eu só conto o que eu vi! (H. de Mendonça, "Saudades" 127–28)

The original "Canção do exílio," published only a generation before, served as an obvious touchstone for H. de Mendonça as she took her first professional steps in her literary career. In her text, she employs a comparable romantic bent, straightforward imagery, and a memorable and popular rhyme scheme as she follows closely the rhetoric of the original. Showing many classic signs of a variation in the positive mode, the text glorifies the author's native region of Goiás in contrast to the capital where her sister lives among the nobles in the imperial court. In H. de Mendonça's divinely blessed Goiás, the birds' songs are more beautiful, the rivers and lakes more vibrant, the beds softer and the fruits more delicious. This text's regional focus, comparing different areas of Brazil to each other, is a common occurrence among the variations, especially those in the positive mode, as authors typically propose the superiority of their specific town or state as a metonym for the superiority of Brazil itself.

According to Eliane Vasconcellos, H. de Mendonça was the first female from Goiás to publish a book of literature (88). Her collection of poems, *A redenção*, published in 1875, and many of her other works appeared in periodicals such as *O Domingo* and the above referenced *Jornal das famílias*. Beginning with the subtitle to the poem above, "Paródia por uma goiana à sua irmã na corte," it is apparent that H. de Mendonça and her sister, who Vasconcellos named as Maria Leonilda Carneiro de Mendonça, were of a more privileged class (89). This upbringing would have allowed H. de Mendonça the opportunity to be educated and less encumbered by domestic responsibilities, giving her comparatively more free time for literary pursuits than most women. Still, this conjecture should not downplay the courage of H. de Mendonça and other pioneering female authors with similar backgrounds; privilege is no guarantee of interest in writing nor publication, nor does it erase other professional challenges and obstacles posed by the patriarchy. Based on her publication record, it is apparent that H. de Mendonça was not only seriously dedicated to the art of literature, but also persistent enough to have her work make its

Chapter Seven

way into print despite the challenges. For this reason, Mendonça's text deserves not only special recognition among the variations, but the author deserves to be included among the growing list of nineteenth-century female writers whose works have been rescued in recent decades through what has been termed a process of "*arqueologia literária*" (Alós 691).

While the most historically significant text of these 103 female-authored texts is H. de Mendonça's from the nineteenth century, the longest female-authored text is from the mid-twentieth century.[7] Published in a newspaper in 1948, Haydee Nicolusi's "Canção do turista malogrado" expresses frustration that the nation cannot capitalize on its own beauty and resources. According to the poem, this shortcoming keeps tourists from discovering Brazil's natural wonders and diminishes potential for profits. In this capitalist light, the text can be read as part of a concerted early twentieth-century modernization effort spearheaded in the 1930s by the Vargas regime to commodify and package Brazil for tourism. According to Skidmore, this effort, including the institutionalization of soccer as the national sport and Carnaval as the nation's yearly cultural celebration, "was clearest after the [Vargas] coup of 1937" and had "an economic rationale (to attract tourism)" while also "help[ing] to soften the dictatorship's image of repression and censorship" (118). By the time Nicolusi published her poem in 1948, the success of Vargas's policies were obvious.[8]

> Canção do Turista Malogrado
>
> Minha terra tem lagos que olham o céu com olhos de novilhas sonhando,
> A água das cascatas tece rendas como a roca das velhas fadas,
> Há regiões que ainda estão nascendo no ventre de florestas meninas,
> Mas para ver tudo isso de perto só falta uma coisa: estradas.
>
> Minha terra tem flores tão raras tais se fossem de prata ou vidro,
> Cada vitória régia em botão é uma pomba de asas fechadas,
> Tem lírios mosqueados como tigres, parasitas-veleiros, navegando,
> Mas para ver tudo isso de perto só falta uma coisa: estradas.
>
> Minha terra tem pássaros que são verdadeiras joias de penas;
> —rolas de âmbar, colibris de opalas, araras de safira e granadas,
> Quando as garças pousam para dormir cada árvore é um ramo branco de noiva,
> Mas para ver tudo isso de perto só falta uma coisa: estradas.

"Sou ali" (1867–2015)

> Minha terra tem cobras grandes que mamam peitos de moça,
> Tem antas que arrasam povoações quando estouram em manadas,
> Tem macacos que riem e choram e papagaios que falam como gente!
> Mas para ver tudo isso de perto só falta uma coisa: estradas.
>
> Minha terra tem arroios de diamantes e serra de ouro sem vulcões,
> Os vales quando estão florindo imitam tapeçarias bordadas,
> Tem grutas que faíscam no escuro que nem broches de brilhantes,
> Mas para ver tudo isso de perto só falta uma coisa: estradas.
>
> Minha terra tem igrejas cor de luar esculpidas por gente sem mãos!
> Tem relíquias de amantes fantasmas. Tem cadeias mal assombradas,
> Tem cidades sepultadas na bruma com mais de trezentos anos.
> Mas para ver tudo isso de perto só falta uma coisa: estradas.
>
> Minha terra tem frutas com coroas e cravos que nem a Cruz,
> Tem pântanos que choram lágrimas de óleo em vez de água estagnada,
> Minha terra tem tudo que há de bom no mundo: tem até homens!
> É nesses que nós pomos nossa última esperança frustrada ...
> (Nicolusi 6)

Divided into seven stanzas of four lines each, the first line of each stanza in "Canção do turista malogrado" approximates the original by repeatedly employing its most common phrase, "minha terra tem." In this way, the poem, as do many others, reads as one long extension of the original's first line. But, in Nicolusi's capitalistic "canção," Gonçalves Dias's "palmeiras" and "sabiá" are substituted by a variety of attractions, both natural and man-made. Among other things, Nicolusi's "terra" has lakes, waterfalls, young forests, rare flowers, birds, snakes, monkeys, diamonds, churches, gold, and buried cities (6). While the mention of "canção" in the title leaves no doubt about the poem's indebtedness to the original, this litany of tokens associated with the original's "palmeiras" also provides a comparable subject matter: Brazil's natural wonders. Yet, the exiled in this poem is not the poet from his native home. It is the tourists from their adventures and subsequently the capitalists from their money. To remedy this, and to facilitate greater extraction of profits, more infrastructure is needed, namely "estradas" (6). And while the fourth line in each stanza except for the last affirms this fact, the last line then reminds us of what is keeping the nation from its capitalistic progress. Tellingly, it is the same factor that stood in the way of the colonizers: "homens" (6). But, somewhat different from the Tupi Guarani and other tribes, this time the men in Nicolusi's poem obstruct the modernizing project through their inept governance and lack of expertise and not through any resistance to the idea.

To balance these longer texts, written in the nineteenth and twentieth centuries, the twenty-first has much shorter poems, all falling well below the average word-count. The shorter texts from the twenty-first century are often composed of only four lines mirroring the first stanza of the original. As an example of a shorter text with a unique subject matter is Guta Gatuna's Twitter-inspired "Gonçalves Dias Revisited" (2009). In this poem, Brazil's "sabiás" do not sing, but tweet: "Minha terra tem palmeiras / Onde twittam os sabiás / As aves que aqui twittam / Não twittam como as de lá" (Gatuna). Emblematic of how the original is inherently shareable, modular, and moldable to new contexts, the verb "twittam" is employed as a neologism based on the popular social media app Twitter, further demonstrating how variations have become even more frequent and more easily circulated as the original is adapted to new media environments.

Although not as diminutive as Gatuna's poem, another female-authored poem in the same new-media vein is Bianca B. Gomes's untitled text from 2012. In Gomes's text, she replaces Gonçalves Dias's "palmeiras" with "Facebook," confirming that it is now through the open-ended virtual environment of the internet that the poem's life will continue to grow:

> Minha terra tem facebook
> onde eu entro sem parar
> sou tão viciada
> que não quero nem estudar.
>
> Posto sempre besteiras
> mas tem várias curtições
> a galera comenta
> e compartilha de montão.
>
> Quando chego da escola
> corro logo pro pc
> entro no facebook
> e esqueço de viver. (24)

Elaine Pauvolid's existentially disruptive poem "Sou ali" from 2005 is another diminutive text which dialogues, although less obviously than most, with Gonçalves Dias's original. Without

Brazil as a referent, this text expresses its uniqueness positioned as an "other" as it manages to achieve the status of variation without employing any of the most frequently borrowed nouns or phrases. Instead, Pauvolid's poem finds itself in conversation with "Canção do exílio" through its syntax and the use of other less commonly borrowed words. With the subtle title, "Sou ali," the poem begins its alternative discourse. Pauvolid's use of the preposition "ali" creatively opens a third space outside of the "cá" / "lá" dialectic of the original. For non-native speakers, the word "ali" translates the same as "lá" as "there," but with a key difference lost in translation: "ali" indicates a space between a more distant "lá" and a close "cá" / "aqui" or "here." In this marginal space, the author can work out her own identity not in relation to the nation, but existentially, as in her relation to life as a poet. Appended to the first-person conjugation of the verb "to be" in the title, the two words together (trans.: "I am there") open a personal space for the poet's succinct rumination. Then, the poem overlaps with the original through the non-traditional uses of the verbs "gorjear" and "cantar." But, instead of indicating the song of the "sabiá" descanting the wonders of Brazil, these verbs hint ironically at an internal silence and nothingness that the author confronts through her poetry. In the closing line, employing the word "onde," the intertextual dialogue concludes by pointing not to the place in the palms where the "sabiá" sings, but to the place where the poet's psychological drama unfolds: in the silence.

> Sou ali
>
> Tudo silencia e gorjeia
> como gorjeasse o nada.
> No entanto, gorjeia tanto este silêncio
> que me tange e não me rompe
> que poeta me vi nascer para cantá-lo.
> Sou o cerne deste silêncio.
> Onde ele toca, aqui estou. (Pauvolid)

As another example of a diminutive female-authored variation, the metaphor in the title of Marta Helena Cocco's hemispherically focused "Versão enlatada do exílio" (2001) sets the tone for its sarcastic message. According to the poem, the siren song of American popular culture and art, conveniently packaged for world consumption, has left an indelible mark on Brazil and

Chapter Seven

veered it from the utopic course laid out by Gonçalves Dias's original. Referencing US cultural expansionism through the filmic genre of Westerns, the poem first proposes Brazilians have been listening too intently to the "som do Sam" (qtd. in Silva Sá 207). These lines are an obvious reference to Uncle Sam who is a personified symbol of American military might going back to the War of 1812.

> Versão enlatada do exílio
>
> Em lá
> sang sung
> som do Sam
> soa bem
> bang bang.
> E cá
> sangue sangue
> sanguessugas
> se dão bem. (qtd. in Silva Sá 6)

Here Uncle Sam's "som," or sound, serving as a translingual homonym for the English word "song," emanates not only from "lá" (the US), but also in the solfege key of "La." Through this creative wordplay, the author reminds us that Brazilian identity in the 20th century, and especially after World War II, instead of being defined by its politico-cultural ties with Portugal and Europe, has been primarily defined by its ties with the US. In this reconfigured dialectic of "cá" (Brazil) and "lá" (United States), the glamorous violence of Western films, depicting the historical lawlessness and genocidal kill-or-be-killed Real Politik of Manifest Destiny, serves as a capitalist metaphor of intercontinental relations. For the author, the results of US expansionism are clear. They compose a violent narrative that has left Brazil in a pool of "blood," both metaphorical and literal, swarmed by its own copy-cat "bloodsuckers": "E cá / sangue sangue / sanguesugas / se dão bem" (qtd. in Silva Sá 6). In this way, the poem reminds us that, if Brazil and other colonies of the Americas were ever inspired by "Uncle Sam" in the nineteenth century to fight for their own independence, then in the twentieth century Brazil has, with the illegal trafficking of America's high caliber rifles and handguns, become one of the most murderous nations on the planet (Hearn).

"Canção do exílio in Japan," published by Marcia Miyasaki in 2008,[9] is a classic example of the utopic moorings of the positive mode. The text closely mirrors the syntax and meaning of the original, but with a modern twist. The author is a "dekassegui," or one of hundreds of thousands of Japanese-Brazilians who, beginning in the late 1980s, returned to Japan in search of a better life. Employing the typical tactic of token substitution, Miyasaki modifies the original to provide a snapshot of popular Brazilian culture, placing it in a positive light in comparison with what she has experienced in Japan. Still, it is no small irony that this example in the positive mode is written by someone who left Brazil because she did not find conditions manageable there. Indeed, as long as there are Brazilians, the fiction of Brazil as a paradise will always persist, even when reality demonstrates otherwise.

The poem begins, as might be expected, with the first two lines of the original, "Minha terra tem palmeiras / Onde canta o sabiá." Then, in the second two lines of the first stanza, the author mimics the unattractive call of the crow instead of the Brazilian thrush: "As aves daqui não gorjeiam / Aqui tem corvo que faz cráá" (Miyasaki). In the second stanza, she hints at a difference in spatial perspectives. She longs for the Brazilian landscape which, in her experience, contrasts with the small homes and tight public spaces typical of urbanized Japan: "Nossas casas tem mais flores / Nossas ruas, mais espaço / Nossos bosques tem mais vida, / Nossa vida, mais sabores." In the next lines, building on the mention of "sabores," the poem covers a number of Brazilian culinary stereotypes, such as "churrasco," "café," and "guaraná." These exist alongside homemade and mass-produced candies, such as the "beijinho," "brigadeiro," and the "Diamante Negro." These popularly consumed items, accompanied by other romanticized Brazilian flora, such as the "laranja," "banana," and "maracujá," complement the "sabiá" and "palmeiras" of the original. The author also goes on to hint at other cultural differences with Japan, such as Brazil's intense Christian traditions of communal worship in contrast to Japan's private Shinto faith. In this vein, she writes: "Quero ir cantar na igreja, / E igreja aqui nem há." The poem then closes with a typical play on words that hints at the assumed "paulista" origins of the writer where there is a significant population of Japanese immigrants. Replacing Gonçalves Dias's "palmeiras" with the three main soccer teams from São Paulo, the first mentioned is the homonymous "Palmeiras," a coincidence which no doubt has precipitated the oft-repeated trope. Then, the author includes "Corinthians" and "São Paulo."[10]

As an example of a female-authored negative variation where a concern for the underrepresented dominates, Porto's "Expropriados" merits a closer look. Written in 2010, this poem adopts the most common tactic among variations, employing the first three words of the original as a template for the elaboration of a list of attributes that, replacing "palmeiras," communicates an entirely different reality for Brazil. Porto's Brazil is a nation filled with violence, exploitation, racism, inequality, and corruption. In the first of three stanzas, she describes the urban realities of the nation's poor, either corralled by the soldier-police in the favelas or homeless and living off scraps. In the second, she rhymes the corrupt "grileiros," who take illegal possession of land and property, with the parasitical "piolho" and "mosca-varejeira," whose larva, once lain in the skin of a host, if undetected, can cause illness and even death. The last stanza paints the stark, yet definitive contrast of haves and have-nots in Brazil. On one hand, the "ricos" have "vantagem / tudo" while the "preto," "pobre," and "puta," instead of the governmental support and resources they need, are given "prison." This drastic contrast with the paradise proposed by the original leads the author to ask in conclusion, "Minha terra?" As seen in Barros's 2009 "Uma canção do exílio," this interrogation of the original's presupposition is a defining feature of variations from the 2000s. Not only is the land not what Gonçalves Dias proposed, for the "expropriated" inhabiting the favelas, the land is not even theirs to contemplate.

> Expropriados
>
> minha terra tem pobreza
> tem soldado na favela
> tem menino na lixeira
> tem esgoto a céu aberto
>
> minha terra tem grileiro
> tem piolho gente astuta
> tem varejeira tem verme
> explorador de viúva
>
> minha terra tem cadeia
> para preto pobre puta
> para rico tem dinheiro

> tem mansão vantagem
> tudo
>
> minha terra? (Porto)

In the "other" mode, there are those texts that, by not articulating Brazil as the referent, offer alternative readings mostly unconditioned by nationalist discourse. Apart from the aforementioned examples about Twitter and Facebook, there are a number of poems in this category, written by both female and male authors, which adapt the original to discuss amorous relationships. The pervasiveness and persistence of the love theme in poetry worldwide coupled with the popularity of "Canção do exílio" in Brazil make this marriage all but an inevitability. As an example of a female-authored text about a relationship is Paula Cajaty's "Desejo de exílio." In an obvious tip of the hat to the original, Gonçalves Dias's "estrelas," "flores," and "palmeiras," among other borrowed terms, are creatively re-appropriated to ruminate on a potential betrayal to take place in the "cama do vizinho."

> Desejo de exílio
>
> dou-lhe uma vida de estrelas,
> ela pede um amor que gorjeie.
> dou-lhe o desfrute das flores,
> ela quer trepar em palmeiras.
> dou-lhe o cantar de um passarinho,
> e ela sonha
> faceira
> com a cama do vizinho. (Cajaty)

"Canto da minha terra," written by Xangô[11] in 2008, is the one variation most easily identifiable as being by an Afro-Brazilian woman. In this poem, which assumes the collective voice of all Brazilians of African descent, the author employs an exilic perspective of an original culture forcibly left behind. In broad strokes, instead of idolizing Brazil, she paints a generally utopic view of the ancestral continent in the pan-African mode, hinting at the rituals and geographies associated with an identity lost to the tragedies of the Middle Passage. As in Gonçalves Dias's original, the utopian qualities of the text are important since "the construction of identity includes the building of a utopia that redeems the

Chapter Seven

community at a symbolic level" (E. Oliveira 36). In this way, the poem becomes part of a wider effort in Brazil beginning in earnest in the 1970s with the *Cadernos negros* to build a black consciousness through literature, an initiative needed to combat the nation's exaggerated racial inequality (E. Oliveira 39).

This text, easily identifiable as a variation of "Canção do exílio," begins in customary fashion with the phrase "Minha terra tem" and then continues with other intertextual echoes, especially the repetition of the "cá" / "lá" dialectic, while advocating for Afro-Brazilians to return to their roots. In this light, the poem references the syncretic religious rituals of Candomblé, which include traditional African music and dance as well as the worship of a pantheon of gods known as "orixás." It also recalls a seventeenth-century war in Palmares[12] where a large community of runaway and emancipated slaves led by Zumbi were besieged and decimated by the Portuguese colonial army, reminding us that the construction of "identity is … a permanent re-telling of the past in which agents reconstruct discourses while envisioning a future" (E. Oliveira 36).

> Canto da minha terra
>
> Minha terra tem cantos e encantos
> Tem dança, música, ritos e rituais
> Onde aqui eu não encontro tudo que tem lá.
> Meu céu tem estrelas lua e luar.
> Minha mata tem verde, tudo que deixei por lá.
> Minha Terra tem Orixás, onde eu canto e
> Toco por eles lá.
> Minha Terra tem lembrança, amizade, amor e tambor
> Onde eu batuco, sempre que posso, toco
> Pra eles nessa banda de cá.
> Minha Terra não tem Palmares, como os daqui
> Lá tem liberdade nos Palmares.
> Terra berço de um povo negro, forte e bravo sempre será
> Povo negro, bravo forte, lutador, rezador e
> Caçador, esperando apenas que o povo de cá
> Reconheça todo esse valor cultural que deixou
> Tudo pra trás. Seja forte e valente a
> Sua vitória está por chegar. (Xangô)

Although there is nothing particularly innovative about Xangô's text in terms of literary form, it is curious that this recently published poem still manages to stand out as the only variation among the 500 texts to deliver a message exclusively about Afro-Brazilian identity. An explanation as to why may rest within the homogenizing force of the original, effecting an erasure of differences as it attempts to join all Brazilians together in a happy uncontentious union much like the "palmeiras" and "sabiá." But, this historical absence of Afro-Brazilian voices also points, as does the absence of female authors prior to 2000, to the subaltern status of blacks in Brazilian society in general, whose representation has been woefully absent in politics and other positions of power. As E. Oliveira argues in *Writing Identity*:

> Confined to underprivileged social conditions, excluded from political channels of participation, inserted in the dominant discourse as the troubled object of study that was either 'inferior' or 'exotic,' stripped of an identity by the presence of the 'mulatto' ideal, blacks [in Brazil] have been denied access to the production of symbolic references that could affirm their identity. (27)

Another standout text from among those of female authorship is Lourenço's "minha terra." Posted online in 2015, along with other variations (which have all been subsequently removed), Lourenço's poem is a bold rebuttal of the endemic misogynist abuses and sexual exploitations of *machismo*, and possibly the one text that best embodies a feminist critique of Brazilian society.

> minha terra
> tem as damas da noite
> que botam pra correr a puta
> que ousar roubar o ponto delas
> tem ponto por debaixo dos panos
> quando um tiozão
> paga por molequinhas virgens
> e por menininhos também
> tem ponto g ignorado
> por trogloditas
> que trepam com suas fêmeas
> como se trepassem
> com uma boneca
> cismo que cismo à noite
> pra ter um pouco de tesão

Chapter Seven

>minha terra
>tem seringueiras sangradas
>pra preservativo virar balão
>minha terra
>não tem papas na língua
>desde que o tupi guarani
>perdeu o posto de língua mãe
>as aves que aqui voejam
>são depenadas no carnaval
>nosso céu de certeza
>só o da nossa boca
>porque contrato com deus
>só no regime celetista
>nossas matas quase mortas
>quase mortos nossos natos
>cismo que cismo à noite
>pra ter um pouco de tesão
>minha terra
>tem seringueiras sangradas
>pra preservativo virar balão.

Dealing with prostitution, pedophilia, and other issues, the poem mixes parasitic atrocities, perpetrated primarily by males, with those of certain damaging environmental practices, animal rights abuses, and even with the extinction of indigenous cultures. Together these offenses offer a sobering counterpoint to the original as they cast a diffuse post-structural light on the dark side of Gonçalves Dias's normative nationalist discourse. The text opposes the original's "palmeiras" and "sabiá" through the presentation of a cast of unwitting and unwilling operatives (i.e., prostitutes fighting over turf) and other downtrodden (exploited children and women tossed around like sex toys) in seemingly inescapable situations of inferiority and domination. With the play on the original's use of the verb "cismar," Lourenço's poem does not anxiously ponder at night her return to the beauties of a Brazilian tropical paradise ("Em cismar sozinho à noite, / Mais prazer encontro eu lá"). Rather, she re-articulates the pleasure principle of Gonçalves Dias's text as a zero-sum power play in which one's enjoyment comes about through another's pain while she anxiously considers whether she is somehow complicit in the Brazilian nightmare she unfolds before us (cismo que cismo à noite / pra ter um pouco de tesão).

"Sou ali" (1867–2015)

To be an exile is to be forcibly placed in a peripheral space. It is the status of not the "one," but an "other" who has been colonized, whether physically or discursively, by an institution (or its agent) in a position of relative power. Thus, while the position in which Gonçalves Dias found himself in 1843 was one of exile, it hardly compares to the tragic circumstances of the sexually exploited "young virgins" of Lourenço's text. Nevertheless, these two subjects still find themselves in dialogue with one another, part of the same exilic discourse. While the first expresses optimism in the nationalist project, the multitudinous perspectives adopted by Lourenço and the other female authors presented in this chapter demonstrate the inherent failure of its heteronormative nationalism, offering in its place a variety of alternative, even if at times painful stories. Thus, while the increase of female-authored "Canção do exilio" variations represents on one hand progress toward Haraway's proto-cyberfeminist world without gender, on the other, the realities communicated through these texts tell us there is still a long path ahead toward achieving equality.

Chapter Eight

"As aves que aqui twittam"
Twitter, Instagram, and Beyond

As Neil Postman posits in *Amusing Ourselves to Death*, the photograph and the text offer two distinct propositions on the world: "the photograph presents the world as object; language, the world as idea ... the photograph documents and celebrates the particularities of [the world's] infinite variety. Language makes them comprehensible" (72). But, even if the two are not the same, they have never really had separate existences. At least since the illuminated manuscripts of early Christian times, created through a painstakingly manual process of applying inks and precious metals to the pages of codices, images have accompanied the written word. Of course, writing itself evolved from what the experimental Portuguese poet Ana Hatherly called a "pintura de signos," or "the painting of signs." In fact, between the interpolation of the world as image, or "object," and the world as text, or "idea," between what our eyes see and what our ears hear—text being the visual representation of a spoken language—all human understanding has evolved.

Today, whether sacred, profane or otherwise, the union of the legible and the visual abounds more than ever. As I have said elsewhere, it is the screen that now unites us. Facilitated by a multitude of digital devices and formats, anyone with access to a smartphone can instantaneously capture and publish modern-day "illuminations" through available social media platforms. In fact, the image and text are the stock-in-trade of social media where photos and quips are uploaded, manipulated, shared in groups, and commented on at-will. On some platforms, such as Snapchat, these posts may quickly disappear. But, on others, such as Instagram and Facebook, they gain a life of their own. Even if Postman would argue that much of the information being shared on new media today is superfluous, I think he would agree that there is a great need for us to comprehend its role in society.

Through standard search engines, such as Google, or through other specialized applications, any enterprising researcher can gather and study these new media "illuminations" and pose questions about society and culture. As discussed in the previous two chapters, since the year 2000, there have been exponentially more "Song of Exile" variations published than in the prior two centuries combined. Furthermore, there are literally thousands upon thousands of intertexts of "Canção do exílio" on Twitter and Instagram alone. Indeed, the ease with which individuals now publish and share online has breathed new life into an already rich intertextual ecosystem, possibly to the point of exacerbation, as we will see in the case of Twitter. Even though almost no posts from Instagram or Twitter were included among the 500 texts, these more recent trends associated with the online community provide fertile ground for further explanation of "Canção do exílio."

When composing the body of 500 texts for analysis, if the general tendency in the years prior to 2000 was toward inclusion, it was necessary post–2000 to use an opposite approach, excluding many texts to keep the corpus at a manageable, yet still robust number. Of course, it also goes without saying that, without the internet, this entire project would have presented itself as too great a challenge since many of the variations, both pre– and post–2000, were discovered in digitized archives and other digital environments. As such, the internet has not only provided the conditions for the poem's continued proliferation but has also created an unprecedented opportunity for its critical study.

Finding its critical orientation somewhere between sociology, visual studies, and literary criticism, one of the minor studies of this project was focused on the relationship between image and text on Instagram and Flickr. The result was an installation for the Bird-watching exhibition entitled "Colors of a Poem," a photographic montage based on 441 photographs uploaded to the above platforms with accompanying texts which borrow from "Canção do exílio" in some way. The process for creating the montage was simple, if time consuming. Similar to those searches conducted in Google Books and the Hemeroteca Digital, research on Instagram and Flickr focused on locating phrases from the original poem in posts and capturing the related text and photos.

"As aves que aqui twittam"

As expected, the best results came from hashtags and comments referencing the first line of the poem, such as #minhaterratem and #minhaterratempalmeiras. Hashtags based on the second line #ondecantaosabiá were also a popular choice among users. (Often this second line was associated with the Escola de Samba Imperatriz Leopoldinense since that line was used as the title of an award-winning samba-enredo from the 1980s. Frequenters of the school's rehearsals now take photos and post them on Instagram with that hashtag.) Other hashtags based on less commonly borrowed lines from the poem, such as "Nossos bosques têm mais vida" and "Não permita Deus que eu morra" likewise produced some results. All in all, more than 550 photographs and accompanying posts were gathered. Although not comprehensive, this number, like that of the 500 intertexts, was sufficiently high to create a preliminary study on the digital relationship between image and text in the poem. (Coincidentally, other Brazilian poems, such as C. D. de Andrade's "Tinha uma pedra," for example, have vibrant lives on Instagram, opening the door for other studies on the visual representation of literature in online communities.)

After being downloaded, these photographs associated with lines from "Canção do exílio" were printed and sorted by hand based on overall color. This artisanal mode of sorting, relying on human perception to differentiate color and image, in comparison to other computer-generated options, was something of a "little data" approach with the goal of placing these visual narratives in dialogue with one another. Put another way, as with many of the texts, these were aggregated visual close readings, albeit hundreds of them. Once printed, the number of photographs was reduced at random from 550 to 441 in order to create a square montage of 21 rows by 21 columns. Already having been assigned a file number, each photograph was organized along a y-axis (top to bottom) based on a spectrum of overall color and, along the x-axis (left to right), from dark to light. Once the montage was complete, the project was returned to the digital, transposing the handcrafted composition into Photoshop based on the position of each file. With each photo digitally reduced to a 2" x 2" square, and with no spaces between them, a Gaussian blur was applied to the montage, eschewing the images and allowing the viewer to focus on the question of color (a reproduction of the montage can be viewed at alainaenslen.com).

Chapter Eight

Three of the four most prominent colors of the montage turned out to be the same as those of the Brazilian flag, namely, blue, green, and yellow, revealing the posts' deep cultural connections with Brazilian identity. As is widely known, the Brazilian flag, like the text of "Canção do exílio," is closely associated with the nation's natural landscape. The green background represents the nation's immense forests; the yellow diamond, its mineral wealth; and the blue circle in the middle, containing the same number of stars as states, represents the night sky. Coincidentally, this constellation in the heart of the flag recalls Gonçalves Dias's line, "Nosso céu tem mais estrelas," just as the green recalls the nation's "palmeiras." Blue, occupying the highest position along the y-axis of the montage, was the most dominant color among the photographs. A total of 147 photographs, or exactly one third of the montage, is primarily this color. The next most prominent color was green with 84 total photographs occupying four rows. Yellow and red tied as the third most prominent colors associated with the poem, with each section taking up three rows of 21 photographs each, or 63 photos per color. The bottom portion of the montage was sorted not based on color *per se*, but on a greyscale. Made up mostly of black and white photographs, this section occupied more space than both the yellow and red sections and the same amount of space as the second most prominent color, green.

An accompanying catalog of numbered QR Codes associated with each photo was created so that visitors to the exhibition could access each of the 441 posts in their original online format. From landscapes to soccer teams and from samba schools to soda cans, all things Brazilian were represented in the photographs and were often able to at least tangentially reproduce the national discourse of the original poem. As might be expected, the primary images found among the 441 photographs mirror the three most frequent nouns in the corpora of 500: "terra," "palmeiras," and "sabiá." Landscapes depicting scenes from the coast to the interior reconfigure in visual form the most frequently repeated noun, "terra." In these landscapes, "sabiás," and especially "palmeiras," are often represented too, and these typically in a favorable light, or positive mode. Thus, as a visual representation of the original, the photography associated with "Canção do exílio" seems to continue primarily in the utopic tradition, reproducing visually the Romantic scenery of the original with rare exception, even while the textual variations have soured toward the negative.

Similar to Instagram and Flickr, Twitter has also been responsible in recent years for a number of new variations of "Canção do exílio," many often bordering on the absurd. In fact, it is very likely that within the last few minutes someone has expanded the poem's intertextual universe by uploading or sharing another variation. Maybe it was a mathematics student posting a useful phrase to friends such as the one mentioned in the introduction: "Minha terra tem palmeiras, / onde canta o sabiá; / SENO A, COSSENO B, / SENO B, COSSENO A." Or maybe someone shared the ridiculous tweet, "Minha terra tem palmeiras onde canta o sabia, mentira não tem mais porque cortei pra fazer papel de troxa [sic]." In this last phrase, "papel de troxa [sic]" constitutes a play on words where "papel" means "paper" made from the chopped down palms, while "papel" also means "role," as in to play the "role of a fool." Another variation is the extremely popular pick-up line, "Minha terra tem palmeiras onde canta o sabiá mas a sua boca e a minha quando que vão se beijar?" This oft repeated tweet is symbolic of the unexpected twists, at times explicit, in the poem's flourishing life on social media. Among the 5932 tweets gathered, the term "beijar," in one form or another (as a verb or noun), appears over 1400 times, with at least one tweet directed at the now-defunct boyband One Direction through the MTV-related hashtag #EMABiggestFans1d.

Over the course of approximately two months in late 2015, with the help of an online tool available at netlytic.org, these 5932 tweets containing the phrase "minha terra tem" were collected in a first attempt to understand the characteristics of the original poem's half-life there. As expected, most tweets gathered with this phrase were clearly related to the original poem. Echoing the other variations, many of these lighthearted texts focused on regional *ufanismos* and subjects like soccer, among other common nationalist themes. Yet, others like those cited above proposed new (if trivial) commentary on daily life. Independent of the subject, though, together these tweets represent the latest trend in the proliferation of an irreverent and diminutive branch of variations that began at least as early as 1849 with this politically charged quatrain: "Minha terra tem palmeiras / Onde canta o sabiá; / Miguelistas, guabirús / Não podem imperar cá" ("Minha terra tem palmeiras" *O Timbyra* 1).[1]

Hypothesizing on the dissemination and survival of cultural trends of all sorts, not just the imitation of poetry, but of the most superficial fads (Beanie Babies) to the most deep-rooted rituals

Chapter Eight

(circumcision), Richard Dawkins in 1976 developed the concept of the "meme." A term adapted from the Greek root *mimeme*, the word is meant to rhyme with the term "gene" as its cultural analog. Defined by Dawkins, a "meme" is a "unit of cultural transmission, or a unit of *imitation*" (192). Dawkins explains, "Examples of memes are tunes, ideas, catch-phrases, clothes fashions, ways of making pots or of building arches. Just as genes propagate themselves in the gene pool ... so memes propagate themselves in the meme pool" (192).

Although the term was coined by Dawkins decades before the internet, it was quickly adapted to the digital age to describe online cultural artifacts that go "viral" as they are shared across a multitude of social media platforms (mostly in the form of misappropriated photos with humorous captions). In an interview for the magazine *Wired*, Dawkins suggested that these "internet memes," as they are called, "instead of mutating by random change and spreading by a form of Darwinian selection ... are altered deliberately by human creativity. Unlike with genes (and Dawkins's original meaning of 'meme'), there is no attempt at accuracy of copying; internet memes are deliberately altered" (Solon). Consequently, many of the tweets gathered for this study represent a "deliberately altered" dramatic departure from the original poem, whose evolution and adaptability has up until now been closely (although not exclusively) tied with the history of the nation. These tweets, true to Dawkins description of internet memes, as suggested, represent a "hijacking of the original idea" (Solon).

Certainly, Gonçalves Dias could not have imagined millennial variations like these:

> From @TheBalboaBruno: "Minha terra tem palmeiras, Onde canta o Sabiá; Bebi muito ontem, E hoje só quero vomitar"

> From @bonfim_andrey: "Minha terra tem palmeiras onde canta o xororó... enquanto vc esta lendo isso mais um gol em Chapecó"[2]

More than just new spins on an old idea, these tweets disregard, or even disrespect outright, the strong connection that the narrative tradition has historically held with the nation itself. Even if there are some examples of these departures written prior to the

2000s, especially among the texts placed in the "other" category, the tweets that inhabit this alternative space now proliferate at an astounding rate. As mentioned, the main body of texts includes only a few tweets in the "other" category, but the ratio of texts in the "other" category is constant across the 500 texts: 50 of 257 from the 19th and 20th centuries and 51 of 243 in this century for a total of 101. Still, it is too early to say if these "anationalist" tweets and the space they inhabit are more global, more local, or something in between. More in-depth studies of these tweets would be a welcome next step, raising interesting questions about national identity and globalization, and about how the nature of literature is evolving in the digital age. To borrow from Manovich's preface to *Instagram and Contemporary Image*, these studies on the evolution of "Song of Exile" in new media serve as a "window into the identities of a young global generation connected by common social media platforms, cultural sensibilities, and visual aesthetics" (4).

Chapter Nine

The Word, the Database, and the Algorithm

> Minha terra tem palmeiras,
> Onde canta o sabiá,
> Se o Haddad é Lula aqui,
> O Lula é Haddad lá.
> (popular chant, 2018 Presidential campaign)

As long as Brazil is, "Canção do exílio" will be its poem. An instant "hit" in the 1840s, the poem has inspired and will continue to inspire thousands more responses. Yet, many critics over the years have downplayed the popularity of the poem, at times even hoping for its demise. In 1932, an anonymous journalist compared "Canção do exílio" with, in his opinion, the far superior work of Olavo Bilac, a Parnassian poet. Wrongfully attributing "Canção do exílio" to the Romantic Casimiro de Abreu, the critic writes:

> Bilac é o Poeta brasileiro ... É o intérprete do anseio nosso. Por isso, não tem época, determinada, no calendário literário. Em 1932, ainda é expoente. Sê-lo-á no ano 2000. O que não será possível é trazermos Casimiro de Abreu, choramingando, para apresentá-lo como um símbolo das nossas letras. Esta história de minha terra tem palmeiras onde canta o sabiá, passou. ("A literatura em 1907 e em 1932")

Half a century earlier, in 1887, the poet and diplomat Lúcio de Mendonça made a similar remark while comparing Gonçalves Dias to Castro Alves. In his short critique, L. de Mendonça declares that the poem "Tyrana da Cachoeira de Paulo Affonso," a poem that few people would remember today, "é muito mais brasileiro e muito mais belo que as ínsulas quadrinhas, não sei porque tão populares: 'Minha terra tem palmeiras / Onde canta o sabiá'" ("Castro Alves" 178). But, despite their assertions to the contrary,

Chapter Nine

these pronouncements only confirm the poem's continued relevance in the Brazilian imaginary. Indeed, as demonstrated in the preceding chapters, the assertion that, by the year 2000, Gonçalves Dias's poem would be long erased from the nation's collective memory could not be further from the truth.

With a referential power in Brazilian culture that is unmatched by any other work of literature, "Canção do exílio" holds the unique position of being the most popular poem in Brazil. Through close readings, distant readings, computational, modal, and algorithmic readings, this study has attempted to systematically represent the characteristics of the metamorphoses of the poem's lines over the course of the last two hundred years. Based on the computational principles of Digital Humanities, as defined by Stephen Ramsay, our experimental readings of the 500 intertexts attempt "to employ the rigid, inexorable, uncompromising logic of algorithmic transformation as the constraint under which critical vision may flourish" (32). Yet, our algorithmic readings (*Syntactic Templates, Modes, Types and Tokens, Frequency Analysis*, etc.), although inspired by or derived from computation, have not worked in opposition to traditional literary readings. Much to the contrary, they have enhanced them. In this vein, Ramsay notes that, while the principal modes of inquiry in the Digital Humanities are computer-based, algorithmic criticism "looks neither to the bare calculating facilities of the mechanism nor to the promise of machine intelligence for its inspiration" (32). He continues, "The hermeneutic proposed by algorithmic criticism does not oppose the practice of conventional critical reading, but … reenvision[s] its logics in extreme and self-conscious forms" (32). Corpora of large numbers of texts are often well served by such a systematic methodology and our algorithmic approaches have helped to normalize the processes of analysis across all 500 texts, making broad perspectives and insights possible.

Guiding our approach to a motley collection of digitized, book-bound, and born-digital texts, the idea of the database has also played an important role in this study's organization. Manovich, speaking of the ways that the digital revolution is re-shaping culture, writes: "a computer database becomes a new metaphor that we use to conceptualize individual and collective cultural memory, a collection of documents or objects, and other phenomena and experiences" (*Language* 215). The logic of the database, that ubiquitous element of new media, is "a cultural form in its own right …

offering a particular model of the world and of the human experience" (*Language* 37). Simply put, this study employs the idea of the database as an unordered collection of discrete items, not favoring any single text over another except for the original. With this idea in mind, the study has gathered a representative sample among thousands of "Canção do exílio" variations and, applying various critical lenses, attempted to group them in meaningful ways for analysis.

Relatedly, it is the idea of the algorithm that serves as inspiration for creating these groups of related texts for analysis, although we do not typically think of conventional critical reading as algorithmic. But let us suppose that an algorithm is to the database what a word is to the alphabet or a melody to a piano keyboard. Manovich makes another analogy: "Just like the game player, the reader of a novel gradually reconstructs the algorithm (here I use the term metaphorically) that the writer used to create the settings, the characters and the events" (*Language* 225). Applying Manovich's metaphor to literary criticism, the critic, through analysis, defines a specific path through a determined text or group of texts to create a reading, distant or close. Emphasizing certain aspects of a text (or texts) over others, she metaphorically defines her path or algorithm. Thus, each reading is an algorithm, which is, in turn, literally and figuratively, a journey through a database of words. Distant readings apply this algorithmic logic to a large group of texts, often with the aid of computers. Or as Moretti put it, distant reading "allows you to focus on units that are much smaller or much larger than the text: devices, themes, tropes—or genres and systems" ("Conjectures" 57) while close reading systematically reorganizes elements of a single text. In the case of "Canção do exílio" and its intertexts, the organization of algorithms, or critical readings, some distant, others close, are meant to offer a comprehensive understanding of the trajectory of the original poem in Brazilian history and culture, examining the emerging narratives from interdisciplinary perspectives.

Another key concept of this study has been Kristeva's "intertextuality." In her original exposé, she offers the "word," or as she put it, the "minimal textual unit" (37), as intertextuality's most basic unit of data for analysis. Applying this logic to the texts at hand, our many analyses have focused on the words of the original "Canção do exílio" as they have traveled through space and time to reappear in subsequent texts. Like the "modularity" of Manovich's new media elements, words from the original poem can be shared and re-combined across a limitless number of subsequent texts which, in turn, represent new cultural and historical realities while still maintaining a relationship to the original text and its context. "Media elements, be they images, sounds, shapes, or behaviors, are represented as collections of discrete samples ... These elements are assembled into larger-scale objects but continue to maintain their separate identities. The objects themselves can be combined into even larger objects—again, without losing their independence" (Manovich *Language* 30).

Thus, the principal hermeneutical task has been to develop a multitude of readings from the reappearances of the words and phrases of the original in later texts, and to consider what these associations tell us about Brazilian culture and identity in the distinct periods under consideration. This methodology has allowed us to directly link nineteenth-century print culture to contemporary digital culture as manifest through the repetition of the original, conceiving each text as a separate data point on a Cartesian plane ordered by similarity to the original (y) and date of publication (x). In this way, Gonçalves Dias's original functions as what I have called a *strategic urtext*, a discrete text in which can be located, in chronological terms, the earliest occurrence of a specific pattern of words. This *strategic urtext* inhabits the gravitational center of a textual universe around which all other texts in the study coalesce in related groups and periods, depending upon the chosen reading, or "algorithm."

Our critical lens has zoomed in on individual texts from specific historical periods, and within those periods, specific words and phrases, while it has also zoomed out to consider trends across the 500 texts as a whole. This dual approach has made the power of counting words, if you will, apparent, showing how the poem rhetorically links Brazil's past and future selves, presenting a grand mise-en-scène of Brazilian identity across a multitude of contexts. Returning to Anita de Melo's quip cited at the beginning of this study, "O Brasil é mesmo uma poesia de Gonçalves Dias até no inferno" (Melo).

In closing, let me provide just two more late examples. As seen in the epigraph which began this chapter, even the 2018 presidential election was not immune to the influence of "Canção do exílio." The poem inspired a popular chant heard in the streets and echoed on Twitter by supporters of Fernando Haddad, the Partido dos Trabalhadores' candidate. Specifically, this variation equated

Haddad with the nation's ex-president Lula da Silva. The "cá" / "lá" dialectic of the original, instead of comparing Portugal to Brazil, communicates the message that Lula, who was "there" in prison in Curitiba and ineligible for election, was represented by Haddad "aqui" among voters on the campaign trail. The campaign's slogan "Haddad é Lula" echoed the same message, denoting that a vote for Haddad, who promised to faithfully carry out the party's agenda focusing on social justice, was the same as a vote for Lula.[1] Linking the campaign to "Canção do exílio" made not only for a catchy rhyme, but also sent the message that today's exaggerated political struggle between the left and right is also a battle over the identity of the nation. Haddad lost the election in a close run-off to Jair Bolsonaro.

Another response that has recently gone "viral" online, composed by two young students from Rio de Janeiro, is a handwritten parody composed, like many other recent variations, in response to a school assignment. First posted in April 2017 by a friend of the students' teacher, the poem was shared over sixteen thousand times on Facebook.[2] Commenting on the violence of the Penha neighborhood in Rio where the two boy authors live, the variation obviously struck a deep chord with Brazilians, who are ever preoccupied with the entrenched violence of the favelas of Rio and other urban peripheries: "Minha terra é a Penha / O medo mora aqui / Todo dia chega a notícia que morreu mais um ali [...] Se cismar em sair à noite / Já não posso mais / Pelo risco de morrer / E não voltar para os meus pais" (qtd. online by Satriano). Nicolás Satriano, in an online report for G1 Rio, considers the reasons for the explosive popularity of this particular response: "[Esta] versão carioca rapidamente comoveu a web: expõe, de modo poético, a triste realidade de quem vive em meio à violência que mata inocentes diariamente—inclusive dentro de colégios, como na morte da menina Maria Eduarda." With the neighborhood of Penha and the fear of a violent death replacing the original's "palmeiras" and "sabiá," this text once more reiterates the poem's uncanny ability to reinvent itself with every generation.

Afterword

Literary Research as Data Art
An Experiment in Critical Reading

I have had the privilege of seeing Joshua Enslen's *Song of Exile: A Cultural History of Brazil's Most Popular Poem, 1846–2018* evolve into its present form[1] as one element within a series of representations, including three site-specific gallery exhibitions and one interactive website. I highlight this book's relation to those other forms of presentation because they must be seen as components of a single project. Not only are they methodologically related—in the sense that the book, exhibitions, and website explore forms of cultural and literary analysis based on computational tools—, but they also make a strong argument for forms of presenting and communicating literary research in visual form, that is, beyond the traditional scholarly monograph. The expressive visualization of textual networks (in analog and digital media) is not incidental or accessory to the project but, on the contrary, is entirely intrinsic to it. The book, exhibitions, and website inform each other and constitute an open-ended exploration of possibilities for relating the verbal and the visual in a media ecology where the digital is both research tool and communication environment. The book's extended argument about "Song of Exile" as the most remixed Brazilian poem is thus framed within what I would call an experiment in critical reading, which calls for hybrid forms of dissemination and public engagement.

This book may be described as an experiment in critical reading in two distinct senses. First, it draws on computational methods for exploring the textual and cultural history of a highly significant Brazilian poem, which had never been studied in this way. For the past decade, such quantitative methods have been variously described as cultural analytics (Manovich 2009), algorithmic criticism (Ramsay 2011), distant reading (Moretti 2013), and macroanalysis (Jockers 2013). Taking advantage of the fact that the ongoing massive digitization of artifacts has made artistic and literary works (and many kinds of social interaction mediated by electronic networks) available as processable digital code, these methods use the encoding of visual, sonic, and verbal artifacts for large-scale automatic analysis. An array of algorithmic techniques can be applied on such datasets, enabling machine analysis of patterns beyond the small set of artifacts that has commonly been the basis for most interpretative action in the arts and humanities.

This book is also an experiment in critical reading insofar as it has based many of its insights and discoveries in practice-based research methods, which turned the analytic process of constructing the poem's intertextual networks into a series of artworks in various analogue and digital media (collages, graphs, montages, film, manifesto, interactive poetry, and sound), as well as a digital visualization in an interactive website. Its practice-based approach expresses its post-digital imagination of literary research as data art and information visualization. Given its focus on the tangibility of its representations, its visualization of various reading strategies is rehearsed as an analogue remodeling of data points, creating an additional level of translation of digital conventions. The exhibition's de-familiarizing effect results from retro-mediating Excel tables and screen digital objects as handcrafted graphs and charts and as collages on walls, plinths, and showcases. Instead of manipulating infographics and digital interfaces, reader-viewers are asked to traverse the de-automated haptic three-dimensional immersive space of visualization in the gallery.

The exhibition's approach uses techniques for expressing textual patterns through visualizations, while drawing attention to the specific heuristics and rhetoric of each visualization. The range of different visual renderings of textual relations foreground the constructed nature of the data used for generating visual forms. Expressive remediation of digital analyses as artworks offers the textual traverse as an embodied experience of the dynamics of literary fields. Current aesthetics of knowledge visualization and related research into the problems of translating various kinds of metrics into structured visual representations provide another relevant context for understanding this project, which can be placed in dialogue with concepts such as visual complexity (Lima), graphesis (Drucker), and instagramism (Manovic, "Instagram").

Manovich describes "information visualization as a mapping between discrete data and a visual representation" ("Visualization"). We could argue that discretization—that is, the process of assigning numerical representations to the modularized components of any digital object—provides the underlying interpretative layer since it determines which units become represented as numerical entities, hence producing a quantized model of its object for digital processing. In the case of the five hundred poems analyzed here, for instance, these units could be letters, words, lines, stanzas, etc. Visualization of such data points, in turn, would be the top interpretative layer whose logic further depends on the system of differences established by its own visual vocabulary and syntax. These could be different colors, shades, and shapes in the graph, the relative distance of a data point from the x- and y-axes in a Cartesian diagram, overlaying effects, etc. Finally, the mapping between metrics and graphics articulates data relations with visual relations, translating the analyses contained in discretization into structures of visual representation.

If data-driven visualization is an aestheticized representation of relational patterns, we could argue that it is an algorithmic analysis of a database which is, in itself, a structured collection of information. So visualization is always the visualization of an interpretation expressed by the data. We could describe visualization as an interpretation of an interpretation—in other words, a structure of signs involved in the general processes of semiosis. Narratives expressed through visualization can obfuscate the fact that data have been generated according to specific methods which were further translated into visual elements. Graphic representation of data, in its turn, follows formal protocols whose relation with the data is necessarily inflected by its own visual vocabulary.

The dynamics between various visual instantiations of its mostly quantitative textual analyses—i.e., its word counts—directs our attention to the relation between datification and visualization instead of reifying the visualization of patterns as objective representations. By *datification* I refer to the ways in which the project has selected and then structured its textual and image corpora according to a number of standard algorithmic techniques, such as string searches in various databases (including social networks like Twitter and Instagram), *String Similarity,* or *Modal Analysis* within the corpus. I use *visualization* to refer to the representation of those datified objetcs as a series of artworks based on graphical structures such as charts and networks, but also through illustrative and metaphorical visual collages. Thus the set of intertextual relations among texts in the corpus—what, strictly speaking, we could describe as its specific literary research—came to be expressed as data art (in this case analogue visual works of art based on digital analyses).

The productivity of Enslen's methodology has to be measured not just against the questions that he has been able to articulate and against the answers digital literary methods have provided, but also in terms of the wider theoretical problems that underlie the framework for this project. Among those theoretical questions I would highlight: What is intertextuality? How do we map intertextual relations? What is a visualization? How should we model a visualization? How do we interpret algorithmic readings? How has the textual landscape around "Song of Exile" been illuminated through this particular study? And how does this research contribute to the advancement of digital humanities methods for literary analysis? What kind of relation between close and distant reading practices can be argued for based on this study?

As a quasi-distant reading of the literary history of a very popular short poem, Enslen's work explores macroanalysis for problems of literary history, in particular the problem of describing textual relations within a given cultural space across a long period of time. His analyses demonstrate the highly generative nature of the "Song of Exile" as textual engine and textual referent for multiple variations and appropriations at different historical moments, from Brazilian Romanticism to Modernism to contemporary ubiquitous social media communication. The timeline distribution of the 500 texts proves the enduring appeal of its motifs and structures for personal and public expression. Why have its simple rhythmic structure and the iconic appeal of its images and feelings as a symbol of national identity been so productive for such a long time? Its formal properties and subject matter alone cannot explain why it became such an imitated, parodied, and remixed text ever since its original publication in mid-nineteenth century Rio de Janeiro. Other social factors may have played a significant role, such as its inclusion in anthologies and textbooks, and its continuing dissemination through the media.

Intertextuality is measured as a certain *string similarity* between the many versions and the original poem, considering features such as occurrence of particular tokens and syntactic templates. Other possibilities can be explored based on those categories of analysis: if we consider not textual overlap and textual proximity but textual divergence and textual distance perhaps it would be possible to distinguish imitations from quotations and allusions and both of those from parody. How explicit does the original have to be in order for a variation to be recognized either as parody or as imitation? Re-contextualization of the most frequent words in more varied lexical and semantic fields may signal formal operations other than imitation and variation. It is probably as difficult to establish a correlation between textual similarity and imitation as to establish a correlation between textual divergence and parody, but analyzing divergence as a form of intertextuality could be a worthy future pursuit.

Song of Exile: A Cultural History of Brazil's Most Popular Poem, 1846–2018 offers a rich and nuanced introduction to Brazilian literary and cultural history through its dynamic, multidimensional, and innovative construction of a network of textual relations. Its method moves between three different levels of analysis: close readings of a significant sample of texts from various historical periods, identifying recurrences and transformations in formal structures and thematic motifs; large-scale readings of a 500-text corpus in search of significant cultural and literary patterns; and contextualized readings of textual forms and their intertextual relations that show how they mediate social, political, and ideological structures at particular moments of production and reception.

The fact that Enslen's corpus is composed of "only" 500 relatively short texts has enabled the entire project to keep the "distant reading" scale relatively near to the "close reading" scale. One of the conceptual challenges of the adoption of macroanalytic approaches by literary studies lies precisely in the problem of integrating distant with close reading approaches. Although an argument can be made for the combination of both scales (Hayles; Eve), they seem to be incommensurate or even mutually exclusive. They cannot be mapped onto each other, offering distinct kinds of cultural mediation. But, we may say that the "machine-readable" and "human-readable" branches of Enslen's methodology are mutually inclusive, i.e., the analyses that resulted in the production of this particular intertextual history are both human- and machine-readable.

The translation of its five categories of macroanalysis (*Significant Words, String Similarity, Syntactic Templates, Word Tokens,* and *Modal Analysis*) into intertextual gallery installations offered an additional analogue close reading of its digital protocols. The interpretative dimension of the metrics-into-graphics rationale of data visualization methods could thus be foregrounded as an aesthetic interpretation of the textual knowledge produced by computing the texts. The material and visual embodiment of intertextual relations as aesthetic interpretation—literary research presented as data art—provides a critique of literal and mechanistic approaches to data visualization as reified knowledge.

As hinted at the beginning of my afterword, for a full appreciation of its contribution as an experiment in critical reading, this book should be read in conjunction with the various instantiations of the related exhibition ("Bird-watching") and with its evolving website. Given its subject-matter and its digital methodologies, this work will be relevant both for scholars of Brazilian literature and culture, and for researchers in digital literary studies and digital humanities. Its artistic practice-based research into data visualization is particularly refreshing as an aesthetic interpretation of a theoretical problem in literary history: How can we generate and represent a network of intertextual relations in ways that offer new insights about textuality and about the social and cultural history they mediate?

An additional contribution of Enslen's work is to revive the notion of intertextuality not only as a dynamic network put in motion by the productivity of writing and reading as social acts, but also as a critical lens for examining textuality as a deeply layered social and historical process. His use of "Song of Exile" as a "strategic urtext" for pinpointing textual relations highlights the heuristic value of intertextual networks for understanding the dynamics of literary production and reception. This particular poem (or rather the discursive network of its many metamorphoses) has become a probe into the multidimensional nature of literary texts. Enslen demonstrates the "poem's continued relevance to representations of national identity" while using its many textual echoes as a fine-grained tool for observing wider cultural transformations.

Another way of highlighting the theoretical and methodological contribution of this study is to say that it offers a convincing answer to this question: What can we learn by counting and visualizing words?

Manuel Portela*
University of Coimbra

*Director of the Materialities of Literature Program at the University of Coimbra, lead researcher for the Livro do Desassossego Digital Archive and author of Scripting Reading Motions (MIT Press, 2013) and Literary Simulation and the Digital Humanities (Bloomsbury, 2022).

Works Cited

Drucker, Johanna. *Graphesis: Visual Forms of Knowledge Production*. Cambridge, MA: Harvard University Press, 2014. www.hup.harvard.edu/catalog.php?isbn=9780674724938.

Eve, Martin Paul. 2019. *Close Reading with Computers: Textual Scholarship, Computational Formalism, and David Mitchell's Cloud Atlas*. Stanford, CA: Stanford University Press, 2019.

Hayles, N. Katherine. "Combining Close and Distant Reading: Jonathan Safran Foer's *Tree of Codes* and the Aesthetic of Bookishness." *PMLA* 128 (1): 226–31, 2013.

Jockers, Matthew L. *Macroanalysis: Digital Methods and Literary History*. Urbana: University of Illinois Press., 2013.

Lima, Manuel. *Visual Complexity: Mapping Patterns of Information*. New York: Princeton Architectural Press, 2011.

Manovich, Lev. "Cultural Analytics: Visualizing Cultural Patterns in the Era of 'More Media.'" *DOMUS*, 2009.

———. "What Is Visualisation?" Visual Studies 26 (1): 36–49, 2011. doi.org/10.1080/1472586X.2011.548488.

———. *Instagram and Contemporary Image*. New York, 2017. manovich.net/content/04-projects/145-instagram-and-contemporary-image/instagram_book_manovich.pdf.

Moretti, Franco. *Distant Reading*. London: Verso, 2013.

Ramsay, Stephen. *Reading Machines: Toward an Algorithmic Criticism*. Urbana: University of Illinois Press, 2011.

Appendix
Table of 500 Texts[1]

Catalog Number	Similarity Coefficient	Year	Author	Title	Mode
1	1	1846	António Gonçalves Dias	Canção do exílio	Positive
2	0.5067	1847	António José Ferreira	A saudade da pátria (imitação)	Positive
3	0.1941	1847	Cherubino Henriques Lagoa	Mez d'abril em Portugal	Positive
4	0.2911	1847	Joaquim Álvaro de Lara e Souza	A minha pátria	Positive
5	0.5046	1848	Anonymous	[Minha terra tem silvados]	Positive
6	0.2213	1849	Anonymous	Epigraph of *O Timbyra*	Positive
7	0.2512	1849	José da Silva Maia Ferreira	Benguelinha	Positive
8	0.1515	1849	José da Silva Maia Ferreira	A minha viagem	Negative
9	0.2921	1849	José da Silva Maia Ferreira	À minha terra	Negative
10	0.0937	1849	José da Silva Maia Ferreira	A minha terra	Negative
11	0.5265	1850	Hypólito Pereira Garcez	Gôa	Positive
12	0.2639	1852	Anonymous	[Minha terra só tem árvores]	Negative
13	0.3214	1852	Itamontanio	Saudades da minha terra	Positive
14	0.4444	1853	R Carlos	Uma resposta	Positive
15	0.2727	1853	Anonymous	Minha terra natal	Negative
16	0.3714	1854	Leandro de Castilho	Minha terra natal	Positive

Table of 500 Texts

Catalog Number	Similarity Coefficient	Year	Author	Title	Mode
17	0.2454	1854	Villela	[Minha terra é mais formosa]	Positive
18	0.399	1855	Casimiro de Abreu	Eu nasci além dos mares	Positive
19	0.2135	1856	Casimiro de Abreu	Suspiros	Positive
20	0.1416	1856	Casimiro de Abreu	Minha terra	Positive
21	0.1698	1857	Anonymous	[A Alemanha tem imprensa]	Negative
22	0.2612	1857	Casimiro de Abreu	Meu lar	Positive
23	0.3062	1857	Casimiro de Abreu	Jurity	Positive
24	0.2154	1857	J F da Silveira Távora	O Brasil	Positive
25	0.2547	1857	Marinho Palhares	Minha terra	Positive
26	0.2953	1858	Anonymous	[Minha terra tem talentos]	Positive
27	0.4093	1858	Trangalão	Coisas do Brasil	Positive
28	0.2672	1860	João Nepomuceno da Silva	Belezas de minha terra	Negative
29	0.1994	1860	Pinto Júnior	Minha pátria	Positive
30	0.3938	1861	Anonymous	Sabiá	Positive
31	0.404	1861	Antero de Quental	A M.E.	Positive
32	0.2587	1862	Anonymous	[Minha terra tem surpresas]	Positive

Table of 500 Texts

Catalog Number	Similarity Coefficient	Year	Author	Title	Mode
33	0.4638	1862	O Muribeca	Gentes dos cajuais alerta!!! canção popular	Negative
34	0.3974	1862	Santos Neves & Oliveira Quintana	Excerpt from Beraldo de Paraná-mirim's Opera	Positive
35	0.3228	1863	F Guarany	Minha terra	Positive
36	0.4371	1863	M A Pinto de Sampaio	Minha terra	Positive
37	0.4662	1864	Sr. R	Pernambuco	Positive
38	0.4289	1865	Alijoense	A minha terra	Positive
39	0.2506	1866	Caetano Candido Alves Martins	O canto dos atins	Other
40	0.6197	1866	J de C Estrela	Minha terra	Positive
41	0.2527	1866	Manoel de Macedo	Corrientes	Positive
42	0.2769	1866	Pedro José Teixeira	Corrientes	Positive
43	0.4344	1867	C Jacarandá	Minha terra (imitação)	Positive
44	0.2806	1867	Honrata Minelvina Carneiro de Mendonça	Saudades da minha terra	Positive
45	0.4515	1867	J F da Cruz	O canto da minha terra	Positive
46	0.1782	1867	Jorge Krauter	Minha terra	Positive

Table of 500 Texts

Catalog Number	Similarity Coefficient	Year	Author	Title	Mode
47	0.4076	1868	Augusto Cavalcanti	Partitura do exílio	Other
48	0.2254	1869	Fabio Ewerton	[Na seta dos meus desejos]	Other
49	0.4152	1870	J A B	Canção do exílio (imitação)	Positive
50	0.2574	1873	Aliquanto	Ao povo maranhense	Other
51	0.2955	1873	Anonymous	D. Octávia Rosata, prima-dona absoluta	Negative
52	0.1023	1873	Cesar Augusto Marques	Discursos e poesias	Other
53	0.3829	1873	D da Silva	Gonçalves Dias	Other
54	0.5422	1873	Estevão de Araújo Pereira Alvim	Portugal	Positive
55	0.1363	1873	Feliciano Caliope Monteiro de Mello	Perante a estátua	Other
56	0.1634	1873	J Auto Pereira	Tributo (a Gonçalves Dias)	Other
57	0.362	1873	J de C Estrela	A Estátua do Exmo. Poeta Maranhense Antônio Gonçalves Dias	Other
58	0.1414	1873	Joaquim Ribeiro Gonçalves	Aos maranhenses	Other
59	0.1244	1873	José E Teixeira de Sousa	Gonçalves Dias: ode	Other

Table of 500 Texts

Catalog Number	Similarity Coefficient	Year	Author	Title	Mode
60	0.3828	1873	Miguel Marques	[Ali vereis no mármore mode-lado]	Other
61	0.3138	1873	Scevalo	Canção do exílio	Negative
62	0.2193	1873	Um Maranhense	Versos na inauguração da estátua de Gonçalves Dias	Other
63	0.6772	1874	João Francisco	Canção do exílio	Negative
64	0.4181	1874	P Mosqueira	A elv	Negative
65	0.4537	1875	Anonymous	Minha terra tem loureiros	Positive
66	0.1956	1875	Anonymous	Dores diplomáticas	Negative
67	0.0914	1875	Machado de Assis	A Gonçalves Dias	Other
68	0.2838	1875	Sena Barbosa	Minha terra	Positive
69	0.4337	1876	Anonymous	Minha terra tem loureiros	Positive
70	0.5677	1877	Dr. Buffon	Paródia dedicada ao delegado de polícia, Pedro Velho Capim de Cheiro	Negative
71	0.2907	1877	Pimpolho	Lá vai obra	Negative
72	0.3906	1879	FJ da Costa	A palmeira	Positive

Table of 500 Texts

Catalog Number	Similarity Coefficient	Year	Author	Title	Mode
73	0.388	1880	MCA	Minha terra	Positive
74	0.4226	1881	François Seul	Canção	Negative
75	0.3761	1882	Anonymous	A vovô	Other
76	0.3979	1884	Bithencourt Sampaio	Gonçalves Dias	Other
77	0.3779	1884	Cezar Osmany	Gonçalves Dias	Other
78	0.4717	1884	José Albano Cordeiro Junior	Canção da morte	Negative
79	0.4637	1884	Lélio	[Minha terra tem cadeiras]	Negative
80	0.3775	1884	Lopes Neves	Nênia (a Gonçalves Dias)	Other
81	0.4267	1884	Violino	[Minha terra tem palmeiras]	Negative
82	0.4416	1886	Demétrio Ferreira Salles	[A minha terra é Sobral]	Positive
83	0.2922	1888	Carlos Perplexo	7a pilheria do sr. bispo	Other
84	0.5	1890	General Degola	Paródia	Negative
85	0.3815	1892	Júlio Camisão	Gonçalves Dias	Other
86	0.2226	1892	Lúcio	O bezouro	Negative
87	0.452	1893	Anonymous	Paródia	Positive
88	0.125	1894	Macamboa	Dominicais	Negative

Table of 500 Texts

Catalog Number	Similarity Coefficient	Year	Author	Title	Mode
89	0.4161	1898	Anonymous	[Faz anos hoje o sr. Dácio Serra]	Other
90	0.2428	1901	Jakson de Figueredo	Minha terra	Positive
91	0.3544	1901	Jakson de Figueredo	A Castro Alves	Other
92	0.3372	1903	JJ Dias do Rego	[Minha terra tem palmeira]	Positive
93	0.2831	1903	Leôncio Correa	Para a galante Maria	Other
94	0.32	1903	Virgílio Brandão	Canção do exílio	Other
95	0.1963	1904	Advertisement	[Vela brasileira]	Positive
96	0.2952	1904	Alcino del Sino	Charada antiga	Negative
97	0.6672	1904	K Móes	Minha terra	Negative
98	0.3884	1905	Luiz de França Pereira	O sabiá da mata	Positive
99	0.3419	1906	Jatye	[Minha querida Antonieta]	Other
100	0.2301	1907	Silvano	[Minha terra tem palmeiras]	Negative
101	0.4359	1907	Dominguinho Trancoso	Cartas de um caipira	Negative
102	0.2768	1907	Fute	[Minha terra tem palmeiras]	Negative
103	0.285	1908	Merlimbar	Crônica	Negative
104	0.2653	1909	Joaquim Osório Duque Estrada	Hino nacional	Positive

Table of 500 Texts

Catalog Number	Similarity Coefficient	Year	Author	Title	Mode
105	0.3252	1910	"Mussiù" Tei Cheira	As sete palmeiras	Negative
106	0.4287	1914	Anonymous	Minha terra tem palmeiras	Other
107	0.386	1914	Catulo de Paixão Cearense	Luar do sertão	Positive
108	0.4732	1914	Telles de Meirelles	Minha terra	Positive
109	0.4081	1915	Juó Bananere	Migna terra	Negative
110	0.4222	1917	Marquez Humorista	Divagando	Negative
111	0.4543	1917	Vicente de Paula Reis	A minha terra	Positive
112	0.1883	1919	Advertisement	Casa Muniz	Positive
113	0.4107	1920	Aquino Correia	Pindorama	Positive
114	0.214	1921	Anonymous	Trovas	Negative
115	0.3865	1922	Anonymous	Do Tejo-Guanabara	Positive
116	0.3643	1923	Advertisement	[Venha venha o guaraná]	Other
117	0.2087	1923	Dr. Zootechnico	Bis-charada 25	Other
118	0.4875	1925	Oswald de Andrade	Canto de regresso à pátria	Negative
119	0.4089	1926	Carlos Drummond de Andrade	Eu protesto	Negative
120	0.2876	1927	Ascenso Ferreira	Minha terra	Positive

Table of 500 Texts

Catalog Number	Similarity Coefficient	Year	Author	Title	Mode
121	0.1939	1927	Conde de [unknown]	A condessa saudosa	Other
122	0.3921	1928	Caio de Freitas	Sururu	Negative
123	0.2856	1929	Napoleão Menezes	Bilhete serrano	Negative
124	0.3749	1929	Violeiro do Norte	Ave tristonha	Positive
125	0.2605	1930	Carlos Drummond de Andrade	Europa França e Bahia	Negative
126	0.2587	1930	Guy	A sociedade sinfonia da cidade	Negative
127	0.4202	1930	Murilo Mendes	Canção do exílio	Negative
128	0.1906	1931	Anonymous	Trovas	Negative
129	0.4029	1931	Artur Coelho	Minha terra	Positive
130	0.2002	1931	Ferreira de Messias	Impressões de viagem	Positive
131	0.5484	1931	J. Paraná	Canção do Exílio	Positive
132	0.3552	1931	Luiz Carlo Peixoto de Castro	Minha terra tem pereira	Positive
133	0.4049	1932	Adelino Maia	São João da Barra	Positive
134	0.4248	1932	Calzans	Alma de Tupi	Positive
135	0.3588	1933	Anonymous	Paisagem brasileira	Negative

Table of 500 Texts

Catalog Number	Similarity Coefficient	Year	Author	Title	Mode
136	0.2095	1933	Guilherme de Almeida	Canção do exílio por Gonçalves Dias, continuada por Guilherme de Almeida	Positive
137	0.3967	1933	Júlio de Castro	Minha terra	Positive
138	0.3897	1933	Sá-Pory	A culpa é de Gonçalves Dias	Other
139	0.3778	1934	[Cartoonist]	[Não se ouve voar uma mosca]	Other
140	0.2496	1936	Felizardo Fontoura	Tesouros de minha terra	Positive
141	0.5179	1936	João de Barro (perf. Carmen Miranda)	Minha terra tem palmeiras	Positive
142	0.3498	1936	Maria Beatriz	Minha terra	Positive
143	0.3427	1937	Haroldo Daltro	Trovas	Other
144	0.4061	1937	Jair Franklin	Minha terra	Positive
145	0.2942	1937	João Accioly	Paulicéia [sic]	Negative
146	0.422	1938	Eustorgio Wanderley	Dádiva do céu	Positive
147	0.14	1939	Anonymous	[Minha terra tem palmeiras]	Negative
148	0.4505	1939	Ribeiro Couto	Modinha do exílio	Negative
149	0.2289	1941	Di Pino	[Palmeira no Palastra]	Other
150	0.4081	1942	David Nasser e Herivelto Martins	Prece da Paz	Negative

Table of 500 Texts

Catalog Number	Similarity Coefficient	Year	Author	Title	Mode
151	0.4049	1942	Lausimar Laus Gomes	Soneto	Other
152	0.4	1943	Anísio de Abreu Neto	Na minha terra	Positive
153	0.458	1943	Carlos Drummond de Andrade	Nova canção do exílio	Negative
154	0.2906	1943	Keeper	Off-side poemas	Other
155	0.378	1944	Guilherme de Almeida	Canção do expedicionário	Positive
156	0.4526	1945	Lygia de Menezes	Coco de Alagoas	Positive
168	0.3849	1945	Manuel Bandeira	Sextilhas românticas	Negative
157	0.4359	1946	Mário Montairo	O nôbo sabiá	Negative
158	0.3858	1947	Barboza Neto	Palmeira	Other
159	0.4443	1947	Camarada Lorotoff	Minha terra tem palmeiras	Negative
160	0.2961	1947	Cassiano Ricardo	Ainda irei a Portugal	Positive
161	0.4138	1947	Gregorian	Notas de um turista sem pressa	Positive
162	0.3206	1948	Camarada Lorotoff	Quadra de onze	Negative
163	0.2357	1948	Haydee Nicolusi	Canção do turista malogrado	Negative
164	0.2643	1948	J Rego Costa	[Minha terra tem palmeiras]	Negative

Table of 500 Texts

Catalog Number	Similarity Coefficient	Year	Author	Title	Mode
165	0.2845	1948	J Rego Costa	[Em meio aos que melhor catam minhoca]	Negative
166	0.3301	1948	J Rego Costa (Moneró Junior)	[Existem aves que cantam]	Negative
167	0.3412	1948	Júlio Pires	Brasil, terra santa	Negative
169	0.1621	1949	Vinícius de Moraes	Pátria minha	Negative
170	0.4615	1949	Wilson Rodrigues	Minha canção do exílio	Positive
171	0.4557	1949	Xerém	No Ceará tem	Positive
172	0.1953	1950	Anonymous	Ditado para matemática	Other
173	0.3161	1950	Luiz Martins	Canção do exílio	Negative
174	0.4491	1950	René Bittencourt	Onde canta o sabiá? Pois sim!	Negative
175	0.2109	1951	Anonymous	Fim de festa	Other
176	0.1969	1951	Tong Tchê	Minha terra	Negative
177	0.4131	1951	Zé Taquara	O pito aceso (trovando trovas)	Negative
178	0.26	1952	Eldes Machado	Palmeiras tristes	Negative
179	0.2153	1953	Anonymous	Pingos	Negative
180	0.257	1953	Jair Silva	[Minha terra tem mendigos]	Negative

Table of 500 Texts

Catalog Number	Similarity Coefficient	Year	Author	Title	Mode
181	0.2222	1954	Anonymous	Versinhos	Other
182	0.239	1955	Anonymous	O que o locutor não disse	Other
183	0.3338	1956	Álvaro Armando	Pingos e respingos	Negative
184	0.2189	1957	Anonymous	Farpas politicas	Negative
185	0.2159	1957	Everardo	Paródia em meia porção	Other
193	0.3915	1957	Rubem Braga	Crônica	Negative
186	0.2131	1958	Anonymous	[Minha terra tem palmeiras]	Negative
187	0.156	1958	Sergio Milliet	Um poeta canta o Rio	Negative
188	0.183	1958	Student Protest Chant	Minha terra tem petróleo	Negative
189	0.4093	1959	Ciro Silva	Trovas paranaenses	Positive
190	0.2588	1959	Dircinha Batista	Minha terra tem palmeiras	Negative
191	0.2346	1960	Anonymous (possibly Carlos Drummond)	Minha terra	Negative
192	0.5665	1960	Candango Forçado	Canção do brasílio	Negative
194	0.1238	1961	Anonymous	Minha terra tem PERNAS DE PAU	Other
195	0.3788	1962	Mario Quintana	Uma canção	Negative

Table of 500 Texts

Catalog Number	Similarity Coefficient	Year	Author	Title	Mode
196	0.22	1962	René Bittencourt	Alo musicistas!	Other
197	0.1741	1963	Fernando Lopes	Minha terra só tem tanques	Negative
198	0.3831	1966	Jonas da Silva	Amazonas	Positive
199	0.2626	1966	Manuel Bandeira	A João Guimarães Rosa	Other
200	0.3368	1964	Armando A.C. Garcia	A minha terra	Positive
201	0.4295	1968	Chico Buarque	Sabiá	Negative
202	0.3875	1968	Gilberto Gil e Torquato Neto	Marginalia II	Negative
261	0.3037	1969	Gilberto Gil & Capinan	Show de me esqueci	Negative
203	0.3851	1970	Chico Buarque	Agora falando sério	Negative
204	0.305	1970	Juca Chaves	Take me back to Piauí	Negative
205	0.1902	1970	Martins d'Alvarez	S. Luís do Maranhão	Positive
206	0.4129	1971	Binho, Ito & Camargo	São Paulo, chapadão de glória	Positive
207	0.2669	1971	Waldemar Machado da Silva	Hino à região do Rio Negro	Positive
208	0.1204	1973	José Paulo Paes	Canção do exílio facilitada	Positive
209	0.3389	1974	Cacaso	Jogos florais II	Negative
210	0.2489	1974	Cacaso	Jogos florais I	Negative

Table of 500 Texts

Catalog Number	Similarity Coefficient	Year	Author	Title	Mode
211	0.6342	1974	LM	Crônica (Nova canção do exílio)	Negative
212	0.2381	1975	Fernando Leite Mendes	Ladainha da implosão	Negative
213	0.2998	1975	Sergio Reis	Saudade de minha terra	Positive
214	0.3695	1975	Taiguara	Terra das palmeiras	Negative
215	0.3945	1977	Carlos Drummond de Andrade	Fazendeiros de cana	Negative
216	0.3808	1978	Alcione	Todos cantam sua terra	Positive
217	0.3956	1978	Pádua & Gismonti (perf. Marilia Barbosa)	Coração de candango	Negative
218	0.2582	1978	Luís Fernando Veríssimo	Nova canção do exílio	Negative
219	0.3826	1978	Vavá & Machado	Na princesa do sertão	Positive
220	0.3455	1979	Nelson Ferreira & Ademar Paiva	Pernambuco você é meu	Positive
221	0.1315	1980	Affonso Romano Sant'Anna	Canção do exílio mais recente	Negative
222	0.4011	1983	Assisão	Sabiá na seca	Other
223	0.3783	1983	Rita Lee	Pirarucu	Negative
224	0.3651	1983	Zé Geraldo	Sabiá	Negative
225	0.3577	1984	Anonymous	Tenho saudade	Positive

Table of 500 Texts

Catalog Number	Similarity Coefficient	Year	Author	Title	Mode
226	0.4145	1984	Anonymous	Boiadeiro	Positive
227	0.3896	1984	Armindo Trevisan	Nova canção no exílio	Negative
228	0.313	1984	Dalton Trevisan	Canção do exílio	Negative
229	0.4084	1984	Flávio Cleto	Versos diversos	Positive
230	0.4035	1984	Moraes Moreira & Beu Machado (perf. Gal Costa)	Ave nossa	Negative
231	0.1047	1984	Poitical Commentary	Minha terra tem dívidas	Negative
232	0.4325	1985	Eduardo Alves da Costa	Outra canção do exílio	Negative
233	0.1183	1986	Antonio Peticov	[Minha terra tem palmeiras]	Other
234	0.3905	1986	Belchior	Retórica sentimental	Negative
236	0.4072	1987	Paulo Leminski	Diversonagens suspersas	Other
237	0.442	1987	Wilson Bueno	Canção sem fronteiras	Negative
238	0.3361	1987	José Paulo Paes	Lisboa: aventuras	Negative
239	0.244	1988	Paulo Mendes Campos	Nova canção do exílio	Negative
240	0.4373	1989	Eduardo Dias	Canção que não é do exílio	Negative
241	0.3882	1990	Edgar Yamagami	Haikai & tempurá	Negative

Table of 500 Texts

Catalog Number	Similarity Coefficient	Year	Author	Title	Mode
242	0.3816	1990	Marcolino Candeias	Aqui não tem sabiá	Negative
243	0.4137	1990	MC Marcinho	Sabiá	Other
244	0.3154	1991	Paulo Frances	Diário da corte	Negative
235	0.3831	1992	Jô Soares	Canção do exílio às avessas	Negative
245	0.3837	1992	Báh	O exílio da canção	Negative
246	0.377	1992	Escola de Samba Rosas de Ouro	Letras samba-enredo	Negative
247	0.3919	1992	Mastruz com Leite	Onde canta o sabiá	Other
248	0.3384	1994	Elton Saldanha	Eu sou do sul	Positive
249	0.3464	1994	Mario Chamie	Ideias fora do lugar	Negative
250	0.2955	1995	Daniel & Samuel	História do Chico	Other
251	0.4164	1995	Daniel Chaves	Canção do martírio	Negative
252	0.0803	1995	Silas Correa Leite	Minha terra tem corinthians, onde canta Rita Lee	Negative
253	0.0887	1995	Silas Correia Leite	Itararé (O céu pode ser lá)	Positive
254	0.6106	1997	Andrey TNT	Canção do exílio à milícia	Negative
255	0.3875	1997	Arnaldo Antunes	Inferno	Negative

Table of 500 Texts

Catalog Number	Similarity Coefficient	Year	Author	Title	Mode
256	0.4299	1999	Fernando Bonassi	Cena 9	Negative
257	0.4086	1999	Luís Antônio Cajazeira Ramos	Canção do exílio	Negative
258	0.1799	2000	Augusto Matos	Magnífico parque	Positive
259	0.3806	2000	Ferreira Gullar	Volta a São Luís	Positive
260	0.4773	2000	Ferreira Gullar	Nova canção do exílio	Other
262	0.2018	2000	Roque Freitas	[Minha terra tem palmeiras]	Positive
263	0.2565	2001	Gustavo Dourado	Sabiá sábia	Other
264	0.3859	2001	Kim	Minha terra	Positive
265	0.1667	2001	Marta Helena Cocco	Versão enlatada do exílio	Negative
266	0.418	2001	Os Monarcas	Pago dileto	Positive
267	0.2997	2002	Antonio Juraci Siqueira	Tem pato na corda	Negative
268	0.4214	2002	Arthur Accioly Pereira	Minha canção do exílio	Negative
269	0.2291	2002	Francisco dos Santos	Poema de domingo	Negative
270	0.423	2002	Sabrina Taury	Canção de retorno	Positive
271	0.4831	2002	Sabrina Taury	Canção de Fuga	Negative
272	0.4726	2002	Sabrina Taury	Apenas canção	Positive

Table of 500 Texts

Catalog Number	Similarity Coefficient	Year	Author	Title	Mode
273	0.4757	2002	Sabrina Taury	Algum cantar	Negative
274	0.2584	2003	Iosif Landau	Exilado	Negative
275	0.5966	2004	Antônio Virgílio de Andrade	Canção do regresso	Positive
276	0.2404	2004	Bom dia DF	Minha terra tem poetas	Other
277	0.399	2004	Cesar Miranda	Minha terra	Negative
278	0.2745	2004	Frederico Barbosa	Mais prazer encontro eu lá	Negative
279	0.3984	2004	Victor e Leo	Paraíso	Positive
280	0.4743	2005	Anonymous	[Minha terra tem palmeiras]	Negative
281	0.4344	2005	Athanazio	Na minha terra tem amendoeira	Negative
282	0.5689	2005	Cleuseni de Oliveira	Canção de uma língua	Positive
283	0.2188	2005	Elaine Pauvolid	Sou ali	Other
284	0.2103	2005	Elizabeth Hazin	Exílio	Negative
285	0.3893	2005	Felipe Stefani	Pátria	Other
286	0.127	2005	Francisco Simões & Alberto Chen	Terra minha	Negative
287	0.3911	2005	Fred Matos	Trinados	Other
288	0.4639	2006	Adames, Dodl, e Hickel	Sujeira brasileira	Negative

Table of 500 Texts

Catalog Number	Similarity Coefficient	Year	Author	Title	Mode
289	0.4245	2006	Alice Bruno Caroline Cassia Marina	O grito da nação	Negative
290	0.3874	2006	Arland Gabriel G. V. Thiago	Minha escola, minha vida	Other
291	0.4011	2006	Bráulio de Castro	Corinthiamo	Other
292	0.3981	2006	Camila, Vanessa, Paulo, Luiza, Vitoria, Paulo	Uma canção	Negative
293	0.4951	2006	Carol, Guilherme, Vicente, Gabriela, Paim, Rodrigues	Canção dos excluídos	Negative
294	0.5749	2006	Carolina, Bianca, Grazieli, Helena, Maria Eduarda, Sara	Canção de uma canção	Positive
295	0.2511	2006	Clevane Pessoa de Araújo Lopes	Um certo sabiá	Other
296	0.4402	2006	Eduardo Becker and Eduardo da Silva Valério	Que país é este	Negative
297	0.5414	2006	Elysa, Isis, Cristian, Júlio and Lucas	Canção da revolta	Negative
298	0.4003	2006	G7 + Henrique	[Que se dane o tal progresso]	Other
299	0.4157	2006	G7 + Henrique	[Pacas tatus cotias]	Other
300	0.4222	2006	G7 + Henrique	[Onde eu penduro minha rede]	Other
301	0.3632	2006	G7 + Henrique	[Mas ele foi rebaixado]	Other

Table of 500 Texts

Catalog Number	Similarity Coefficient	Year	Author	Title	Mode
302	0.453	2006	G7 + Henrique	[Mas elas não tem opinião mobilizada]	Other
303	0.418	2006	G7 + Henrique	[Dignas de cartão postal]	Other
304	0.408	2006	G7 + Henrique	[Belchior não entra lá]	Other
305	0.4428	2006	Heber Bensi	São Paulo	Positive
306	0.6424	2006	Hênio dos Santos	Canção do novo exílio	Negative
307	0.4412	2006	Porto, Sens, Coelho, Sousa	Último suspiro	Negative
308	0.4557	2006	Santiago, Kappel, Dau, Vanessa, Rockenbach	Outro lugar	Negative
309	0.4181	2006	Valéria Fagundes	Minha terra	Positive
310	0.4	2006	Zedio Alvarez	Minha terra	Positive
312	0.4382	2007	George Carvalho	Minha canção do exílio	Negative
313	0.3957	2007	Jussara Godinho	Amor a Caxias do Sul	Positive
314	0.4041	2007	Paralelo Nobre	Vou me embora	Positive
315	0.2048	2007	Rosa Pena	[Em sonhar, sozinha, … noite]	Other
316	0.5101	2007	Thássius Veloso	Canção do martírio	Negative
317	0.3224	2008	Al-Chaer	Laranjas laranjeiras laranjais	Negative

Table of 500 Texts

Catalog Number	Similarity Coefficient	Year	Author	Title	Mode
318	0.3586	2008	Benedita Azevedo	A minha terra	Positive
319	0.3708	2008	Elsa Villon	Minha terra tem buzinas	Negative
320	0.3394	2008	Forro DanadodeBom	Bahia	Positive
321	0.6948	2008	Galadriel'ves	Canção do exílio	Other
322	0.4136	2008	Gustavo Ganso	Minha terra não tem mais palmeiras	Negative
323	0.2015	2008	José Orestes de Albuquerque	Minha terra	Positive
324	0.2142	2008	Liria Porto	Onde cantam os bem-te-vis	Positive
325	0.3418	2008	Lourdes Bernadete C Bispo	Minha terra	Negative
326	0.4056	2008	Manoel Virgílio	Minha terra	Positive
327	0.598	2008	Marcia Miyasaki	Canção do exílio in Japan	Positive
328	0.5852	2008	Miriam Panighel Carvalho	Paráfrase da canção do exílio	Negative
329	0.2576	2008	Rodrigo de Souza Leão	Gaiola	Other
346	0.454	2008	Irene de Xangô	Canto da minha terra	Positive
330	0.2149	2009	Adriano Nunes	Era para ser uma canção de exílio	Other
331	0.4351	2009	Ana Guimaraes Brito	Minha canção do exílio	Positive

Table of 500 Texts

Catalog Number	Similarity Coefficient	Year	Author	Title	Mode
332	0.3667	2009	Aníbal Beça	São sabiá	Other
333	0.435	2009	Aníbal Beça	Sabiá	Other
334	0.1356	2009	Aníbal Beça	Haicai	Other
335	0.1895	2009	Anonymous	Nação corinthiana	Positive
336	0.3071	2009	Antonio Mariano	Do impossível exílio	Negative
337	0.3111	2009	Cesar Cardoso	Porque me ufano de minha terra	Other
338	0.1567	2009	Cesar Cardoso	Exílios, canções	Negative
339	0.3891	2009	Cesar Cardoso	Cadernos de exercícios literários	Negative
340	0.4254	2009	Ceumar & Mathilda Kovak	Oração do anjo	Other
341	0.5852	2009	FTNT (Caio Muriel Sostisso)	Canção de exílio moderno	Negative
342	0.4588	2009	Gabriel Rezende Mota	Canção do Brasil	Negative
343	0.2241	2009	Gilberlândio	[Estrela]	Positive
344	0.234	2009	Guta Gatuna	Gonçalves dias revisited	Other
345	0.2188	2009	Horácio Costa	Sobre canários e presidentes	Negative
347	0.3586	2009	João de Abreu Borges	Minha terra sem palmeiras	Negative

Table of 500 Texts

Catalog Number	Similarity Coefficient	Year	Author	Title	Mode
348	0.5906	2009	João Guilherme	Canção do exílio na cidade dos automóveis	Negative
349	0.378	2009	João Rodrigues	Meu sabiá	Positive
350	0.3138	2009	José Aloise Bahia	josé murilo gonçalves aloise mendes dias bahia	Negative
351	0.3673	2009	Judith de Souza	Exílio de ti	Other
352	0.4228	2009	Kelly Brandão	Minha terra	Positive
353	0.4783	2009	Kennedy Aranha	Terra das palmeiras	Positive
354	0.3557	2009	Lou Vilela	Indulto	Other
355	0.231	2009	Lucas Carrasco	Chega de saudade	Negative
356	0.4237	2009	Luci Collin	Poema sintônico	Negative
357	0.417	2009	Marco di Aurélio	[Em minha terra tem de tudo...]	Positive
358	0.2328	2009	Munir Jacob	Minha terra	Positive
359	0.6743	2009	Narlan Teixeira	Canção do exílio	Positive
360	0.4711	2009	Osmar Reyex	Canção do exilado	Negative
361	0.2844	2009	Paula Cajaty	Desejo de exílio	Other
362	0.3458	2009	Paulo Briguet	Canção do exíguo	Negative

Table of 500 Texts

Catalog Number	Similarity Coefficient	Year	Author	Title	Mode
363	0.561	2009	Pedro Fontes	Exílio do sabiá	Negative
364	0.1841	2009	Pedro Sette Câmara	[Minha terra tem esquerdas]	Negative
365	0.3945	2009	Reginaldo Francisco de Oliveira	Minha terra	Positive
366	0.2388	2009	Renan Nuernberger	Canção do exílio	Other
367	0.6813	2009	Reynaldo Bessa & Marcelo Alvarez	Canção do exílio	Negative
368	0.4077	2009	Ribeiro de Castro	Terra azul	Positive
369	0.1986	2009	Ricardo Alfaya	Reflexão no. 1	Negative
370	0.3892	2009	Ricardo Domeneck	Cão são da ex-ilha	Other
371	0.7346	2009	Robertson Frizero Barros	Uma canção do exílio	Negative
372	0.4524	2009	Robertson Frizero Barros	Novíssima canção do exílio	Positive
373	0.571	2009	Rogério Miranzelo	Canção destorcida	Positive
374	0.3857	2009	Rosane Villela	Exílio de amor	Other
375	0.4014	2009	Rose Felliciano	Minha terra tem	Positive
376	0.1532	2009	Sandro Fortes	Do exílio	Negative
377	0.4037	2009	Trixie Hachi-Roku	[Minha terra tem corruptos]	Negative
378	0.6205	2009	Wilson Roberto de Carvalho Almeida	Canção do martírio	Negative

Table of 500 Texts

Catalog Number	Similarity Coefficient	Year	Author	Title	Mode
380	0.6234	2010	Laelio Ferreira de Melo	Canção do exílio araqueado	Negative
381	0.3572	2010	liria porto	expropriados	Negative
382	0.7197	2010	Raquela Maythenand	Canção do exílio	Negative
383	0.5845	2010	Sergio Silva	Canção para o exílio	Negative
384	0.297	2010	Telma Ellos	Canto do sabiá	Positive
385	0.4788	2011	Caroline Lima Franca Andreza	Paródia II	Negative
386	0.39	2011	Chal	Sabiá	Positive
388	0.7305	2011	Juliana da Conceição David	Canção do carioca	Negative
389	0.447	2011	Maria Mogorim	Canção do martírio	Negative
390	0.4554	2011	Neves, Henrique & Mendonça	Paródia I	Negative
391	0.1473	2012	Éder Vieira	[Onde eu moro]	Negative
392	0.35	2012	Adrielly de Almeida Silva	[Minha terra tem bananeiras]	Negative
393	0.5038	2012	Ana Rute	Canção do bairro	Negative
394	0.1995	2012	Andréa Délis	[Minha terra tem novas tecnologias]	Other
395	0.698	2012	Awdrey Lorenna	[A minha terra tem cerejeiras]	Positive

Table of 500 Texts

Catalog Number	Similarity Coefficient	Year	Author	Title	Mode
396	0.3322	2012	Beatriz Mirella	[Minha terra tem areia]	Positive
397	0.222	2012	Beatriz Teixeira	[Na minha terra não tem palmeiras]	Negative
398	0.3344	2012	Bianca B.Gomes	[Minha terra tem facebook]	Other
399	0.4313	2012	Claudio Fernando	[Minha terra tem poluição]	Negative
400	0.4433	2012	Cleiton Cunha	[Em minha terra tinha palmeiras]	Negative
401	0.3272	2012	Clériston Felipe	[Na minha cidade tem palmeiras]	Positive
402	0.5072	2012	Daniela Brito	Era uma vez uma terra	Negative
403	0.5679	2012	Derik Pádua	[Minha terra tem coqueiros]	Positive
404	0.1902	2012	Elizama Ferreira	[Na minha terra tem belezas]	Other
405	0.637	2012	Elzimara Souza	A terra que há	Negative
406	0.2242	2012	Erison Santiago	[Na minha terra tem tristeza]	Negative
407	0.4245	2012	Eudes Malheiro da Silva	[Na minha terra tem jaqueira]	Positive
408	0.2544	2012	Fernanda	[Nosso céu tem mais estrela]	Positive
409	0.1957	2012	Franklin Castro	[Minha terra tem fumaça]	Negative

Table of 500 Texts

Catalog Number	Similarity Coefficient	Year	Author	Title	Mode
410	0.5955	2012	Gabriel Macedo	Canção das favelas	Negative
411	0.2189	2012	Gabriela Pereira	[A minha terra é de muitos amores]	Other
412	0.1973	2012	Geovane César	[Na minha terra tem "cabra macho"]	Negative
413	0.514	2012	Gustavo Silva	[Na minha terra tem viciados]	Negative
414	0.4	2012	Heloisa Cristina Teixeira da Silva	[Minha terra tem algumas árvores]	Negative
415	0.3173	2012	Humberto Mendes de Paula Neto	[Minha terra tem praias lindas]	Negative
416	0.296	2012	Ingrind Caroline	[Na minha terra tem gente que veio pra ficar]	Negative
417	0.257	2012	Isabelle Thonyson	[Minha terra tem palmeiras]	Negative
418	0.3158	2012	Jease Bernardo	[Na minha terra tem mangueiras]	Positive
419	0.3063	2012	Jeisiele Pereira	[Minha terra tem pirulito]	Positive
420	0.3356	2012	João Carlos	[Minha terra tem bananeira]	Negative
421	0.2134	2012	Jonas F. Souza	[Na minha casa tem goteiras]	Negative
422	0.1802	2012	Jonathan César	[A espera de um exílio]	Other

Table of 500 Texts

Catalog Number	Similarity Coefficient	Year	Author	Title	Mode
423	0.4064	2012	Jonny Pádua	[Minha terra tem palmeiras]	Positive
424	0.25	2012	José André	[Na minha escola tem palmeiras]	Other
425	0.4087	2012	José Carlos de Lima Neto	[Vivo no meio do mato]	Negative
426	0.1836	2012	José Demétrio	[Minha terra tem amores]	Other
427	0.3784	2012	José Lucas Lopes	[Em terra de palmeiras]	Positive
428	0.3074	2012	José Sidney	[Jaboatão terra de grandes]	Negative
429	0.1916	2012	Joyce Lourenco	[Minha terra tem cantores]	Other
430	0.1959	2012	Joyce Maria	[Minha terra tem palmeiras]	Positive
431	0.2726	2012	Juarez Junior	[Nosso céu tem mais estrelas]	Other
432	0.4718	2012	Jucileide Conceição	Cidade SSA	Negative
433	0.2065	2012	Kathiana Lima	[Minha terra tem lindas praias]	Positive
434	0.1966	2012	Kevellen Mayara	[Na minha terra tem flores]	Positive
435	0.5314	2012	Lanai Raquiele	Canção do martírio	Negative
436	0.1781	2012	Lays Grazielle	[Ao ficar sozinho a noite]	Other
437	0.2783	2012	Layse Oliveira	[Onde eu moro tem muitas árvores]	Positive

Table of 500 Texts

Catalog Number	Similarity Coefficient	Year	Author	Title	Mode
438	0.3985	2012	Leandro José Arruda	[Minha terra tem bambu]	Negative
439	0.3729	2012	Lucas Vinícius	[Meu antigo bairro não tem palmeiras]	Negative
440	0.3097	2012	Lucimar	Meu Tocantins	Positive
441	0.1682	2012	Luiz	[Eu moro numa terra que]	Negative
442	0.3884	2012	Marcos Paulo	[Na minha terra não tem palmeiras]	Negative
443	0.3012	2012	Marilia Miguel	[Na minha terra tem praias]	Positive
444	0.1843	2012	Mikaela Conceição	[Minha terra tem brigadeiro]	Other
445	0.4279	2012	Mylena Maria	[Minha terra tem roseiras]	Positive
446	0.3721	2012	Nadianne Galvão	[Na minha casa tem um bateria]	Other
447	0.2146	2012	Nara Natália	[Só de ficar sozinho a noite]	Other
448	0.3377	2012	Rafael Henrique	[Minha terra tem bananeiras]	Negative
449	0.176	2012	Ramon Barros	[Minha terra tem Sport, Náutico e Ceará]	Other
450	0.2362	2012	Renailson	[Na minha terra não tem palmeiras]	Negative

Table of 500 Texts

Catalog Number	Similarity Coefficient	Year	Author	Title	Mode
451	0.1581	2012	Renata Ferreira	[Minha infância divertida]	Other
452	0.4695	2012	Ronaldo Costa Fernandes	Canção do exílio	Negative
453	0.1639	2012	Thalyta Kattiane	[Minha terra tem pobreza]	Negative
454	0.3707	2012	Tiago Santos	[Minha terra tem mais alegria]	Positive
455	0.1935	2012	Vitor Monteiro	[Minha terra tem o náutico]	Other
456	0.1877	2012	Willyana Oliveira	[Minha terra tem cadeira]	Other
457	0.4149	2013	Angela Beatriz	Chão verde	Negative
458	0.3138	2013	Anonymous	Canção da injustiça	Negative
459	0.4476	2013	Breno Lobato e Samara Cristina	[Minha terra tem o brega]	Positive
460	0.4843	2013	Célia Monteiro	[Minha tem açaí]	Positive
461	0.387	2013	Eliane Pereira Tavares	[Meu lugar tem mais verde]	Negative
462	0.5774	2013	José Augusto Botelho	[Minha terra tem um time]	Positive
463	0.4285	2013	Ligia Silva Dias	[Minha terra tem problemas]	Negative
464	0.4962	2013	Maria Riciene Santos and Janeth Lúcia	[Minha rua tem crianças]	Negative
465	0.5911	2013	Pamela Berger	Canção da corrupção	Negative

Table of 500 Texts

Catalog Number	Similarity Coefficient	Year	Author	Title	Mode
466	0.6477	2013	Selma	[Meu pará tem palmeiras]	Positive
467	0.3627	2013	Vanderleia	[Minha terra tem muralhas]	Negative
468	0.3633	2013	Venâncio Paz	Nas asas da imaginação	Negative
469	0.4069	2014	Amanda Afonso	[Minha terra tem estádios]	Negative
470	0.326	2014	Escola de Samba Rosas de Ouro	Inesquecível	Positive
471	0.708	2014	Luís Tavares	Canção do exílio (poemas para almas apressadas)	Positive
472	0.557	2015	Adriana Aneli Costa Lagrasta	Exílio dos sabiás	Other
473	0.5221	2015	Adriane Garcia	E o sabiá?	Negative
474	0.1843	2015	Arnaldo Sisson	Minha terra tem uns mares	Positive
475	0.4223	2015	Beatriz Lourenço	Minha terra	Negative
476	0.5158	2015	Carvalho Junior	Canção de um filho	Positive
477	0.4176	2015	Chris Herrmann	Sabiás e palmeiras	Positive
478	0.2427	2015	Elke Lubitz	O sabiá	Negative
479	0.3705	2015	Eloí Elisabete Bocheco	Minha terra tem chagas na alma e chora	Negative
480	0.3594	2015	Fabíola Mazzini Leone	Canção do exílio do menino	Negative

Table of 500 Texts

Catalog Number	Similarity Coefficient	Year	Author	Title	Mode
481	0.3016	2015	Flavia D'Ângelo	Refúgio	Negative
482	0.6276	2015	Groisman Themis	Minha alma	Positive
483	0.4921	2015	Gustavo Terra	Canção da anistia	Negative
484	0.3816	2015	Helena da Rosa	Exílio é para quem fica	Negative
485	0.6857	2015	Inês Santos	Cidade cinza	Negative
486	0.3982	2015	Joelma Bittencourt	Poema pré-alfabetizado	Negative
487	0.4142	2015	Jorge Nagão	Canção do (ex)sírio	Negative
488	0.3845	2015	Jose Couto	Canção da extinção	Negative
489	0.554	2015	Jose Regí Poesia	Utopia	Negative
490	0.3515	2015	Lorenza Junqueira	Sabiá	Other
491	0.3227	2015	Lourença Lou	Cantiga de quem não se exilou	Negative
492	0.41	2015	Lourença Lou	Canção dos contrários	Negative
493	0.4139	2015	Luciane Lopes	Canção do exílio de dentro	Negative
494	0.6265	2015	Luiz Alexandre Cruz Ferreira	Ode ao exílio	Negative
495	0.4213	2015	Marcelo Adifa	Das dores, o exílio	Positive
496	0.4295	2015	Monica Martins	Infância do exílio	Negative

Table of 500 Texts

Catalog Number	Similarity Coefficient	Year	Author	Title	Mode
497	0.3945	2015	Nil Kremer	Minha terra incompreendida	Negative
498	0.3931	2015	Paulo Becker	Exílio na rua cipó	Negative
499	0.4764	2015	Paulo Betancur	Exílio da Canção	Positive
500	0.3465	2015	Paulo George	De Gonçalves Dias ao tempo da utopia	Negative
501	0.3977	2015	Raimundo Fontenele	Segunda canção do exílio	Negative
502	0.3005	2015	Tere Tavares	Extinção do empecilho	Negative
503	0.3746	2015	Wander Porto	Canção sem brilho	Negative

Note

1. This appendix is intended as a complement to the book's close readings and literary analysis. It conveys the main features of the quantitative analysis of the 500 texts and provides historical context in a statistical format. The categories represented by each column are textual similarity, date of publication (or best estimate), author(s), title (or first line), and modal analysis. The gender of the authors, another important feature of analysis discussed in Chapter 7, can be assumed based on the names of the authors. The data art installation "Graph of 500 Texts" was largely based on the data in this appendix. A time-lapse video of the construction of this graph can be found here: https://youtu.be/G5uewutXd3M. It is also important to note that, although references to many of these texts can be found in the Works Cited, others can be read online at sites such as the literary journal Germina: Revista de Literatura e Arte. Germina maintains a collection of well-known variations and many lesser known contemporary variations curated by the editor Silvana Guimarães (https://www.germinaliteratura.com.br/sabiaseexilios/asavesqueaquigorjeiam_1.htm). The discovery of the Germina site was important to the early development of this project. I have since shared texts with the editor for inclusion in this collection and appreciate the collaboration. Also, most titles listed under the year 2012 were published in a single volume found here: https://www.scribd.com/document/109651993/Cancao-do-Exilio-Revisitada. Other less exhaustive collections abound across the web on blogs and other sites. For the purpose of dates and the Works Cited, I have made every effort to locate the earliest version of all texts, although this can be difficult at times, especially for the born-digital ones. The remainder of the 500 texts can be read from various sources to include websites, online digital archives, and in traditional print. For example, many texts were found via the search engine of the Hemeroteca Digital of the Biblioteca Nacional Brasileira or on Google books.

Notes

Chapter One

1. Gonçalves Dias went on to have a short, but illustrious career before tragically dying in a shipwreck off the coast of his home state of Maranhão in 1864.

2. "The history of the world is the slaughterhouse of the world, reads a famous Hegelian aphorism; and of literature. The majority of books disappear forever—and 'majority' actually misses the point: if we set today's canon of nineteenth-century British novels at two hundred titles (which is a very high figure), they would still be only about *0.5 percent* of all published novels. And the other 99.5 percent? This is the question behind this article, and behind the larger idea of literary history that is now taking shape in the work of several critics—most recently Sylvie Thorel-Cailleteau, Katie Trumpener, and Margaret Cohen" (Moretti, "The Slaughterhouse" 207).

3. For one possible example, see the Google N-Gram Viewer: books.google.com/ngrams (Michel, Jean Baptiste et al.).

4. "The United States is the country of close reading, so I don't expect this idea to be particularly popular. But the trouble with close reading (in all of its incarnations, from the new criticism to deconstruction) is that it necessarily depends on an extremely small canon. This may have become an unconscious and invisible premise by now, but it is an iron one nonetheless: you invest so much in individual texts *only* if you think that very few of them really matter. Otherwise, it doesn't make sense. And if you want to look beyond the canon (and of course, world literature will do so: it would be absurd if it didn't!) close reading will not do it. It's not designed to do it, it's designed to do the opposite. At bottom, it's a theological exercise—very solemn treatment of very few texts taken very seriously—whereas what we really need is a little pact with the devil: we know how to read texts, now let's learn how *not* to read them. Distant reading: where distance, let me repeat it, *is a condition of knowledge*: it allows you to focus on units that are much smaller or much larger than the text: devices, themes, tropes—or genres and systems. And if, between the very small and the very large, the text itself disappears, well, it is one of those cases when one can justifiably say, Less is more. If we want to understand the system in its entirety, we must accept losing something. We always pay a price for theoretical knowledge: reality is infinitely rich; concepts are abstract, are poor. But it's precisely this 'poverty' that makes it possible to handle them, and therefore to know. This is why less is actually more" (Moretti, "Conjectures" 57).

5. Much appreciation and credit are due to the engineering professor Ledlie Klosky and mathematician Jocelyn Bell for their many helpful ideas and feedback in the early stages of this study as we articulated together these categories of analysis.

Chapter Three

1. Regarding the relation of the author to the nation during the Romantic period, Alfredo Bosi writes: "O fulcro da visão romântica do mundo é o sujeito" (Bosi, *História concisa* 93) and "A nação afigura-se ao patriota do século XIX como uma idéia-força que tudo vivifica (*História* 95). Even though Brazil and Portugal are never mentioned explicitly by name in "Canção do exílio," the context of the poem, being written in Portugal by a Brazilian, and the general Romantic sentiment of the period, which was especially concerned with narrating national identity, has led the poem's interpreters from the beginning to read it as an autobiographical text. The apologetic personal footnote in the original version of the poem supports this interpretation, indicating that Gonçalves Dias was, like other Romantics, interested in using literature to define the Brazilian nation and the place of the individual within it. Specifically, when writing "Canção do exílio," Gonçalves Dias had his home state of Maranhão in mind: "Quando eu compus esta canção, ou como melhor se chame, tinha apenas visto algumas províncias do norte do Brasil" (*Primeiros cantos* 2). Thus, the first-person perspective of the poem can easily be read as autobiographical, and not the voice of some other poetic "I," and the two nations being narrated are in fact Brazil, corresponding to "lá" in the text, and Portugal corresponding to "cá." Not coincidentally, the autobiographical nature of the poem's responses has been a constant from the nineteenth century to today, as those who write variations continue to work out their place within the nation by adapting and dialoguing with Gonçalves Dias.

2. The majority of these sixteen texts are of Portuguese authorship, but technically this is a coincidence, albeit an almost inevitable one. Portuguese authorship was not a requirement, or even a consideration, for the inclusion of any of these poems. The main criterion for selection of these Portuguese responses was based on content. Once having established a textual link with "Canção do exílio" and included in the group of 500, it was determined whether the focus of the poem— the specific land being missed, possessed, glorified, etc.—was Portugal instead of Brazil.

3. In addition to these Portuguese responses, there is also another noteworthy group of Brazilian-themed poems that can be read, to some degree or another, as responses to the Portuguese, such as: "Minha terra tem talentos," written in 1858 by an unknown author; Manuel Bandeira's "Sextilhas românticas" from 1945; Vinicius de Moraes's "Pátria minha" from 1949; Waldemar Machado da Silva's "Hino à região do Rio Negro" from 1971; and Jose Aloise Bahia's conglomerated "josé murilo gonçalves aloise mendes dias bahia" from 2009. A discussion of the intertextual relations that these poems have with the Portuguese responses begins with their inclusion of the word "rouxinol." In the 1858 response, an unknown poet wrote a direct response to the Portuguese poet opening with these lines: "Minha terra tem talentos / Que ainda brilham como um sol / Tem um estro mui subido / Que vence o do rouxinol." The poem also includes a footnote placed at the end of this stanza that declares unequivocally that the piece should be read as a response to A. J. Ferreira's original 1847 parody. Almost ninety years later, the "rouxinol" would continue to echo in Brazilian poetry as a Portuguese referent. Bandeira opens "Sextilhas românticas" with the lines: "Paisagens da minha terra, / Onde o rouxinol não canta." The poet then goes on to describe a Brazil that, although indebted to the Romantic poets whom he mentions by name, is neither dependent on Dias's "sabiá" nor the Portuguese alternative. Four years after "Sextilhas românticas," Moraes wrote "Pátria minha" while working abroad as a diplomat in Los Angeles. Employing the word "exílio" in the opening lines, Moraes formulates his very own twentieth-century "Canção do exílio" that describes a Brazilian cultural dependency not on Europe, but on a neo-colonial economic master, the United States. The poem closes by describing a complicated attempt to reconnect with his nation through an "avigrama" transmitted not only by the Brazilian "sabiá," but also by the European "rouxinol" and the "cotovia": "Agora chamarei a amiga cotovia / E pedirei que peça ao rouxinol do dia / Que peça ao sabiá / Para levar-te presto este avigrama: / 'pátria minha, saudades de quem te ama... / vinicius de moraes" (Moraes, "Pátria" 385). "By inventing a fantastic mode of transmitting his letter which ends with the song of the *sabiá*, Moraes points to a communication breakdown between writer and nation that has taken place over the decades since Gonçalves Dias' 'Canção do exílio'" (Enslen, "Vinícius" 425). Here, whether the use of the term "rouxinol" tells us that Vinícius was aware of the Portuguese responses to "Canção do exílio" is not the point. At the very least, he would have been aware of the nightingale's strong relation to the European canon of which Portuguese poetry was a part. It is also well-documented that Moraes was thinking of "Canção do exílio" during this post-war period. For example, in a "crônica" entitled "Meu Deus, não seja já," written from Hollywood in 1946, Moraes makes numerous references to "Canção do exílio" while communicating all the many things he misses in Brazil. As one example, he references the second stanza of the original, closing the first paragraph of the crônica with the line: "Hollywood é bonito, não há dúvida, mas não tem essas estrelas flores vidas amores" (Moraes, "Meu Deus" 1).

4. After appearing in *Lisia poética*, "A saudade da pátria" was also reprinted at least one other time on February 18, 1852 in the Brazilian newspaper *O mercantil*.

5. I am not proposing here that A. J. Ferreira's poem is definitely the first parody or imitation, but only the earliest confirmed in this study. As a slightly earlier poem entitled "Lyra: Como é bela a minha pátria" intimates, written by C. A. de Sá and published in the *O mercantil* on September 25, 1847, it is quite possible that other parodies already existed by November 1847 and that they may have already evoked the "rouxinol" as the Portuguese counterpart of the "sabiá." The Brazilian Sá writes, "Não temos o rouxinol, / Tal cantor não há; / Mas que importa, possuimos / Mavioso sabiá, / Como encanta nosso ouvido, / Gaturamo tão sentido!" (3). On the

other hand, it is unlikely that any of these earlier imitations, if they exist, had the same influence as Ferreira's poem, based on the evidence at hand.

6. "Recordações de Portugal" was written on November 20, 1847.

7. Credit is due to the mathematician, Jocelyn Bell, for helping me define the term "syntactic template."

8. See discussion in previous chapter of Bosi's *Colony, Cult, Culture* wherein he demonstrates the etymological relationship these words share with the land.

9. The seventeen unique nouns and the first nine most frequent nouns in the 500 texts come from among these seventeen. In order of appearance, these seventeen nouns in the original are: "canção," "exílio," "terra," "palmeiras," "sabiá," "aves," "céu," "estrelas," "várzeas," "flores," "bosques," "vida," "amores," "noite," "prazer," "primores," and "deus." "Terra" appears 1245 times in the 500 texts. "Sabiá" appears 417 times. "Palmeiras" is mentioned 372 times. And "deus," "céu," "amores," "vida," "noite," and "flores" appear 206, 194, 189, 182, 164, and 140 times, respectively.

Chapter Four

1. "Gilberto Freyre was right to advocate for the need to build an original tropical civilization in Brazil: 'Brazil does not want to be sub-European in its appearance or anti-European in its attitudes but rather to join its European heritage with tropical values to thus form a new style of civilization'" (qtd in Sachs 75).

2. The quotation marks from "Canção do exílio" are employed in the version found in official government documents, but if the intention was to give full credit to Gonçalves Dias, there is an omission since the phrase "têm mais flores" should also appear in quotes.

3. Author's translation.

4. Based on references in the newspapers of the time, Múcio Teixeira was a colorful figure whose acts and utterances were criticized and praised with equal zeal: memoria.bn.br/docreader/089842_02/368. Due to his divisive popularity, he even had to go so far as to request the daily protection of the police from those who were angered by his prophecies: memoria.bn.br/docreader/089842_02/344 and memoria.bn.br/docreader/089842_02/1393.

5. "Uma digna ociosidade sempre pareceu mais excelente, e até mais nobilitante, a um bom português, ou a um espanhol, do que a luta insana pelo pão de cada dia ... a atividade produtora é, em si, menos valiosa que a contemplação e o amor" (Holanda, *Raízes* 38).

6. Even prior to these poems about Bahia, an adapted version of Gonçalves Dias's opening stanza was already circulating in Maranhão in 1849 as the epigraph of a political periodical. The first two lines of the four-line epigraph affirm the glory and beauty of Brazil represented by its "palmeiras" and "sabiás" while the last two complain about the Empire. Included in the second issue of *O timbyra* (and all subsequent issues), it reads as follows: "Minha terra tem palmeiras / Onde canta o sabiá; / Miguelistas, guabirús / Não podem imperar cá" ("Minha terra tem palmeiras" *O timbyra* 1). A year after the

Praieira Revolution in Pernambuco, this Northeastern publication's content complains of increased regulation at the ports and other governmental interventions and the reference to the "Miguelistas, guabirús" was a thumbing of the nose toward perceived abuses of imperial power. "Miguelistas" was a term used to refer to the defeated absolutist monarchy of Miguel I in Portugal while "guabirús" is an indigenous term for rats, leaving the implication obvious. (Dom Pedro I, the first emperor of Brazil, had abdicated his reign to return to Portugal to defeat his brother Miguel I and install a constitutional monarchy that would limit the powers of the throne.) If first used to refer to the supporters of Miguel I's absolutist monarchy, this Brazilian publication's slogan used the term "miguelistas" as a pejorative reference for all meddling and overbearing imperial officials.

7. A transcription of the original manifesto can be read here: edisciplinas.usp.br/pluginfile.php/3817523/mod_resource/content/2/manifesto%20republicano%201870.pdf

8. A preliminary search reveals that the Castro Barbosa mentioned here is possibly the same as a popular singer from the time.

9. Relatedly, the earliest known text rendered in a language other than Portuguese that I have so far uncovered is by Ludwig Ferdinand Schmid, written in German, that reads as a loose translation with significant departures. Originally published in Germany's *Allemeigne Deutsche Zeutung* and transposed in Rio's *O mercantil* on October 31, 1883 (memoria.bn.br/DocReader/376493/2731).

10. A previous version of this paragraph was first published in Joshua and Alaina Enslen's "Bird-watching: Visualizing the Influence of Gonçalves Dias''Canção do exílio.'"

11. Among the 500 texts studied here, Carlos Drummond de Andrade is responsible for at least four variations and a possible fifth, an anonymous text from 1960 entitled "Minha terra," discussed in Chapter 5. See Appendix for more details.

Chapter Five

1. "Although Tropicália coalesced as a formal movement only in the realm of popular music, it was a cultural phenomenon manifest in film, theater, visual arts, and literature. The dialogic impulse behind Tropicália would generate an extraordinary flourish of artistic innovation during a period of political and cultural conflict in Brazil" (Dunn 2). "The tropicalist movement coalesced toward the end of a tumultuous decade marked by the intensification of left-wing activism and a reactionary military coup in 1964 aimed at preempting any movement for radical social transformation. Debates over the proper role of the artist in relation to progressive social and political movements oriented much of the cultural production during this period" (37).

2. The 50 texts under consideration in this chapter published from 1960 to 1989 are listed here in chronological order: "Minha terra," possibly authored by C. D. de Andrade, Candango Forçado's (pseud.) "Canção do

brasílio," and a "crônica" from Rubem Braga were all published in 1960; a newspaper blurb from 1961 which begins, "Minha terra tem pernas de pau"; René Bittencourt's "Alô musicistas!" and Mario Quintana's "Uma canção," both from 1962; Fernando Lopes's "Minha terra só tem tanques que ameaçam atirar" from 1963; Jonas da Silva's "Amazonas" from 1966; Manuel Bandeira's "A João Guimarães Rosa" from the same year; Armando Garcia's Portuguese response from 1967 entitled "Minha terra"; Chico Buarque's famous "Sabiá" from 1968; Gilberto Gil and Torquato Neto's "Marginália II," also from 1968; Gilberto Gil and Capinan's "Show de me esqueci" from 1969; Chico Buarque's "Agora falando sério," Juca Chaves's "Take me back to Piaui," Martins D'Alvarez's "S. Luis do Maranhão," all from 1970; Binho, Ito and Camargo's "São Paulo, chapadão de glória" from 1971; Waldemar Machado da Silva's "Lyra da saudade" from 1971; José Paulo Paes's "Canção do exílio facilitada" from 1973; Cacaso's "Jogos florais I" and "Jogos florais II," both from 1974; L.M.'s "Nova canção do exílio" from 1974; Fernando Leite Mendes's "Ladainha da implosão," Sergio Reis's "Saudade de minha terra," and Taiguara's "Terra das palmeiras," all from 1975; C. D. de Andrade's "Fazendeiros de cana" (1977); Alcione's "Todos cantam sua terra" (1978); José Carlos Pádua and Egberto Gismonti's "Coração de candango" (1978); Luiz Fernando Veríssimo's "Nova canção do exílio" (1978); Vavá and Machado's "Na princesa do sertão" (1978); Nelson Ferreira and Aldemar Paiva's "Pernambuco você é meu" from 1979; Affonso Romano Sant'anna's "Canção do exílio mais recente" from 1980; Assisão's "Sabiá na seca," Rita Lee's "Pirarucu," and Zé Geraldo's "Sabiá," all from 1983; from 1984, "Tenho saudade," "Boiadeiro," Armindo Trevisan's "Nova canção no exílio," Dalton Trevisan's "Canção do exílio," Flávio Cleto's "Veros diversos," Gal Costa's song "Ave nossa," written by Moraes Moreira and Beu Machado, and a brief two-line political commentary, beginning with the line, "Minha terra tem dívidas"; Eduardo Alves da Costa's "Outra canção do exílio" (1985); Belchior's "Retórica sentimental" and António Peticov's untitled text from 1986; Paulo Leminski's "Diversonagens dispersas" and Wilson Bueno's "Canção sem fronteiras" from 1987; José Paulo Paes's "Lisboa: aventuras" from 1987; Paulo Mendes Campos's "Nova canção do exílio" from 1988; and Eduardo Dias's "Canção que não é do exílio" from 1989.

3. With three texts from 1963 and 1986 serving as bookends—Fernando Lopes's "Minha terra só tem tanques," an important harbinger from late 1963, Belchior's famous "Retórica sentimental" and António Peticov's untitled text from 1986—the number of texts from the period comes to 39.

4. "The word *crônica* has no exact equivalent in English. Somewhat similar to our newspaper column, it is a short composition, often humorous in tone, that may at times resemble a short story or an essay while commenting on almost any subject that interests the author" (*Crônicas brasileiras* xv).

5. The only non-stop words to appear more frequently than "terra" are the verb "tem" (90) and the possessive "minha" (74) while the subject pronoun "eu" appears a comparable 59 times. As mentioned elsewhere, the presence of "minha" and "tem" in comparable frequency to "terra" is not surprising. Together with "terra," these two words form the ubiquitous trio, "minha terra tem," by far the most common phrase from the original among the 500 texts. The same is true in the 39 texts as the phrase appears 46 times with little variation.

The high frequency of the word "eu" is also an important consideration since, in the original text, the subject pronoun appears even more frequently than "terra." In fact, it appears five times whereas "terra," "palmeiras," and "sabiá" appear only 4 times each. In the 500 variations, "eu" is more frequent than "sabiá" and "palmeiras," appearing 573 times, but far less frequent than "terra," which appears more than a thousand times. Although lacking substantive specificity, the high frequency of "eu" points to a grand consistency in language and meaning coursing through the corpora. As these poetic protagonists propound in the first person those things that "minha terra tem," they express a deep and abiding concern for the welfare of the land and especially for the place of the individual or citizen within it, reinforcing the personalized nature of most variations.

6. The tokens from the poem Armando A.C. Garcia's "Minha terra" (1967) were not included in this list since the focus of the poem is not Brazil, but Portugal.

Chapter Six

1. For reference, below are the titles, authors, and publication dates of the 61 texts from the three categories delineated above. Some texts have been included in more than one category. Every effort has been made to find the earliest and most reliable source for the dates of publication for each of these texts; however, due to the information bounce inherent in new media, many of these texts appear in many places on the web. This fact, along with other bibliographic challenges presented by the internet, mean that, while the majority of dates is reliable, some dates may not be exact.

The *Environmentalism* category has 31 texts: one from 2002 (Sabrina Taury, "Algum cantar"); one from 2005 (Francisco Simões and Alberto Chen, "Terra minha"); four from 2006 (Various, "O grito da nação," Clevane Pessoa de Araújo Lopes, "Um certo sabiá," Henio dos Santos, "Canção do novo exílio," Various, "Outro lugar"); three from 2008 (Gustavo Ganso, "Na minha terra não tem mais palmeiras"; Lourdes Bernadete C Bispo, "Minha terra"; Miriam Panighel Carvalho, "Paráfrase da canção do exílio"); four from 2009 (Caio Muriel Sostisso, "Canção de exílio moderno"; João de Abreu Borges, "Minha terra sem palmeiras"; Reynaldo Bessa and Marcelo Álvarez, "Canção do exílio"; Wilson Roberto de Carvalho Almeida, "Canção do martírio"); one from 2010 (Raquela Maythenand, "Canção do exílio"); one from 2011 (Maria Mogorim, "Canção do martírio"); six from 2012 (Cláudio Fernando, "[Minha terra tem poluição]"; Daniela Brito, "Era uma vez uma terra"; Elzimara Souza, "A terra que há"; Humberto Mendes de Paula Neto, "[Minha terra tem praias lindas]"; José Carlos de Lima Neto, "[Vivo no meio do mato]"; Marcos Paulo, "[Na minha terra não tem palmeiras]); two from

207

2013 (Ligia Silva Dias, "[Minha terra tem problemas]"; Venâncio Paz, "Nas asas da imaginação"); and eight from 2015 (Adriane Garcia, "E o sabiá"; Beatriz Lourenço, "Minha terra"; Eloí Elisabete Bocheco, "[Minha terra tem chagas na alma e chora]"; Helena da Rosa, "Exílio é para quem fica"; Inês Santos, "Cidade cinza"; José Couto, "Canção da extinção"; Lourença Lou, "Canção dos contrários"; Paulo Becker, "Exílio na Rua Cipó").

The *Literatura Marginal* category has 29 texts: one from 1999 (Fernando Bonassi, "Cena 9"); one from 2001 (Marta Helena Cocco, "Versão enlatada do exílio"); two from 2002 (Francisco dos Santos, "Poema de domingo"; Sabrina Taury, "Canção de fuga"); one from 2003 (Iosif Landau, "Exilado"); one from 2005 (Francisco Simões and Alberto Chen, "Terra minha"); four from 2006 (Adames Hickel, "Sujeira brasileira"; Various, "Uma canção"; Various, "Canção dos excluídos"; Porto Sens Coelho Sousa, "Último suspiro"); one from 2008 (Lourdes Bernadete C Bispo, "Minha terra"); one from 2009 (Gabriel Rezende Mota, "Canção do Brasil"); one from 2010 (Liria Porto, "Expropriados"); two from 2011 (Various, "Paródia I"; Various, "Paródia II"); seven from 2012 (Ana Rute, "Canção do bairro"; Gabriel Macedo, "Canção das favelas"; Gustavo Silva, "[Na minha terra tem viciados]"; Jucileide Conceição, "Cidade SSA"; Leandro José Arruda, "[Minha terra tem bambu]"; Thalyta Kattiane, "[Minha terra tem pobreza]"; Éder Vieira, "[Onde eu moro]"); two from 2013 (Lígia Silva Dias, "[Minha terra tem problemas]"; Maria Riciene N. Santos and Janeth Lúcia, "[Minha rua tem crianças]"); and five from 2015 (Beatriz Lourenço, "Minha terra"; Fabíola Mazzini Leone, "Canção do exílio do menino"; Joelma Bittencourt, "Poema pré-Alfabetizado"; Lourença Lou, "Cantiga de quem não se exilou"; Mônica Martins, "Infância do exílio").

The *Corruption* category has 14 texts: one from 2005 (Francisco Simões and Alberto Chen, "Terra minha"); two from 2006 (Eduardo Becker and Eduardo da Silva Valerio, "Que país é este"; Various, "Canção da revolta"); two from 2009 (Paulo Briguet, "Canção do exíguo"; Trixie Hachi-Roku, "[Minha terra tem corruptos roubando adoidado]") one from 2011 (Maria Mogorim, "Canção do martírio"); three from 2012 (Ana Rute, "Canção do bairro"; Beatriz Teixeira, "[Na minha terra não tem palmeiras]"; Jucileide Conceição, "Cidade SSA"); two from 2013 (Pamela Berger, "Canção da corrupção"; Unknown, "Canção da injustiça"); one from 2014 (Amanda Afonso, "[Minha terra tem estádios]"); two from 2015 (Jose Regí Poesia, "Utopia"; Tere Tavares, "Extinção do empecilho").

2. As just one example of the hundreds of "Canção do exílio" variations not able to be included in this study, Dilercy Aragão Adler and Leopoldo Gil Dulcio Vaz published an anthology of poetry containing 1000 poems aptly titled, *Mil Poemas para Gonçalves Dias*. None of these poems were included in the group of 500.

3. As described on the website: "This tool uses fuzzy comparisons functions between strings. It is derived from GNU diff and analyze.c. The basic algorithm is described in: 'An O(ND) Difference Algorithm and its Variations,' Eugene Myers; the basic algorithm was independently discovered as described in: 'Algorithms for Approximate String Matching,' E. Ukkonen." (www.tools4noobs.com/online_tools/string_similarity/)

4. See Appendix.

5. The bulk of the poems in the latter category come from the texts surrounding the dedication of Gonçalves Dias's monument.

6. The idea behind a modal analysis was inspired by the Greek musical modes. Related to the seven notes in the Western major scale, the Greek modes, such as Aeolian, Lydian or Dorian, each named after a region of Ancient Greece, are all based on the same seven notes, also known as the Ionian mode. Yet, each of these modes begins from a different note within the same scale. For example, if the seven note Ionian mode were the all-natural C Major scale (C D E F G A B), then the Dorian pattern would be based on the second tone of that scale, rendering the mode as D E F G A B C. The Mixolydian mode, based on the fifth note, would then be G A B C D E F. The importance of explaining this system is that the relative "feeling," or sound, of each of these modes is quite different from the original Ionian scale, although they all share the same notes in common. Thus, each mode within a single major scale, although it contains the same notes as the others, has its own unique tonal characteristics derived from the relationship between the root or first note of the mode and the other six notes. With notes as words, a similar logic organizes our modal analysis of the texts. But, instead of seven modes, we have established only three: positive, negative, and other. Of course, the textual modes here are not nearly as predictable or formulaic as the Greek modes, but as a rule each of the texts falls under one of three modal categories based on its semantic relationship with the "feeling" of the original.

7. According to the author's online notes, the quoted portion of the poem is from one of his own "crônicas" entitled, "Tempos de corvos," from 1998.

8. For further discussion of Bonassi's text, see also Enslen, "Birdwatching."

9. This poem along with Liria Porto's "Expropriados" are discussed in more detail in the chapter on female authors.

10. As just one of many possible examples, see: www.washingtonpost.com/news/morning-mix/wp/2015/08/27/why-are-brazils-environmentalists-being-murdered/

Chapter Seven

1. The five female-authored texts published before 2000 and included in the main body of 500 are, in chronological order: Honrata Minelvina Carneiro de Mendonça's "Saudades da minha terra" from 1867; Maria Beatriz's "Minha terra," from 1936; Lygia de Menezes's "Coco de Alagoas," from 1945; Haydee Nicolusi's "Canção do turista malogrado," from 1948; and Rita Lee's "Pirarucu," from 1983. The breakdown by year of the number of texts with at least one female author in the 2000s is as follows:

2000 – 0, 2001 – 1, 2002 – 4, 2003 – 0, 2004 – 0, 2005 – 3, 2006 – 7, 2007 – 2, 2008 – 6, 2009 – 11, 2010 – 3, 2011 – 4, 2012 – 34, 2013 – 9, 2014 – 1, 2015 – 13. The determination of an author's gender was based on name. All collaboratively authored texts—a growing trend in the new millennium—with at least one female author were included in the list of female-authored texts.

2. A similar trend emerges regarding the digital-print dichotomy. With the majority of all variations being published more or less freely online, the last variation in print (newspapers, books, etc.) would not be long hence, if the trend continues. Yet, this scenario is also not likely since new and old media are by no means mutually exclusive.

3. I am borrowing this term from computer science since it will only be through digitization and algorithmic searches that such a totalizing scenario would take place.

4. In the 103 texts, there are 8982 words in total, making the average poem 87 words in length. This number is roughly equivalent to the 91-word average of the 242 texts from the post-1999 group, but significantly smaller than the 160-word average of the pre-millennial texts. (The average length of all 500 texts is 126 words.)

5. As a reminder, the 12 most frequent nouns from the 2000s as a whole are: "terra" (485), "sabiá" (174), "palmeiras" (161), "noite" (103), "vida" (100), "deus" (90), "céu" (74), "amores" (67), "canção" (66), "exílio" (57), "estrelas" (52), and "aves" (50). In the female-authored texts, there is a tie for the twelfth most frequent noun between "amor," from the original, and "lugar," not from the original. If we include by exception "amor" in light of this tie, then the only three most frequent nouns not shared by the two groups are "aves," "vida," and "flores." The first two are from the list of most frequent nouns of all texts from the 2000s and the last one is only most frequent in the female-authored texts.

6. The following is a list of the female-authored titles in the negative mode. In those texts with no title, the first lines were used and, in order to conserve space, the names of the authors for texts with three or more authors were listed parenthetically as "various." A more detailed table is available in the Appendix: one from 1948 ("Canção do turista malogrado," Haydee Nicolusi); one from 1983 ("Pirarucu," Rita Lee); one from 2001 ("Versão enlatada do exílio," Marta Helena Cocco); two from 2002 ("Canção de fuga," Sabrina Taury; "Algum cantar," Sabrina Taury); one from 2005 ("Exílio," Elizabeth Hazin); four from 2006 ("O grito da nação," Various; "Uma canção," Various; "Canção dos excluídos," Various; "Canção da revolta," Various); three from 2008 ("Minha terra tem buzinas," Elsa Villon; "Minha terra," Lourdes Bernadete C. Bispo; "Paráfrase da canção do exílio," Miriam Carvalho); two from 2009 ("Poema sintônico," Luci Collin; "Minha terra tem corruptos," Trixie Hachi-Roku); two from 2010 ("expropriados," líria porto; "Canção do exílio," Raquela Maythenand); four from 2011 ("Paródia II," Various; "Canção do carioca," Juliana da Conceição David; "Canção do martírio," Maria Mogorim; "Paródia I," Various); eleven from

2012 ("Minha terra tem bananeiras," Adrielly Silva; "Canção do bairro," Ana Rute; "Na minha terra não tem palmeiras," Beatriz Teixeira; "Era uma vez uma terra," Daniela Brito; "A terra que há," Elzimara Souza; "Minha terra tem algumas árvores," Heloisa Cristina Teixeira da Silva; "Na minha terra tem gente que veio pra ficar," Ingrind Caroline; "Minha terra tem palmeiras," Isabelle Thonyson; "Cidade SSA," Jucileide Conceição; "Canção do martírio," Lanai Raquiele; "Minha terra tem pobreza," Thalyta Kattiane); six from 2013 ("Chão verde," Angela Beatriz; "Meu lugar tem mais verde," Eliane Tavares; "Minha terra tem problemas," Ligia Silva Dias; "Minha rua tem crianças," Maria Riciene N. Santos & Janeth Lúcia; "Canção da corrupção," Pamela Berger; "Minha terra tem muralhas," Vanderléia); one from 2014 ("Minha terra tem estádios," Amanda Afonso); and eleven from 2015 ("E o sabiá?" Adriane Garcia; "Minha terra," Beatriz Lourenço; "Canção do exílio do menino," Fabíola Leone; "Refúgio," Flávia d'Angelo; "Exílio é para quem fica," Helena da Rosa; "Cidade cinza," Inês Santos; "Poema pré-alfabetizado," Joelma Bittencourt; "Cantiga de quem não se exilou," Lourença Lou; "Canção dos contrários," Lourença Lou; "Canção do exílio de dentro," Luciane Lopes; "Infância do exílio," Monica Martins).

7. Mendonça's text from 1867, written in the generally verbose Romantic mode, is 270 words in length and Nicolusi's text, the longest of all female-authored texts, is 320 words in length.

8. The Vargas era is discussed in greater detail in Chapter 4.

9. This is an estimated date of publication based on occurrences online.

10. It may be worth mentioning that soccer, as a vastly male-dominated sport, is one of those popular athletic traditions that, although immensely cherished by people of all genders, in large part supports the patriarchal norms underlying the unifying national discourse of Gonçalves Dias's original, as evidenced by the sport's promotion and co-optation by the Vargas dictatorship.

11. The author's surname, Xangô, is the name of the primary god, or "Orixá," of the Candomblé tradition.

12. O. de Andrade's famous "Canto de regresso à pátria," discussed in Chapter 4, also references this important conflict.

Chapter Eight

1. See Chapter 4, note 6.

2. Written at the height of the club's season prior to the fateful plane crash that tragically killed most of the players and coaches.

Chapter Nine

1. One can find versions of this chant on Twitter and it is also mentioned in this article, "Fernando Haddad faz caminhada com apoiadores pelo Centro de Goiânia," by Bárbara Zeiden, published online on September 28, 2018 in *Mais Goias* (www.emaisgoias.com.br).

2. See Satriano.

Afterword

1. It was originally developed as a post-doctoral project within the "Digital Mediation and Materialities of Literature" research group of the Center for Portuguese Literature at the University of Coimbra in 2015–16. The first stage of research culminated in an exhibition, "Bird-Watching", by Joshua Enslen and Alaina Enslen, at the Science Museum of the University in June 2016. An article related to the exhibition can be found at Enslen, Joshua A and Alaina Enslen. "Bird-watching: Visualizing the Influence of Gonçalves Dias's 'Canção do exílio'." Chiricu 1.2, 2017, 127–48. Videos related to the exhibitions can be found at tinyurl.com/y9fqeyjr.

Works Cited

"A literatura em 1907 e em 1932." *Fon Fon.* Rio de Janeiro, 16 Apr. 1932. memoria.bn.br/DocReader/259063/79699

Accioly, João. "Paulicéia." *Olho d'Agua.* 3rd ed. São Paulo: Saraiva & Companhia, 1947. 121–23.

Alencar, José de. "Carta ao dr. Jaguaribe." *Iracema.* Ministério da Cultura: Fundação Biblioteca Nacional. Accessed 21 May 2017. objdigital.bn.br/Acervo_Digital/livros_eletronicos/iracema.pdf

Alfaro, María Jesús Martínez. "Intertextuality: Origins and Development of the Concept." *Atlantis,* vol. 18, no. 1/2, 1996. 268–85. jstor.org/stable/41054827.

Alijoense (pseud.). "À minha terra," *Jornal do comércio.* Rio de Janeiro. 12 Nov. 1865. 2. memoria.bn.br/DocReader/364568_05/9368

Almino, João. "The Myth of Brasília and Literature." *João Almino.* Accessed 4 Jun. 2017. www.joaoalmino.com/en/omito/

Alós, Anselmo Peres. "Um passo além: o resgate de escritoras brasileiras do século XIX." *Revista Estudos Feministas,* vol. 16, no. 2, 2008. 691–93. dx.doi.org/10.1590/S0104-026X2008000200025

Andrade, Carlos Drummond. "Europa, França e Bahia." *Alguma poesia.* São Paulo: Companhia das Letras, 2013. 19.

———."Fazendeiros de cana." *Jornal do Brasil.* Rio de Janeiro, 19 Mar. 1977. 6. memoria.bn.br/DocReader/030015_09/157662

Andrade, Oswald de. "Canto de regresso à pátria." *Obras completas: poesias reunidas,* vol. 7. Rio de Janeiro: Civilização Brasileira, 1971. 144.

Andrey TNT (pseud.). "Canção do exílio à milícia." *Eu, Multívolo!?!...* Brasília: Thesaurus Editora, 1997. 56. books.google.com/books?id=jX3fO2dm9yUC&lpg

Antologia Mil poemas para Gonçalves Dias. Eds. Dilercy Aragão Adler and Leopoldo Gil Dulcio Vaz. São Luís: EDUFMA, 2013.

Araújo Pereira Alvim, Estevão de. "Portugal." *Cancioneiro de músicas populares.* Ed. Cesar das Neves. Porto: Typografia Occidental, 1893. 179.

———. "Portugal." *O sexo feminino.* Rio de Janeiro, 18 Oct. 1873. 3. memoria.bn.br/DocReader/706868/25

"As sete palmeiras." *Correio da manhã.* Rio de Janeiro, 30 Jan. 1910. 8. memoria.bn.br/DocReader/089842_02/284

Assis Figueiredo Júnior, Afonso Celso de. *Porque me ufano de meu país.* Rio de Janeiro: Laemert & C, 1901. hdl.handle.net/2027/nyp.33433081695128

Assisão. "Sabiá na seca." *Casamento aprissiguido.* Beverly, 1983.

Works Cited

B.C.S. "Adeus a Coimbra." *Almanach madeirense para o anno 1892*. Madeira: Antonio Francisco Monteiro, 1891. 105–07.

Bahia, José Aloise. "josé murilo gonçalves aloise dias mendes bahia." *Germina: revista de literatura e arte*. Accessed 1 Feb. 2015. www.germinaliteratura.com.br/sabiaseexilios/asavesqueaquigorjeiam_6.htm

"Balada dos estudantes." *Cancioneiro de músicas populares*, vol. 1. Ed. Cesar das Neves. Porto: Typographia Ocidental, 1893. 140–41.

Bananère, Juó (pseud.). "Migna terra." *O Pirralho*, 3 May 1913. memoria.bn.br/DocReader/213101/2082

Bandeira, Manuel. "Sextilhas românticas." *Correio da manhã*. Rio de Janeiro, 27 May 1945. 1. memoria.bn.br/DocReader/089842_05/26134

Barros, Robertson Frizero. "Uma canção do exílio." *Germina: revista de literatura e arte*, 14 Jun. 2017. www.germinaliteratura.com.br/sabiaseexilios/asavesqueaquigorjeiam_9.htm

Basto, Evaristo. "A partida." *Lisia poetica ou coleção de poesias modernas*, vol. 1. Ed. José Ferreira Monteiro. Rio de Janeiro: Typographia Commercial, 1848. 9.

Beatriz Lourenço, Beatriz. "Minha terra." *O Alvoradense*. 6 Jan. 2016. oalvoradense.com.br/blogs/josecouto/

Berrini, Beatriz. *Utopias, utopias*. São Paulo: EDUC, 1997.

"Bis-charada: Calendário do Zé Povo." *O malho*. Rio de Janeiro. 14 Oct. 1916. memoria.bn.br/docreader/116300/32962

Bocheco, Eloí Elisabete. "Minha terra tem chagas na alma." *O Alvoradense*. 6 Jan. 2016. oalvoradense.com.br/blogs/josecouto/

"Boiadeiro." *Recordar é viver: cancioneiro popular*. Org. Ivo Inácio Bersch. São Paulo: Edições Loyola, 1984. 84.

Bonassi, Fernando. "15 cenas de descobrimento de Brasis." *Os cem melhores contos brasileiros do século*. Org. Ítalo Moriconi. Rio de Janeiro: Editora Objetiva, 2000. 604–09

@bonfim_andrey. "Minha terra tem palmeiras onde canta o xororó ... enquanto vc esta lendo isso mais um gol em Chapecó." *Twitter*. 5 Oct. 2015. twitter.com/bonfim_andrey/statuses/651189442326102016

Bosi, Alfredo. *Colony, Cult, Culture*. Trans. Robert P. Newcomb. East Providence: U Mass Dartmouth, 2008.

———. *História concisa da literatura brasileira*. São Paulo: Editora Cultrix, 1994.

Braga, Rubem. "Fim de semana na fazenda." *Ai de ti, Copacabana*. 28th ed. Rio de Janeiro & São Paulo: Editora Record, 2010. 28–30.

Works Cited

Brasil, José. "A volta de Gonçalves Dias." *Jornal do Maranhão.* São Luís do Maranhão. 8 Dec. 1968. 5 memoria.bn.br/DocReader/112135/4316

Brito, Antônio Carlos de [Cacaso]. "Jogos florais I." *Beijo na boca e outros poemas.* São Paulo: Brasilense, 1985. 110.

Bueno, Eva P. "Caipira Culture: The Politics of Nation in Mazzaropi's Films." *Imagination Beyond Nation: Latin American Popular Culture.* Eds. Eva P. Bueno and Terry Caesar. Pittsburgh: U of Pittsburgh P, 41–63. www.jstor.org/stable/j.ctt5hjp98.5

Cajaty, Paula. "Desejo de exílio." *Germina: revista de literatura e arte.* Accessed 6 Jun. 2017. www.germinaliteratura.com.br/sabiaseexilios/asavesqueaquigorjeiam_8.htm

Caminha, Pero Vaz de. "A Carta de Pero Vaz de Caminha." *Ministério da Cultura: Fundação Biblioteca Nacional.* Accessed 17 Nov. 2016. objdigital.bn.br/Acervo_Digital/livros_eletronicos/carta.pdf

Camões, Luís de. *Os lusíadas.* Lisboa: António Gonçalves Impressor, 1572. purl.pt/1/4/cam-3-p_PDF/cam-3-p_PDF_24-C-R0150/cam-3-p_0000_capa-capa_t24-C-R0150.pdf

———. "Sôbolos rios que vão." *Obras completas: volume I: redondilhas e sonetos.* Lisboa: Livraria Sá da Costa. 101–18.

Candango Forçado (pseud.). "Canção do brasílio." *Correio da manhã.* Rio de Janeiro, 10 Jun. 1960. 1. memoria.bn.br/DocReader/089842_07/6046

Carlos, R. "Uma resposta." *Periódico dos pobres.* Rio de Janeiro, 27 Oct. 1853. 5. memoria.bn.br/DocReader/709697/2073

Carvalho, José Murilo de. "500 anos de ilusão." *Folha online,* 8 Aug. 1999. Accessed 14 Jun. 2017. www1.folha.uol.com.br/fol/brasil500/dc_6_6.htm

"Casa Muniz." *Correio da Manhã.* Rio de Janeiro, 4 May 1919. 2. memoria.bn.br/docreader/DocReader.aspx?bib=089842_02&PagFis=39097

Castello, José. *Vinícius de Moraes: o poeta da paixão.* São Paulo: Companhia das Letras, 1994.

Castro, Júlio de. "Minha terra." *Blog de albergaria.* 2008. Accessed 18 Nov. 2016. blogdealbergaria.blogspot.com/2008/06/minha-terra-de-jlio-de-castro-1933.html

Castro, Thaís Isabel. "De *Minha terra tem palmeiras* a *Alguma poesia.*" *Em Tese,* vol. 9, 2005. 263–72.

Castro Rocha, João Cezar de. "A lírica do exílio e a cultura brasileira." *Leituras desauratizadas: tempos precários, ensaios provisórios.* Org. Valdir Prigol. Recife: UFPE, 2017. 359–68.

———. *O exílio do homem cordial: ensaios e revisões.* Rio de Janeiro: Museu da República, 2004.

Works Cited

Chalmers, Vera Maria. "A crônica humorística de 'O Pirralho.'" *Revista de Letras*, no. 30, 1990. 33–42. www.jstor.org/stable/27666542

Chaves, Juca. "Take Me Back to Piauí." *Muito vivo*. Premier, 1970.

Chazkel, Amy. "Beyond Law and Order: The Origins of the 'Jogo Do Bicho' in Republican Rio de Janeiro." *Journal of Latin American Studies*, vol. 39, no. 3, 2007. 535-65. www. jstor.org/stable/40056543

Clayton, Jay and Eric Rothstein. *Influence and Intertextuality in Literary History*. Madison: U of Wisconsin P, 1991.

Confete, Rubem. "Taiguara (em guarani: cidadão livre)." *Tribuna da imprensa: Suplemento da tribuna*, no. 910. Aug. 1975. 2. memoria.bn.br/DocReader/DocReader.aspx?bib=154083_03&PagFis=20829

Costa, Eduardo Alves da. "Outra canção do exílio." *Escritas*. Accessed 21 Apr. 2017. www.escritas.org/pt/eduardo-alves-da-costa.

Costa, Gal. "Ave nossa," written by Moraes Moreira and Béu Machado, *Profana*, RCA, 1984.

Costa, J. Rego. "Em meio aos que melhor catam minhoca." *Diário de S. Luiz*. São Luis de Maranhão, 12 Sep. 1948. 3. memoria.bn.br/DocReader/093874/11064

———. "Existem aves que cantam." *Diário de São Luiz*. São Luís de Maranhão. 12 Sep. 1948. 3. memoria.bn.br/DocReader/093874/11064

Couto Monteiro, A.M. "Coimbra." *O trovador: coleção de poesias contemporâneas*. Coimbra: Imprensa de E. Trovão, 1848. 52–55

Cristina, Samara and Breno Lobato. "Minha terra tem o brega." *Silene Faro: Língua e Literatura*. Accessed 17 Dec. 2021. infolaboratorio.blogspot.com/2013/03/parodia-da-cancao-do-exilio.html

Cowdery, James R. "A Fresh Look at the Concepto of Tune Family." *Ethnomusicology*, vol. 28, no. 3, 1984. 495–504. www.jstor.org/stable/851236

Crônicas brasileiras: Nova fase. Eds. Richard A. Preto-Rodas, Alfred Hower and Charles A. Perrone. Gainesville: UP Florida, 1994.

Danescu-Niculescu-Mizil, Cristian, Justin Cheng, John Kleinberg and Lillian Lee. "You Had Me at Hello: How Phrasing Affects Memorability." Cornell U Library, 30 Apr. 2012. Accessed 15 Jun. 2017. arxiv.org/abs/1203.6360

Dawkins, Richard. *The Selfish Gene*. 30th Anniversary Edition. Oxford and New York: Oxford UP, 1989

Di Pino. "Bolas." *O Dia*. Curitiba, 11 May 1941. memoria.bn.br/DocReader/092932/43660

Dias, Galadriel'ves (pseud.). "Canção do exílio." *Vilmar: onde a luz do Antigo oeste ainda vive*, 4 Jun. 2008. Accessed 15 Jun 2017. www.valinor.com.br

"Divagando." *Jornal das moça*, no. 87. Rio de Janeiro. memoria.bn.br/DocReader/111031_01/3540

"Do Tejo-Guanabara." *A noite*. Rio de Janeiro, 16 May 1922. 2. memoria.bn.br/DocReader/348970_02/5837

Drucker, Johanna. *Graphesis: Visual Forms of Knowledge Production*. Cambridge: Harvard UP, 2014.

Dunn, Christopher. *Brutality Garden: Tropicália and the Emergence of a Brazilian Counterculture*. Chapel Hill: U of North Carolina P, 2001. www.jstor.org/stable/10.5149/9781469615707_dunn

Elysa, Isis, Cristian, Júlio, and Lucas. "Canção da revolta." *Germina: revista de literatura e arte*. Accessed 14 Jun. 2017. www.germinaliteratura.com.br/sabiaseexilios/asavesqueaquigorjeiam_3.htm

Enslen, Joshua A. "Vinícius de Moraes and 'Pátria minha': The Politics of Writing in Post-War Brazil." *Hispania*, vol. 94, no. 3, 2011. 416–28.

Enslen, Joshua A. and Alaina Enslen. "Bird-watching: Visualizing the Influence of Gonçalves Dias' 'Canção do Exílio.'" *Chiricu*, vol. 1, no. 2, 2017. 127–48.

@f_rancisunior. "Minha terra tem palmeiras onde canta o sabia, mentira não tem mais porque cortei pra fazer papel de troxa." *Twitter*, 6 Oct. 2015. twitter.com/f_rancisjunior/statuses/651579727174631424

"Farpas políticas." *A tarde*. Curitiba, 4 Oct. 1957. 1. memoria.bn.br/DocReader/797596/13806

Fausto, Boris. *História Concisa do Brasil*. São Paulo: EDUSP, 2014.

Fernandes, Dmitri Cerboncini. "'E fez-se o samba': condicionantes intelectuaisda música popular no Brasil." *Latin American Music Review*, vol. 32, no. 1, 2011. 39–58. muse.jhu.edu/article/448416

Ferraz, Gabriel. "Heitor Villa–Lobos e Getúlio Vargas: doutrinando crianças por meio da educação musical." *Latin American Music Review*, vol. 34 no. 2, 2013. 162–95. www.jstor.org/stable/43282553

Ferreira, António José. "Recordações de Portugal." *Lisia poética*, vol. 1. Ed. José Ferreira Monteiro. Rio de Janeiro: Typografia Commercial, 1848. 109–13. books.google.com

———. "A saudade da pátria (imitação)." *Lisia poética*, vol.1. Ed. José Ferreira Monteiro. Rio de Janeiro: Typografia Commercial, 1848. 43–44. books.google.com/

Ferreira, José Maia. "A minha terra." *Espontaneidades da minha alma*. Luanda: Imprensa do Governo, 1849. 12–18. books.google.com/

Ferreira, Nelson and Aldemar Paiva. "Pernambuco você é meu." *Jornal do Brasil*. Rio de Janeiro, 22 Feb. 1979. memoria.bn.br/DocReader/030015_09/189963

"Fim de festa." *Governador*. São Paulo, 2 Aug. 1951. 12. memoria.bn.br/DocReader/104795/1104

Works Cited

Fonseca, André Azevedo da. "Eduardo Palmério, um perfil intelectual: humorismo e cultura política nas crônicas da imprensa paulista dos anos 1940." *Intercom–RBCC*, vol. 35, no. 2, 2012. 61–84. www.scielo.br/pdf/interc/v35n2/04.pdf

Francisco, João. "Canção do exílio." *Jornal do Recife*, no. 179, 10 Aug. 1874. 5. memoria.bn.br/DocReader/705110/9548

Freyre, Gilberto. *Casa grande e senzala*. São Paulo: Global Editora, 2014.

Fute (pseud.). "Cartas a uma noiva." *Gutenberg*. Maceió, 31 Aug. 1907. memoria.bn.br/DocReader/809250/7860

Garcez, Hypollito Pereira. "Gôa." *Almanach de lembranças luso-brasileiro para o anno 1860*. Lisboa: Typografia Franco-Portugueza, 1859. 356. books.google.com/books?id=4J4DAAAAYAAJ

Garcia, Armando A. C. "Minha terra." *Recanto das letras*. 17 May 1964. Accessed 15 Oct. 2015. www.recantodasletras.com.br/poesias/171260

Gatuna, Guta. "Gonçalves Dias Revisited." *O bloguette*, 1 May 2009. Accessed 30 Nov. 2015. www.germinaliteratura.com.br/sabiaseexilios/asavesqueaquigorjeiam_5.htm

Geraldo, Zé. "Sabiá." *Caminhos de Minas*. Magazine, 1983.

Gil, Gilberto, and Capinam. "Show de me esqueci." *Brasil, Ano 2000* (trilha sonora). Forma, 1969.

Gil, Gilberto, and Torquato Neto. "Marginália II." *Gilberto Gil*. Universal, 1968. www.gilbertogil.com.br

Gilman, Bruce. "The Politics of Samba." *Georgetown Journal of International Affairs*, vol. 2, no.2, 2001. 67–72. www.jstor.org/stable/43134029

Gomes, Bianca B. "Minha terra tem Facebook." *Canção do exílio revisitada: processos de intertextualidade-intertextos*. Jaboatão dos Guararapes, PE: Organização, 2012. 24. www.scribd.com/document/109651993/Cancao-do-Exilio-Revisitada

Gonçalves Dias, Antônio. "Canção do exílio." *Primeiros cantos: poesias*. Rio de Janeiro: E. and H. Laemmert, 1846. 9–10. books.google.com/books?id=ma5OAQAAIAAJ

———. *Primeiros cantos: poesias*. Rio de Janeiro: E. e H. Laemmert, 1846. books.google.com/books?id=ma5OAQAAIAAJ

Gonçalves de Magalhães, Domingos. "O dia 7 de abril, em Paris." *Suspiros poéticos e saudades*. Rio de Janeiro: Casa do Senhor João Pedro da Veiga, 1836. 325–30

Guy. "A sociedade: symphonia da cidade." *Estado de São Paulo*. São Paulo,3 Oct. 1930. 2. acervo.estadao.com.br/pagina/#!/19301003-18667-nac-0002-999-2-not

Works Cited

Hanley, Anne G. "Financing Brazil's Industrialization." *Reconceptualizing the Industrial Revolution*. Eds. Jeff Horn, et al., 2010. 251–70. www.jstor.org/stable/j.cH5hhgmdm.16

Haraway, Donna J. "A Cyborg Manifesto." *Simians, Cyborgs and Women: The Reinvention of Nature*. NY: Routledge, 1991. 149–82.

Hausser, Roland. *Foundations of Computational Linguistics*. New York: Springer, 1998.

Hearn, Kelly. "The NRA Takes on Gun Control—in Brazil." *Alternet*, 5 Oct. 2005. Accessed 17 Jun. 2008 www.bbc.com/portuguese/noticias/2014/01/140113_armas_crime_gl_cc.

Hearst, Marti A. "Exploratory Text Analysis and the Middle Distance." *UC Berkeley*, 14 Jun. 2017. people.ischool.berkeley.edu/~hearst/talks/dm-middle-distance.pdf.

Herculano, Alexandre. "Futuro literário de Portugal e do Brasil." *Gonçalves Dias: poesia completa e prosa escolhida*. Rio de Janeiro: Editora José Aguiar, Ltda., 1959. 96–98.

Holanda, Aurélio Buarque de. "À margem da 'Canção do exílio.'" *Correio da Manhã*. Rio de Janerio, 30 Apr. 1944. memoria.bn.br/DocReader/089842_05/20487

Holanda, Chico Buarque de. "Agora falando sério." *Chico Buarque de Holanda—Volume 4*. CBD/Philips Records, 1970. www.chico-buarque.com.br/discos/mestre.asp?pg=chico_70.htm

Holanda, Chico Buarque de and Antônio Carlos (Tom) Jobim. "Sabiá." *Chico Buarque de Holanda—Volume 4*. CBD/Philips Records, 1970. www.chicobuarque.com.br/discos/mestre.asp?pg=chico_70.htm

Holanda, Sérgio Buarque de. *Raízes do Brasil*. São Paulo: Companhia das Letras, 1995.

Hutcheon, Linda. *The Politics of Postmodernism*. New York: Routledge, 1989.

@IvanNunes_cfc. "Minha terra tem palmeiras, / onde canta o sabiá; / SENO A, COSSENO B, / SENO B, COSSENO A." *Twitter*, 6 Sep. 2015. twitter.com/IvanNunes_cfc/statuses/640717229278015488

João III. "Carta régia a Martim Affonso." *História geral do Brasil*. 3rd Edition. Ed. Francisco Adolfo de Varnhagem. Rio de Janeiro: Companhia Typográfrica do Brasil, 1906. 192–94. books.google.com/books?id=dJAgAQAAIAAJ

Keeper (pseud.). "Off-side poemas." *Jornal dos sports*. Rio de Janeiro, 4 Mar. 1943. memoria.bn.br/DocReader/112518_01/20209

Kristeva, Julia. "Word, Dialogue and Novel." *The Kristeva Reader*. Ed. Toril Moi. New York: Columbia UP, 1986. 34–61.

Works Cited

Lagoa, Cherubino Henriques. "Mez d'abril em Portugal." *Lisia poética*, vol. 1. Ed. José Ferreira Monteiro. Rio de Janeiro: Typografia Commercial, 1848. 30-33. books.google.com/books?id=GzY-AAAAIAAJ

Landau, Iosif. "Exilado." *Gigi e Myra: conversa entre irmãos*, 19 Mar. 2010. Accessed 15 Jun. 2017. gigi-e-myra.blogspot.pt/2010/03/exilado-eu-vi-2003-iosif-landau.html

Lara e Souza, Joaquim Álvaro de. "A minha pátria." *Lisia poética*, vol. 1. Ed. José Ferreira Monteiro. Rio de Janeiro: Typografia Commercial, 1848. 102–04. books.google.com/books?id=GzY-AAAAIAAJ

Leacock, Ruth. *Requiem for Revolution: The United States and Brazil, 1961–1969*. Kent, Ohio & London: Kent State UP, 1990.

Lee, Rita, and Roberto de Carvalho. "Pirarucu." *Bom Bom*. Universal Music, 1983.

Lemos, João de. "O Sino da Minha Terra." *O trovador: coleção de poesias contemporâneas*. Coimbra: Imprensa de E. Trovão, 1848. 24–25.

L. M. (pseud.). "Crônica: nova canção de exílio." *Estado de São Paulo*. São Paulo, 24 Jul. 1974. 8.

Lopes, Fernando. "Minha terra só tem tanques e que ameaçam atirar." *Tribuna da imprensa*, 7 Oct. 1963. memoria.bn.br/DocReader/154083_02/13813

Lopes, José Sérgio Leite. "Class, Ethnicity and Color in the Making of Brazilian Football." *Daedulus*, vol. 129, no. 2, 2000. 239–70.

Lourenço, Beatriz. "Minha terra." *O Alvoradense*, 6 Jan. 2016. oalvoradense.com.br

Lúcio (pseud.). "O Bezouro." *O tempo*. Rio de Janeiro. 9 Nov. 1892. 8. memoria.bn.br/DocReader/218731/1757

Machado de Assis, Joaquim Maria. "O espelho." *50 contos de Machado de Assis*. Ed. John Gledson. Rio de Janeiro: Companhia das Letras, 2007. 154–62.

———. "O jogo do bicho." *Portal Domínio Público*, 15 Sep. 2018. www.dominiopublico.gov.br/download/texto/fs000198.pdf

Magalhães Júnior, Raimundo. "Minha terra tem palmeiras." *A noite*. Rio de Janeiro, 7 Jan. 1937. 1. memoria.bn.br/docreader/348970_03/38845

Majoy (pseud.). "Minha terra tem palmeiras." *Correio da manhã*. Rio de Janeiro, 12 Nov. 1939. 2. memoria.bn.br/DocReader/089842_04/54959

Manovich, Lev. *Instagram and Contemporary Image*, 2017. manovich.net/index.php/projects/instagram-and-contemporary-image

———. *The Language of New Media*. Cambridge: MIT Press, 2001.

@MarciaGpuava "Minha terra tem palmeiras, / Onde canta o sabiá / Se o Lula aqui é Haddad / O Haddad é Lula lá" *Twitter*. 14 Sep. 2018. twitter.com/MarciaGpuava/status/1040594621175406592

Marquês, Wilton. "O poema e a metáfora." *Revista letras*, no. 60, 2003. 79–93. www.ufscar.br/~neo/Estudos/arquivos/opoemaeametafora.pdf

Matos, Gregório de. "Adeus Coimbra." *Florilégio da poesia brasileira*, vol. 1. Ed. Francisco Adolfo de Varnhagem. Lisbon: Imprensa Nacional, 1850. 20–21.

Matos, Gregório de and Eusébio de Matos. "Em quarta-feira de cinzas." *Florilégio da poesia brasileira*, vol. 1. Ed. Francisco Adolfo de Varnhagem. Lisbon: Imprensa Nacional, 1850. 123–26.

Meade, Teresa. "'Civilizing Rio De Janeiro': The Public Health Campaign and the Riot of 1904." *Journal of Social History*, vol. 20, no. 2, 1986. 301–22. www.jstor.org/stable/3787709

Melo, Anita de. Electronic conversation with author, 21 May 2016.

Mendes, Fernando Leite. "Ladainha da implosão." *Diário de notícias*. Rio de Janeiro, 22 Nov. 1975. 9. memoria.bn.br/DocReader/093718_05/41360

Mendes, Murilo. "Canção do exílio." *Os cem melhores poemas do século*. Org. Ítalo Moriconi. Rio de Janeiro: Objetiva, 2001. 33.

Mendonça, Honorata Minelvina Carneiro de. "Saudades da minha terra." *Jornal das famílias*, no. 6, Feb. 1868. 127–28. memoria.bn.br/DocReader/docreader.aspx?bib=339776&PagFis=2003

Mendonça, Lúcio de. "Castro Alves e G. Dias." *A Semana*. 4 Jun. 1887. Rio de Janeiro. 177–78. memoria.bn.br/DocReader/383422/1021

Michel, Jean Baptiste, et al. "Quantitative Analysis of Culture Using Millions of Digitized Books." *Science*, no. 331, 2011. 176–82.

"Minha terra." *Mundo ilustrado*. Rio de Janeiro, 3 Dec. 1960. 21. memoria.bn.br/DocReader/119601/22137

"Minha terra natal." *Marmota fluminense*. Rio de Janeiro, 25 Nov. 1853. 2. memoria.bn.br/DocReader/706906/1720

"Minha terra tem loureiros," *Trovador: coleção de modinhas, recitativos, árias, lundús, etc*, vol. 3. Rio de Janeiro: Na Livraria de A.A. da Cruz Coutinho, 1876. 71–72. books.google.pt/books?id=pkAzAAAAIAAJ

"Minha terra tem loureiros." *Trovador brasileiro*. Rio de Janeiro: Livraria de A.T. de Castro Dias, 1875. 60–61. books.google.com/books?id=YqjuAAAAMAAJ

"Minha terra tem palmeiras..." *Pharol*. Juíz de Fora, 17 Mar. 1914. 2. memoria.bn.br/DocReader/258822/31427

"Minha terra tem palmeiras." *Diário de S. Luiz*. São Luis de Maranhão, 12 Sep. 1948. 3. memoria.bn.br/DocReader/093874/11064

"Minha terra tem palmeiras." *O timbyra*. Maranhão, 24 May 1849. 1. memoria.bn.br/DocReader/718092/2

Works Cited

"Minha terra tem petróleo." *O semanário*. Rio de Janeiro, 26 Feb–4 Mar 1958. 7. memoria.bn.br/DocReader/149322/2293

"Minha terra tem talentos." *Correio paulistano*. São Paulo, 13 Jan. 1858. 3. memoria.bn.br/DocReader/090972_01/5201

Miranda, Carmen. "Minha terra tem palmeiras." Odeon, 1936. dicionariompb.com.br/carmen-miranda/discografia

Miyasaki, Márcia. "Canção do exílio in Japan." *Recanto das palavras*, 23 Jun. 2008. Accessed 16 Jun. 2017. recantodaspalavras.wordpress.com/2008/06/23/uma-verso-da-cano-do-exlio-por-uma-brasileira-no-japo/

Mões, K. (pseud.). "Minha terra." *O malho*. Rio de Janeiro, 14 May 1904. 18. memoria.bn.br/DocReader/116300/2622

Montairo, Mário. "O nôbo sabiá." *A manhã*, 18 Apr. 1946. 5. memoria.bn.br/DocReader/720984/2938

Monteiro, José Ferreira. "Introdução." *Lisia poética*, vol. 1. Ed. José Ferreira Monteiro. Rio de Janeiro: Typografia Commercial, 1848. i–iii. books.google.com/books?id=GzY-AAAAIAAJ

Monteiro, José Ferreira, ed. *Lisia poética, ou Coleção de poesias modernas de autores portuguesas*, vol. 1. Rio de Janeiro: Typografia Commercial, 1848. books.google.com/books?id=GzYAAAAIAAJ

Moraes, Vinícius de. "Meu Deus, não seja já." *Diário carioca*. Rio de Janeiro, 29 Dec. 1946. 1. memoria.bn.br/DocReader/093092_03/27177

———. "Pátria minha." *Vinícius de Moraes: poesia completa e prosa*. Ed. Alexei Bueno. Rio de Janeiro: Nova Aguilar, 1998. 383–85.

Moraes Moreira and Béu Machado. "Ave nossa." perf. Gal Costa. *Profana*. RCA, 1984.

Moretti, Franco. "Conjectures on World Literature." *New Left Review*, no. 1, Jan–Feb 2000, 54–68. newleftreview.org/II/1/franco-moretti-conjectures-on-world-literature

———. "The Slaughterhouse of Literature." *Modern Language Quarterly*, vol. 61, no. 1, Mar. 2000. 207–27.

Moser, Robert H. *The Carnivalesque Defunto: Death and the Dead in Modern Brazilian Literature*. Athens: Ohio UP, 2008.

Munhoz, Sidnei J. "At the Onset of the Cold War: The USA and the Repression of Communism in Brazil." *Brazil-United States Relations: XX and XXI Centuries*. Maringá: SciELO—EDUEM, 2013. 129–164. www.jstor.org/stable/10.7476/9788576-286592.7

Murad, Maurício. "O futebol no Brasil: reflexões sociológicas." *Caravelle* no. 89, Dec. 2007, 109–28.

Muribeca (pseud.). "Gentes dos cajuais alerta!!!" *Pedro II*. Fortaleza, 6 Oct. 1862. 3. memoria.bn.br/DocReader/216828/6735

Nicolusi, Haydee. "Canção do turista malogrado." *Estado de São Paulo*, 10 Apr. 1948. 6.

Novais, Faustino Xavier de. "Introdução." *O bardo: jornal de poesias inéditas*. Editors Faustino Xavier de Novais and António Pinheiro Caldas. Porto: F. Gomes da Fonseca, 1857. 3–6. babel.hathitrust.org/cgi/pt?id=inu.39000004496175;view=1up;seq=7

Nunes, Rosana Barbosa. "Portuguese Migration to Rio De Janeiro, 1822–1850." *The Americas,* vol. 57, no.1, 2000, 37–61. www.jstor.org/stable/1007711.

"O 13 de maio atual!" *Estado de São Paulo*. São Paulo, 13 May 1923. 8. acervo.estadao.com.br/pagina/#!/19230513-16176-nac-0008-999-8-not

"O acerto de contas." *Folha de São Paulo*. São Paulo, 23 Mar. 2013. arte.folha.uol.com.br/especiais/2014/03/23/o-golpe-e-a-ditadura-militar/o-acerto-de-contas.html

"O que o locutor não disse." *Jornal das Moças*. Rio de Janeiro, 19 May 1955. 70. memoria.bn.br/DocReader/111031_05/17658

Oliveira, Emanuelle K. *Writing Identity: The Politics of Contemporary Afro-Brazilian Literature*. West Lafayette: Purdue UP, 2007.

Oliveira, Hugo. "Fernando Haddad faz caminhada com apoiadores pelo Centro de Goiânia." *Mais Goiás: você e ponto*, 29 Sep. 2018. www.emaisgoias.com.br

Oliveira, José Carlos. "Tropicalismo: por uma nova canção do exílio." *Jornal do Brasil*. Rio de Janeiro, 16 Mar. 1968. 3. memoria.bn.br/DocReader/030015_08/112656

Oliveira, Manuel Botelho de. "Descrição da ilha de Itaparica." *Florilégio da poesia brasileira*, vol. 1. Ed. Francisco Adolfo de Varnhagem. Lisbon: Imprensa Nacional, 1850. 158–73.

Oliveira, Manuel Botelho de. "A ilha da Maré." *Florilégio da poesia brasileira*, vol. 1. Ed. Francisco Adolfo de Varnhagem. Lisbon: Imprensa Nacional, 1850. 134–44.

Pádua, José Carlos and Egberto Gismonti. "Coração de candango." Perf. Marília Barbosa. *Filme Nacional*. Som Livre, 1978.

Paes, José Paulo. "Lisboa aventuras." *Jornal do Brasil*. Rio de Janeiro, 20 Jun. 1987. 6. memoria.bn.br/DocReader/030015_10/141399

Palmério, Eduardo. "Minha terra tem palmeiras." *Diário da noite*. Rio de Janeiro, 28 May 1947. 2. memoria.bn.br/DocReader/221961_02/39114

———. "Quadra de onze." *Diário da noite*. Rio de Janeiro. 17 Apr. 1948. 4. memoria.bn.br/DocReader/221961_02/43842

"Palmeiras imperiais se iluminam com neon." *Jornal do Brasil*. Rio de Janeiro, 17 Dec. 1986. 4. memoria.bn.br/DocReader/030015_10/128945

Works Cited

Palmeirim, Luiz Agosto Xavier de. "Recordação da infância." *Lisia poetica ou coleção de poesias modernas*, vol. 1. Ed. José Ferreira Monteiro. Rio de Janeiro: Typographia Commercial, 1848. 157–60.

Parker, Phyllis R. *Brazil and the Quiet Intervention, 1964*. Austin & London: U of Texas P, 1979.

Pauvolid. Elaine. "Sou ali." *Germina: revista de literatura e arte*, 16 Jun. 2017. www.germinaliteratura.com.br/sabiaseexilios/asavesqueaquigorjeiam_4.htm

Pena, Rosa. "*." *Germina: revista de literatura e arte*, 1 Nov. 2017. www.germinaliteratura.com.br/sabiaseexilios/asavesqueaquigorjeiam_9.htm

Pereira de Castro. "Primores da minha terra." *Jaguanary*. Porto Alegre, 20 Dec. 1860. memoria.bn.br/DocReader/DocReaderMobile.aspx?bib=766585&pasta=&pagfis=10&pesq=

Pereira, Lúcia Miguel. *A vida de Gonçalves Dias*. Rio de Janeiro: Editora José Olympio, Ltda., 1943.

Pergher, Paulo Henrique. "Múcio Teixeira: o sacrifício do poeta ao hierofante."*Mafuá*, no. 28, 2017. mafua.ufsc.br/2017/mucio-teixeira-o-sacrificio-do-poeta-ao-hierofante/

Pimpolho (pseud.). "Lá vai obra." *O binóculo*. Salvador da Bahia, 27 Jun. 1877. 2. memoria.bn.br/DocReader/817813/2

Pinto de Sampaio, M A. "Minha terra." *O constitucional*. São Luis, 7 Mar. 1863. 3–4. memoria.bn.br/DocReader/docreader.aspx?bib=748501&PagFis=36

Porto, Liria. "Expropriados." *Tanto mar*, 26 Jun. 2010. Accessed 15 Jun. 2017. liriaporto.blogspot.com/2009/09/desigualdades.html

Postman. Neil. *Amusing Ourselves to Death: Public Discourse in the Age of Show Business*. New York: Penguin, 1985.

Quental, Antero de. "A M.E." *Raios de extinta luz*. Lisboa: M. Gomes, 1892. 221–22. purl.pt/3470/6/l-8924-p_PDF/l-8924-p_PDF_24-C-R0150/l-8924-p_0000_capa-260_t24-C-R0150.pdf

Quintana, Mario. "Uma canção." *Poesia completa*. Org. Tânia Franco Carvalhal. Rio de Janeiro: Editora Nova Aguilar, 2006. 443.

R. V. "Saudades do Tejo." *O bardo: jornal de poesias inéditas*. Eds. Faustino Xavier de Novais and António Pinheiro Caldas. Porto: F. Gomes da Fonseca, 1857. 289–91. babel.hathitrust.org/cgi/pt?id=inu.39000004496175;view=1up;seq=7

Ramsay, Stephen. *Reading Machines: Towards an Algorithmic Criticism*. Champaign: U of Illinois P, 2011.

@rangump. "Minha terra tem palmeiras onde canta o sabiá mas a sua boca e a minha quando que vão se beijar?" *Twitter*. 12 Sep. 2015. twitter.com/tuddoshit/statuses/642896756859105280

Rebelo, Marques. "Uma senhora." *Os cem melhores contos brasileiros do século*.

Org. Ítalo Moriconi. Rio de Janeiro: Editora Objetiva, 2000. 100–03.

"Recordações da pátria." *O correio da tarde*. Rio de Janeiro, 5 Jan. 1848. 3. memoria.bn.br/DocReader/616028/11

Reipert, Fabíola. "SBT veta história de paixão antiga de Manoel Carlos." *R7*, 26 Nov. 2009. entretenimento.r7.com/blogs/fabiola-reipert

Ricardo, Cassiano. "Ainda irei a Portugal." *Um dia depois do outro*. São Paulo: Companhia Nacional, 1947. 49–52.

Rio, João do. "O bebê de tarlatana rosa." *Os cem melhores contos brasileiros do século*. Org. Ítalo Moriconi. Rio de Janeiro: Editora Objetiva, 2000.

Rosa, Helena da. "Exílio é para quem fica." *O Alvoradense*, 6 Jan. 2016. oalvoradense.com.br

Sá, C. A. de. "Lyra: como é bela a minha pátria." *O mercantil*. Rio de Janeiro, 25 Sep. 1847. 3. memoria.bn.br/DocReader/docreader.aspx?bib=228133&PagFis=4475

Sachs, Ignacy. "Quo Vadis, Brasil?" *Brazil: A Century of Change*. Eds. Ignacy Sachs, Jorge Wilheim, Paulo Sérgio Pinheiro. Raleigh: U North Carolina P, 2009. 332–44. www.jstor.org/stable/10.5149/9780807894118_sachs.19

Sadlier, Darlene J. *Brazil Imagined: 1500 to Present*. Austin: UT Press, 2008.

Sampaio, Theodoro. "O tupy na geographia nacional." *Jornal do Recife*. Recife, 1 Feb. 1930. memoria.bn.br/DocReader/705110/109631

Sant'anna, Affonso Romano. "O múltiplo Caetano." *Jornal do Brasil*. Rio de Janeiro, 10 Mar. 1973. memoria.bn.br/DocReader/030015_09/79850

Santa Rita Durão, José de. "Descobrimento do Brasil." *Florilégio da poesia brasileira*, vol. 1. Ed. Francisco Adolfo de Varnhagem. Lisbon: Imprensa Nacional, 1850. 350–59.

Satriano, Nicolás. "Minha terra tem horrores: versão de poema feita por alunos do rio causa comoção nas redes sociais." *G1 Rio*. Rio de Janeiro, 7 Apr. 2017. g1.globo.com

Scevola (pseud.). "Canção do exílio." *O cearense*. Fortaleza, 1 Jan. 1873. 3–4. memoria.bn.br/DocReader/709506/10052

Schmid, Ludwig Ferdinand. "Lied aus der Verbannung." *O mercantil*. Rio de Janeiro, 31 Oct. 1883. Memoria.bn.br/DocReader/376493/2731

Scott, Joan W. "Deconstructing Equality-versus-Difference: Or, the Uses of Poststructuralist Theory for Feminism." *Feminist Studies*, vol. 14, no. 1, 1988. 32–50.

Shaw, Lisa. "São coisas nossas: Samba and Identity in the Vargas Era (1930–45)." *Portuguese Studies*, no. 14, 1998. 152–69. www.jstor.org/stable/41105089

Silva, Gustavo. "Na minha terra têm viciados." *Canção do exílio revisitada: processos de intertextualidade-intertextos*. Jaboatão dos Guararapes: Organização, 2012. 17. www.scribd.com/document/109651993/Cancao-do-Exilio-Revisitada

Silva, Jair. "Minha terra tem mendigos." *Gazeta de Paraopeba*. Paraopeba, 9 Apr. 1953. memoria.bn.br/DocReader/830232/2351

Silva, João Nepomuceno da. "Belezas de minha terra." *Gazeta oficial*, vol. 3, no. 90. Belém do Pará, 21 Apr. 1860. memoria.bn.br/DocReader/720836/1507

Silva, Vanderson Teófilo da and Marcos Vinicius Lopes. "Minha terra é a Penha." *Facebook*, 3 Apr. 2017. Accessed 4 Apr. 2017. www.facebook.com/elenferreira/

Silva, Waldemar Machado da. "Hino à região do Rio Negro." *Jornal do Comércio*. Manaus, AM, 15 Dec. 1971. 5. memoria.bn.br/DocReader/170054_01/160587

Silva Sá, Roberto Boaventura da. "Do canto dos sabiás à trama silenciosa dos pombos na 'Versão enlatada do exílio.'" *Polifonia*, no. 7, 2003. 205–15. periodicoscientificos.ufmt.br/ojs/index.php/polifonia/article/download/1147/911

Simões, Francisco. "Terra minha." *Francisco Simões*, Sept. 2005. Accessed 15 Jun. 2017. www.francisco-simoes.com/terraminha.htm

Sino, Alcino del. "Charada antiga." *Tagarela*, no. 142. Rio de Janeiro, 10 Nov. 1904. memoria.bn.br/DocReader/709689/2041

Skidmore, Thomas. *Brazil: Five Centuries of Change*. New York: Oxford U P, 1999.

Soares, Jô. "Canção do exílio às avessas." *Veja*, 16 Sep. 1992. 15.

Solon, Olivia. "Richard Dawkins on the Internet's Hijacking of the Word 'Meme.'" *Wired*, 20 Jun. 2013. www.wired.co.uk/article/richard-dawkins-memes

Sommer, Doris. "Irresistible Romance: The Foundational Fictions of Latin America." *Nation and Narration*. Ed. Homi K. Bhabha. New York: Routledge and Keegan Paul, 1990. 71–98.

Sostisso, Caio Muriel [pseud. FTNT]. "Canção do exílio moderno." *Travian Forum*, 16 Feb. 2009. Accessed 15 Jun. 2017. forum.travian.com.br/showthread.php?t=14286

Souza, Elzimara. "A terra que há." *Escritores do Odette*, 3 Apr. 2012. Accessed 15 Jun. 2017. escritoresdoodette.blogspot.com/2012/04/parodias-da-cancao-do-exilio-dos-alunos.html

Souza, Pero Lopes de. *Diário da navegação da armada que foi à terra do Brasil*. Org. Francisco Adolfo de Varnhagen. Lisboa: Typografia de Sociedade Propagadora dos Conhecimentos Úteis, 1839. books.google.com/books?id=-F8CAAAAYAAJ

Souza Silva, Joaquim Norberto de. "Uma tarde em Nighteroy." *Modulações poéticas*. Rio de Janeiro: Typographia Franceza, 1841. 147–55.

Taiguara. "Terra das palmeiras." *Lar Futuro*. EMI/Odeon, 1975.

Tavares, Tere. "Extinção do empecilho." *O Alvoradense*. 6 Jan 2016. oalvoradense.com.br

Taquara, Zé (pseud.). "O pito aceso: trovando trovas." *O Governador*. São Paulo. 30 Aug. 1951. memoria.bn.br/DocReader/104795/1147

@temerpoeta. "Minha terra tem calheiros / Onde canta o jucás / Das aves que aqui gorgeiam / A mais linda é satanás." *Twitter*, 20 May 2016. twitter.com/temerpoeta/status/733716418051645440

"Tenho saudade." *Recordar é viver: cancioneiro popular*. Org. Ivo Inácio Bersch. São Paulo: Edições Loyola, 1984. 94.

@TheBalboa Bruno. "Minha terra tem palmeiras, Onde canta o Sabiá; Bebi muito ontem, E hoje só quero vomitar." *Twitter*, 7 Oct. 2015. twitter.com/TheBalboaBruno/statuses/651931235174981632

Thery, Hervé. "A Cartographic and Statistical Portrait of Twentieth-Century Brazil." *Brazil: A Century of Change*. Eds. Ignacy Sachs, Jorge Wilheim, Paulo Sérgio Pinheiro. Raleigh: U North Carolina P, 2009. 1–19. www.jstor.org/stable/10.5149/9780807894118_sachs.6

Trancoso, Dominguinho. "Cartas de um caipira." *O olho da rua*. Curitiba, 8 Jun. 1907. memoria.bn.br/DocReader/240818/128

Trevisan, Dalton. "Canção de exílio." *Estado de São Paulo: suplemento cultural*. São Paulo, 5 Aug. 1984. 12.

"Trovas." *Careta*. Rio de Janeiro. 2 Jul. 1921. memoria.bn.br/DocReader/083712/26002

"Um quinteto de rainhas!" *A noite*. Rio de Janeiro, 3 Feb. 1937. memoria.bn.br/docreader/348970_03/39959

Varnhagem, Francisco Adolfo de, ed. *Florilégio da poesia brasileira*, vol. 1. Lisbon: Imprensa Nacional, 1850.

Vasconcellos, Eliane. "Percursos da literatura goiana." *Revista UFG* 12.8, 2010, 87–100.

"Vela Brasileira." *A Província*. Recife, 29 Jan. 1904. 1. memoria.bn.br/DocReader/128066_01/14586

Veríssimo, Luis Fernando. "Nova canção do exílio." *Jornal do Brasil*. Rio de Janeiro, 19 Nov. 1978. memoria.bn.br/DocReader/030015_09/189963

Vieira, Éder. "Onde eu moro." *Canção do exílio revisitada: processos de intertextualidade-intertextos*. Jaboatão dos Guararapes, PE: Organização, 2012. 43. www.scribd.com/document/109651993/Cancao-do-Exilio-Revisitada

Works Cited

Villaça, Alcides. "'O espelho': superfície e corrosão." *Luso-Brazilian Review*, vol. 46, no. 1, 2009. 93–105. www.jstor.org/stable/25654812.

"Votos pitorescos dividiram juízes: uns acharam graça e outros não gostaramnada." *Jornal do Brasil*, 12 Oct. 1958. 5. memoria.bn.br/DocReader/030015_07/93826

Xangô, Irene de. "Canto da minha terra." *Garganta da serpente*. 9 Oct. 2008. Accessed 16 Jun. 2017. www.gargantadaserpente.com/toca/poetas/irenedexango.php?poema=1

Zootechnico, Dr. (pseud.). "Bis-Charada." *O Malho*. Rio de Janeiro, 19 May 1923. memoria.bn.br/DocReader/116300/49943

Index

Abolition, 68-9, 76
Afonso, Martim, 27-28
Afro-Brazilians, 59, 69, 144-46
Alagoas, 64, 67, 84
Alencar, José de, 17
Amazon, 85, 99-100, 122
Andrade, Carlos Drummond de, 75-76, 85, 88
Andrade, Oswald, 6, 33, 56-57, 59, 73-6
Angola, 3, 49
Anthropophagy (Cannibalist Manifesto), 56, 76-77
Ato Institucional 5, 80-1
Authoritarianism, 55, 79-80, 95, 97
Azores, 3, 48-49

Bahia, 19, 61, 65-67
Berrini, 30, 48
Bilac, Olavo, 157
binomial pair
    palmeiras / sabiá, 81-85, 88, 90-91, 95-97
    loureiros / rouxinol, 3, 7, 34-35, 37-40, 82
Bolsonaro, Jair, 161
Bonassi, Fernando, 101, 112, 115, 120
Bosi, Alfredo, 15-17
Braga, Rubem, 82-83
brazilwood (pau brasil), 85
Buarque de Holanda, Aurélio, 16
Buarque de Holanda, Francisco (Chico Buarque), 91-93
Buarque de Holanda, Sérgio, 65-66

"cá" / "lá" dialectic, 20, 36, 57, 121, 139, 140, 145, 161
Cabral, Pedro Álvares, 15, 17-19, 27, 73, 85, 120
Caminha, Pero Vaz de, 17-18,
Camões, 16-18, 25-26, 145, 73

Candomblé, 145
Carnaval, 58-63, 87, 136
Castelo Branco, 78-79, 84
Castro Rocha, João Cezar de, 16-18, 20-21, 24
censorship (censura), 56, 80-81, 93, 95
Coimbra, 1, 3, 7, 20-22, 48,
Communism, 55-56
Corinthians (soccer), 71, 95-96, 142
Corruption, 67, 101, 119, 122-123, 142
crônica, 82-83, 85, 93, 100, 112-13

database, 158-59, 165,
Dawkins, Richard, 154
distant reading, 5, 105, 158-59, 163, 166-67,
Douro (region), 22-23, 27, 38
Drucker, Johanna, 9, 164

environmentalism, 93, 100, 119, 121-22, 147
Esperanto, 56, 69, 73

Ferreira, António José de, 3, 31-39
Figueiredo (General), 80
Figueiredo Jr., Afonso Celso de, 99
First Republic (Primeira república), 68
Freyre, Gilberto, 56
futebol (soccer), 56, 71, 87, 94-95, 136, 142, 153

Gil, Gilberto, 87, 90, 92, 93
Gôa, 3, 110
Goiás, 133-35
Gonçalves de Magalhães, 17, 21, 24-25
Goulart, João, 79-80
grand ubertext, 14

Index

Grito do Ipiranga, 57
Guanabara Bay, 31, 50-51, 99
Guarani (language), 138, 147

Haddad, Fernando, 157, 161
Haraway, Donna, 125, 148
Herculano, Alexandre, 28-29

immigration (migration), 56, 75,
   Japan, 141-42
   Portugal, 29, 50
independence (Brazil), 2, 17, 37-38, 43-44, 49, 57, 85
Indianismo, 17
Industrialization, 68-69, 75-76
intertextuality, 12-14

João do Rio, 63
João III (King of Portugal), 27-28
Jobim, Antônio Carlos, 91, 95
Jockers, Matthew, 164
jogo do bicho, 56, 69-70

Kristeva, Julia, 12-14, 159
Kubitschek, Juscelino, 84

Lisbon, 20, 22, 28, 50, 51, 80
literatura marginal, 101, 120-21, 146-47
Luiz Inácio Lula da Silva, 123, 157, 161

Machado de Assis, Joaquim Maria, 11, 70
Magalhães Jr., Raimundo, 60
Manifesto antropófago (see anthropophagy)
Manovich, Lev, 125, 155, 158-60, 163, 165
Matos, Gregório de, 20, 25
memes, 154
Mendonça, Honorata Minelvina Carneiro de, 133-36
Mendonça, Lúcio de, 157
Mensalão, 123

military regime (dictatorship), 79-81, 97-98
Minho (region), 27, 53
Miranda, Carmen, 61
miscegenation, 48, 56
modal analysis, 5-6, 63-65, 81-82, 90, 98, 110-113, 152-53
Modernismo, 56-57, 59, 74-77
Moraes, Vinícius, 80-81
Moretti, Franco, 4-5, 159, 163

national anthem (Brazil), 57-58, 61

Oliveira, Emanuelle, 144-146
Oliveira, Manuel Botelho de, 17-19
Operação Lava Jato, 123

Palmares, 6, 74, 145
Pedro I (Emperor of Brazil), 57
Pedro II (Emperor of Brazil), 2, 50, 55, 66-67, 68, 133-34
Petrobrás, 123
Plate River, 28
Porto, 22-23
português macarrônico, 57, 73
Postman, Neil, 149

Quadros, Jânio, 79, 84

race, 59, 69, 121, 126, 144-46
Ramsay, Stephen, 158, 163
Rebelo, Marques, 63
Recife, 63-64, 67,
Ricardo, Cassiano, 52-53
Rio de Janeiro, 29-31, 34, 51, 59-60, 65, 70, 99, 161
Romanticism, 2, 15, 17, 20-21, 28
Rousseff, Dilma, 4, 101, 123

samba, 58-61, 94, 151
Santa Rita Durão, 17-19
São Paulo, 27, 71-76, 142
significant words, 5-6, 38, 44, 45, 82, 87, 108, 127
soccer (see futebol)

Sousa Silva, 21
strategic urtext, 14, 160, 168,
string similarity, 5-6, 63, 105-07, 111, 165, 167
syntactic templates, 5-6, 16, 35-36, 46-47

Tejo, 24, 50,
Temer, Michel, 4
Tio Sam (Uncle Sam), 140-41
Torquato Neto, 90
Tropicália, 74, 81, 91-93
tune families, 41
types and tokens, 5-6, 7, 36, 46-47, 51, 74-75, 82, 88-90, 115-19, 130-33, 158, 167

Vaccine Revolts (Rio de Janeiro), 65
Vargas, Getúlio, 55-56, 58-59, 62-63, 136
Varnhagem, Adolfo de, 18, 28
Veloso, Caetano, 74, 93
Verissimo, Luiz Fernando, 94-95
Villa-Lobos, Heitor, 58-59

word frequency (see significant words)
word tokens (see types and tokens)

Zumbi dos Palmares, 6, 74, 145

About the Book

Song of Exile: A Cultural History of Brazil's Most Popular Poem (1846–2018) (with an afterword by Manuel Portela) is the first comprehensive study of the influence of Antônio Gonçalves Dias's "Canção do exílio" (or "Song of Exile"), one of the most imitated poems in the world. Written in Coimbra, Portugal in 1843 by the Brazilian poet and published three years later in the state of Rio de Janeiro, "Song of Exile" has inspired thousands of parodies and pastiches over the last almost 200 years with new variations appearing all the time. In every Brazilian generation, writers, canonical and otherwise, have adapted the poem's verses, glorifying the wonders of the nation, its culture and geography, or written parodies of it to criticize Brazil, exposing a litany of the nation's issues. Yet, only in recent times, with the availability of digital archives, such as the Hemeroteca Digital Brasileira and Google Books, has it become possible to take a comprehensive view of the poem's influence. Based on a core of 500 texts, this book catalogues the networks of the poem's re-invention as pastiche and parody in Brazilian print culture from nineteenth-century periodicals to new media. With chapters dedicated to the early reception of the poem among Portuguese immigrants in nineteenth-century Rio, its proliferation in the First Republic (1889-1930) through the Vargas Era (1930-1945), its re-invention during the military regime (1964-1985), its continued adaptation to Brazil's most recent crises in new media, and another to the specific contributions of female authors, this study maps the re-occurrences of the original's keywords and phrases through both distant and close readings, uncovering how the poem has become a palimpsest upon which successive generations write and re-write the nation's history and culture within the context of their own time. This process of reinvention has guaranteed the permanency of "Song of Exile" in Brazilian culture, making it not only the nation's most popular poem, but one of the most imitated in the world.

About the Author

Joshua Alma Enslen is an Associate Professor in the Department of Foreign Languages at West Point, where he teaches courses in Portuguese as a second language and in Brazilian literature and culture. He holds a PhD from the University of Georgia (2008) and a Post-Doctoral Certificate of Studies (2016) from the University of Coimbra's Materialities of Literature program. His current research focuses on exploring, in visual and narrative modes, the intertextual influence of Gonçalves Dias' "Canção do Exílio" (1843), one of the world's most imitated poems. His works of data-driven art conveying the influence of Gonçalves Dias' poem, and created in collaboration with visual artist Alaina Enslen, have been featured in solo exhibitions at the historic University of Coimbra's Museum of Science (2016), later nominated for an APOM 2017, at FOLIO 2016 (Óbidos), and at U Lisbon's Caleidoscópio (2017). Apart from his book on the influence of "Song of Exile," he has published numerous essays on varied topics in Brazilian literature and culture in academic journals such as the *Luso-Brazilian Review*, *Hispania*, and *Portuguese Literary and Cultural Studies*.

"In this carefully crafted study, Joshua Enslen chronicles the allure and cultural impact of Brazil's most iconic and imitated poem. Penned in Coimbra, Portugal, in 1843 by Brazilian Antônio Gonçalves Dias, 'Song of Exile' inspired Brazilians to reimagine their nation's landscape and history. References to it abound in popular culture and music. For nearly two centuries, the poem has been invoked by political regimes and actors, including protestors during Brazil's 2018 presidential election. 'Song of Exile' idealized Brazil as an Edenic garden and offered fertile ground for subsequent writers to imitate or challenge Gonçalves Dias's utopic vision."
—Luciana Namorato, Indiana University

CPSIA information can be obtained
at www.ICGtesting.com
Printed in the USA
LVHW012152230622
721997LV00002B/227